BASIC
English
Grammar
*for Speaking & Writing*

2권

## BASIC English Grammar
## for Speaking & Writing 2권

**2025년 01월 02일 인쇄**
**2025년 01월 10일 발행**

지 은 이   E & C
발 행 인   Chris Suh
발 행 처   **MENT🅞RS**

경기도 성남시 분당구 황새울로 335번길 10 598
TEL 031-604-0025 FAX 031-696-5221
mentors.co.kr
blog.naver.com/mentorsbook
* Play 스토어 및 App 스토어에서 '멘토스북' 검색해 어플다운받기!

등록일자   2005년 7월 27일
등록번호   제 2009-000027호
I S B N   979-11-94467-22-9
          979-11-94467-19-9(세트)
가     격   16,000원(정답 및 해설 PDF 무료다운로드)

# BASIC
# English
# Grammar
*for Speaking & Writing*

# 머리말

## ▶ 문법이란?

문법이란 문장을 만들어 말을 하고(speaking) 또한 문장을 만드는(writing) 것을 말한다. 모국어를 하는데는 그리 많은 문법이 필요하지 않는다. 어머니 뱃속에서부터 히어링을 하면서 모국어를 익히기 때문에 저절로 알게 되며 나중에 문법의 체계화를 위해 후천적으로 문법을 약간 학습할 뿐이다. 그러나 모국어가 아닌 외국어로 영어를 배우는 과정은 모국어 습득과 정반대가 된다.

## ▶ 외국어로 영어배우기는…

우리는 영어듣기와 영어말하기에 먼지 노출될 수 없기에 역으로 영문법을 통해서 영어를 말하고 쓰게 되는 과정을 밟아간다. 즉 한 언어, 즉 여기서는 영어를 문법을 통해서 이해하고 이를 발판으로 해서 영어회화, 영어작문 그리고 영어듣기 등에 많은 시간을 쏟고 주구장창 몰두하게 된다. 모국어로 영어를 배우는 네이티브와는 비교될 수 없는 싸움을 하는 것이다. 미국이나 영국에서 네이티브들과 소통하면서 몇년 살면 저절로 배워지는 영어지만 다 그럴 수 없기 때문에 우리는 어쩔 수 없이 비효율적인 방법으로 영어로 익힐 수밖에 없다. 여기에 문법의 중요성이 생기게 된다.

## ▶ 문법에만 흠뻑 빠지면 안돼…

여기서 한가지 범하기 쉬운 오류가 있다. 문법이 외국어를 배우는 최초의 단계임에는 분명하지만 너무 문법에 사로잡혀서 그래서 완벽한 문장 아니면 말을 하지 못하는 어리석음에 놓일 수가 있다. 언어는 시대에 따라 시시각각 변하고 이를 밑받침하는 문법 역시 계속 변화가 된다. 역으로 생각을 해보자. 우리가 특히 일상생활에서 우리말을 할 때 얼마나 국문법 규칙을 지키면서 말하는지 말이다. 이 말은 문법을 꼭 알아야 하지만 너무 문법에 얽매이면 안된다는 얘기이다.

## ▶ 이거 알면 남들보다 앞서가…

이 책 <BASIC English Grammar 1권, 2권>과 <SMART English Grammar 1권, 2권>은 지금 시대에 가장 잘 맞는 그리고 꼭 알아야 하는 문법규칙들을 무겁지 않게 정리하여 문법을 공부하는 사람들이 부담스럽지 않게 학습할 수 있도록 꾸며져 있다. 또한 이를 각종 Test들로 확인하게 되어 이를 다 풀고 나면 남들보다는 한두단계 영어에서 앞서 갈 수 있을 것이라 확신한다.

# New Grammar is About

## 1 실용영어를 위한 문법

문법도 실용영어를 하는데 필요한 최소한의 도구이다. 따라서 문법을 위한 문법이 아닌 '실용영어를 위한 문법' 이란 캐치프레이즈를 내걸고 실제로 영어를 읽고 말하는 데 필요한 영어문법 사항들만을 정리하였다. 가장 실용적인 영어회화문(Dialogue)을 통해 우리가 학습해야 할 문법사항을 언급하는 것 또한 '지금,' '현재' 쓰이고 있는 문법을 지향하기 위함이다.

## 2 영어회화를 위한 문법

실용영어의 목적은 영어로 하는 의사소통이다. '영어말하기' 란 목표를 달성하기 위해 문법에 영어회화를 접목해본다. 문법을 단순한 지식으로 책상에서만 필요한 것이 아니라 실제 영어로 말하는데 활용할 수 있도록 매 Unit별로 학습한 문법지식을 바탕으로 다양한 문장을 영어로 옮겨보는 훈련을 해보며 간접적인 영어회화훈련을 시도해본다. 이는 또한 점점 실용화되고 있는 영어시험자격증인 TOEFL, TOEIC, IELT 등에서 고득점을 취할 수 있는 기본 베이스가 될 수 있을 것이다.

## 3 다양한 테스트

학습한 문법사항은 연습을 통해 훈련하지 않으면 다 날아가버린다. 이런 과오를 범하지 않기 위해 각 Unit마다 다양한 연습문제를 그리고 각 Chapter가 끝날 때마다 Review Test를 통해 이중으로 테스트를 해보며 머리 속에 오래도록 각인해본다. '영어말하기' 뿐만 아니라 각종 시험에서도 높은 점수를 받을 수 있을 것이다.

# New Grammar is Organized

## 1 Chapter

명사와 관사로부터 시작해서 대명사, 형용사와 부사, 비교, 접속사, 전치사구, 관계사구, 가정법 및 일치와 특수구문 등 총 9개의 Chapter로 실용영문법의 엑기스만을 집중 구분하여 정리하였다.

### 총 9개의 Chapters

Chapter 01 | 명사와 관사
Chapter 02 | 대명사
Chapter 03 | 형용사와 부사
Chapter 04 | 비교
Chapter 05 | 접속사
Chapter 06 | 전치사구
Chapter 07 | 관계사구
Chapter 08 | 가정법
Chapter 09 | 일치와 특수구문

## 2 Unit

Chapter는 다시 세분되어 각 Chapter별로 2~7개의 Unit로 정리된다. 따라서 총 9개의 Chapter는 총 34개의 Unit로 구성되어 있으며 각 Unit는 다시 Grammar in Practice, Grammar in Use, Unit Test, Writing Pattern Practice 등으로 나누어 진다.

### 각 Unit의 구성

Grammar in Practice
Grammar in Use
Unit Test
Writing Pattern Practice

## 3 Review

각 Chapter가 끝날 때마다 Chapter에서 학습한 내용을 다시 복습할 공간을 마련하였다. Review 1, 2에서 종합적으로 문제를 풀어보면서 자신이 학습한 내용을 얼마나 습득하였는지를 확인해볼 수 있다.

## 4 정답 및 해설

각 Unit의 테스트와 Review의 문제에 대한 정답을 별도의 부록 처리하여 문제를 풀 때 정답에 접근하는 것을 어렵게 하여 가급적 스스로 풀어보도록 꾸며졌다.

# How to Use this Book

영어회화와 문법을 접목시키는 부분. 각 Unit에서 학습할 문법사항이 실제 영어회화에서는 어떻게 쓰이는지 보면서 문법을 왜 배워야 하는지를 느껴본다.

**Grammar in Use**

역시 실용성에 focus를 맞춰 불필요한 문법지식을 다 걷어내고 오직 실제로 영어를 말하고 쓰는데 필요한 문법엑기스만을 간단하지만 밀도있게 서술하고 있는 부분이다.

**More Tips**

Grammar in Use에서 못다한 추가정보를 그때그때마다 간략이 설명해준다.

**Unit Test**

각 Unit마다 학습한 문법사항을 바로 확인해보는 자리이다. 다양한 형태의 테스트를 통해 학습한 문법지식을 머리 속에 차곡차곡 잊지 않고 기억해둘 수 있다.

**Writing Pattern Practice**

이번에는 좀 더 적극적으로 문법과 영어회화를 접목시키는 공간이다. 학습한 문법사항을 실제로 영어말하는데 활용해 볼 수 있는 공간으로 문법이 살아있음을 느낄 수 있다.

## Review

각 Chapter별로 제공되는 테스트시간으로 일종의 종합문제이나. 이미 Unit Test로 한번 확인한 문법을 다시 한번 꼭꼭 기억할 수 있는 공간이다.

## Wrap UP

군데군데 혼란스럽거나 복잡해보일 때마다 일목 요연하게 1페이지로 학습내용을 깔끔하게 정리하였다.

# New Grammar Level 1-B
# Contents

# *Chapter 1 │ 명사와 관사

# Unit 01 | 명사의 쓰임

A: Who is he?
B: He's my brother.
A: What's his name?
B: His name is Jack Daniel.
A: Where does he live?
B: He lives in Vancouver.
A: What hobbies does he have?
B: He likes swimming and surfing.

**1.** 명사란 사람이나 사물, 장소 등의 이름을 나타내는 말이다.
**Jenny** stayed at **the Hilton** in **Hawaii.** Jenny는 Hawaii에서 Hilton 호텔에 머물렀다.
My favorite **sport** is **soccer.** 내 좋아하는 스포츠는 축구이다.

**2.** 명사는 문장 안에서 주어, 목적어, 보어, 전치사의 목적어 역할을 한다.

● 주어 역할
The **weather** is nice. 날씨가 좋다.
My **sisters** are twins. 여동생들은 쌍둥이다.

● 목적어 역할
People watch **television** a lot. 사람들은 TV를 많이 본다.
Jane loves her **parents.** Jane은 부모님을 사랑한다.

● 보어 역할
Today is **Monday.** (주격보어) 오늘은 월요일이다.
People call me **a fool.** (목적격보어) 사람들은 나를 바보라고 부른다.

● 전치사의 목적어
Look at **that girl.** 저 소녀를 봐.
We're waiting for **the bus.** 우리는 버스를 기다리고 있다.

# Unit Test

**1.** 각 문장에서 명사를 찾아 모두 동그라미 하시오.

1. Ann is in good health.

2. Money is very important in life.

3. Sally likes classical music.

4. The sky is blue and the sun is shining.

5. Tokyo is the capital of Japan.

6. Money doesn't always bring happiness.

7. We need friends.

8. My father is a lawyer.

9. Ann works at a restaurant.

10. It's a secret.

**2.** 밑줄 친 명사가 주어이면 S, 목적이이면 O, 보어이면 C로 쓰시오.

1. I don't eat <u>meat</u> very often.
   (    )

2. <u>The weather</u> is very good.
   (    )

3. Do you wear <u>glasses</u>?
   (    )

4. People call me <u>Katie</u>.
   (    )

5. <u>The police</u> are here.
   (    )

6. <u>Europe</u> is bigger than Australia.
   (    )

7. I finish <u>work</u> at 6 o'clock.
   (    )

8. Jerry is <u>a vegetarian</u>.
   (    )

9. My favorite <u>sports</u> are tennis and badminton.
   (    )

10. My favorite sports are <u>tennis and badminton</u>.
    (    )

# Writing Pattern Practice

**1.** 「명사(주어) + 동사」

날씨가 좋아.(nice)

내 여동생들은 쌍둥이야.(twins)

장미는 아름다워.(Roses~)

Eric은 내 남자친구야.

Jenny는 Hilton 호텔에서 머물렀어.

**2.** 「주어 + 동사 + 명사(목적어)」

나는 스포츠를 좋아해.

Jane은 부모님을 사랑해.

Daniel은 책을 썼어.

코끼리는 긴 코를 가지고 있지.(An~)

사람들은 TV를 많이 본다.(a lot of)

**3.** 「주어 + 동사 + 명사(주격보어)」

나는 학생이야.

오늘은 월요일이야.

내 좋아하는 스포츠는 축구야.(favorite)

어제는 내 생일이었어.

**4.** 「주어 + 동사 + 목적어 + 명사(목적격보어)」

나를 David 이라고 불러줘.

사람들은 나를 바보라고 불러.(a fool)

**5.** 「~전치사 + 명사(전치사의 목적어)」

나는 음악에 관심이 있어.(interested)

저 소녀를 봐.(Look at~)

우리는 버스를 기다리고 있어.(wait for)

나는 내 핸드폰을 찾고 있어.(look for)

Unit

# 02 | 명사의 소유격

Grammar
in
Practice

A: Can I use your cell phone?
B: I'm sorry, but I didn't bring it today.
    Why don't you use Mike's?
A: Is this Mike's cell phone?
B: Yes, it is.

Grammar
in
Use

**1.** 명사의 소유격은 살아있는 생물체의 경우 명사에 's를 붙이는 것이 원칙이다.
Is that **Tom's** car? 저것은 Tom의 자동차예요?
These are **women's** clothes. 이것들은 여성의류이다.
**The men's** room is right there. 남자 화장실은 바로 저기예요.
David has a **driver's** license. David은 운전면허증이 있다.

**2.** −s로 끝나는 복수명사일 경우, 뒤에 apostrophe( ' )만 붙인다.
**a girls'** school 여학교
**my parents'** car 부모님 차

**3.** 무생물의 소유격은 A의 B일 때 〈B of A〉 형태로 쓴다.
**the principal of the school** 학교의 교장
What's **the title of this song**? 이 노래 제목이 뭐지?
Hurry up, or we'll miss **the beginning of the movie**.
서둘러, 그렇지 않으면 우리는 영화 시작부분을 못 볼 거야.

**4.** 명사 없이 소유격만 썼을 때는 소유대명사 '∼의 것'의 뜻이다.
This computer is **Tom's** (computer). 이 컴퓨터는 Mike의 것이다.
We'll meet at **Mary's** (house). 우리는 Mary 집에서 만날 거야.

## Unit Test

**1.** 다음 명사의 소유격을 쓰시오.

girls -_____     Judy -_____     women -_____     men -_____

mother -_____     children -_____     baby -_____     Scott -_____

**2.** 알맞은 명사의 소유격에 동그라미 치시오.

1. There is no (womens'/ women's) room on the first floor.
2. We sell (mens'/ men's) clothing.
3. Is this (Mike's/ Mike') computer?
4. Susan goes to a (girls'/ girls's) middle school.
5. My (teacher's/ teacher') first name is Molly.

**3.** 문장을 읽어보고 어색한 곳을 찾아 고치시오.

1. The bag is Jacks. _____
2. I'm at Janets. _____
3. Is the lady Mr. Kim wife? _____
4. Do you know Cindy phone number? _____
5. Are you going to Sally birthday party? _____

**4.** 밑줄 친 곳이 맞으면 O표 하고, 틀리면 X표 하고 고쳐 쓰시오.

1. <u>The favorite food of Peter</u> is spaghetti.

       (     ) → _____

2. I sat in <u>the front of the classroom</u>.

             (     ) → _____

3. What's <u>the name of this song</u>?

            (     ) → _____

4. "Where are you?" I'm at <u>the house of my parents</u>.

                  (     ) → _____

5. <u>The end of the movie</u> was very shocking.

       (     ) → _____

6. I'm leaving for China at <u>the end of this year</u>.

                (     ) → _____

7. Tell me <u>the phone number of your sister</u>.

           (     ) → _____

8. What's <u>the nickname of Kate</u>?

        (     ) → _____

# Writing Pattern Practice

**1.** 「**명사(사람)'s + 명사**」 'A의 B'
　　　 A　　　　 B

Tom의 자동차

저것은 Tom의 자동차니?

여자 옷들(clothes)

이것들은 여자들 옷이야.

운전면허증(driver's license)

David은 운전면허증이 있어.

Tim의 핸드폰

이것은 Tim의 핸드폰이야.

Jane의 집

Jane의 집은 우체국 옆에 있어.(next to)


**2.** 「**명사 + of + 명사(무생물)**」 'A의 B'
　　　 B　　　 A

이 노래 제목

이 노래 제목이 뭐지?

영화의 시작(the beginning)

서둘러, 그렇지 않으면 우리는 영화 시작을 못 볼 거야.(miss)

이 책의 작가(author)

이 책의 작가를 나에게 얘기해줘.


**3.** 「**명사's**」 'A의 것'
　　　 A

Mike의 것

이 컴퓨터는 Mike의 것이다.

Mary의 것

너는 Mary의 것을 써도 좋아.(can)

Shakespeare의 것

이 극은 Shakespeare의 것이니?(play)

# 03 | 셀 수 있는 명사와 셀 수 없는 명사

Grammar
in
Practice

A: What did you buy?
B: I bought some vegetables.
A: We're running out of rice. Did you buy some?
B: Yes, I did.

Grammar
in
Use

**1.** 셀 수 있는 명사는 사물, 사람 등 구체적인 명사를 말한다. a/an을 붙일 수 있으며 단수와 복수
의 구별이 있다.

**I have an apple and some pears.** 나는 사과 한 개와 몇 개의 배를 가지고 있다.

● 셀 수 있는 명사

apple, desk, boy, city, book, dog, day, week, month 등
a flower / some flowers 한 송이 꽃/ 약간의 꽃들
a week/ two weeks 한 주/ 두 주

**2.** 셀 수 없는 명사는 추상적인 개념(love, happiness 등)이나 하나씩 분리하기 어려운 것들(gold,
air 등)이다. 항상 단수형을 쓰고 단수취급 한다.

● 셀 수 없는 명사

추상적 개념 – peace, art, beauty, death 등
액체 – water, oil, gasoline, blood 등
고체 – ice, gold, iron, silver, glass, paper, wood, cotton 등
기체 – steam, air, oxygen, nitrogen, smoke, smog, pollution 등
음식 – coffee, tea, soup, bread, butter, cheese, meat 등
자연 – weather, dew, fog, hail, heat, humidity, lightning, rain, snow, wind 등
범주 – furniture, food, clothing, money 등

**3.** 셀 수 없는 명사는 직접 세지 못하고 담는 용기나 단위를 통하여 센다.

예 We bought a furniture(x)　　some furnitures(x)　　two piece of furnitures(X)
　　　a piece of furniture(O)　　some furniture(O)　　two pieces of furniture(O)

a **piece**(two pieces) of paper/furniture/cake/advice
a **cup**(two cups) of tea/coffee
a **spoonful**(two spoonfuls) of sugar/salt
a **box**(two boxes) of cereal/flour
a **bag**(two bags) of flour
a **glass**(two glasses) of water/juice
a **bottle**(two bottles) of beer/soda
a **bar**(two bars) of chocolate
a **loaf**(two loaves) of bread/meat
a **cut**(two cuts) of meat
a **bunch**(two bunches) of bananas/grapes

# Unit Test

**1.** 다음 중 셀 수 있는 명사에 C(countable) 셀 수 없는 명사에 U(uncountable)를 써 넣으시오.

| | | | |
|---|---|---|---|
| star ( ) | ink ( ) | apple ( ) | car ( ) |
| money ( ) | bread ( ) | furniture ( ) | advice ( ) |
| music ( ) | book ( ) | salt ( ) | information ( ) |
| water ( ) | eye ( ) | foot ( ) | tooth ( ) |
| chair ( ) | man ( ) | boy ( ) | perfume ( ) |
| love ( ) | happiness ( ) | friend ( ) | key ( ) |

**2.** 그림을 보고 보기와 같이 빈칸에 쓰시오.

보기 |  It's a book.    It's bread.

1. _____
2. _____
3. _____
4. _____
5. _____

**3.** 다음 둘 중 알맞은 것에 동그라미 하시오.

1. I need some (money/ moneys).
2. You can get some (information/ informations) over there.
3. Janet has (a long/ long) hair.
4. Ted never wears (a hat/ hat).
5. Can you drive (a car/ car)?
6. Jon brought me (a flower/ flower).
7. Are you looking for (a job/ job)?
8. Are you sleepy? Drink some (coffee/ coffees)
9. (A money/ Money) isn't everything.
10. I don't eat (a meat/ meat)

# Writing Pattern Practice

**1.** 「I need a(n) + 셀 수 있는 명사(단수형)」

나는 사과 하나가 필요해. _____

나는 여자친구가 한사람 필요해. _____

나는 핸드폰이 하나 필요해. _____

나는 한달이 필요해. _____

**2.** 「I need two/three~ + 셀 수 있는 명사(복수형)」

나는 의자가 두 개 필요해. _____

나는 펜이 두 개 필요해. _____

나는 책이 두 권 필요해. _____

나는 두 주가 필요해. _____

**3.** 「I need + 셀 수 없는 명사」

나는 돈이 필요해. _____

나는 음식이 필요해. _____

나는 종이가 필요해. _____

나는 신선한 공기가 필요해.(fresh) _____

**4.** 「I need a piece/cup/spoonful/box/glass/bottle/loaf/box/bunch of + 셀 수 없는 명사」

나는 커피 한 잔이 필요해. _____

나는 종이 한 장이 필요해. _____

나는 물 한 잔이 필요해. _____

나는 설탕 한 스푼이 필요해. _____

**5.** 「I need two/three~ pieces/cups/spoonfuls/glasses/bottles/bars/loaves/boxes/bunches of + 셀 수 없는 명사」

나는 빵 두덩어리가 필요해. _____

나는 시리얼 두 박스가 필요해. _____

나는 콜라 두 병이 필요해. _____

나는 포도 두 송이가 필요해. _____

Unit

# 04 | 명사의 복수형

Grammar in Practice

A: I need my glasses, but I can't find them.
B: They are on the desk.
A: Where are my shirt and jeans?
B: I put them on your bed.

Grammar in Use

**1.** 명사의 복수형을 만드는 방법은 다음과 같다.

● **규칙**

| | |
|---|---|
| • 대부분의 명사에 –s를 붙인다. | flower→flowers week→weeks hat→hats chair→chairs |
| • –s, –x, –sh, –ch, –o로 끝나는 명사는 –es를 붙인다. | bus→buses box→boxes dish→dishes church→churches potato→potatoes tomato→tomatoes 예외: pianos photos radios 등 |
| • 「자음+y」로 끝나는 단어는 y를 i로 고치고, –es를 붙인다. | baby→babies lady→ladies dictionary→dictionaries |
| • –f, –fe는 v로 바꾸고, –es를 붙인다. | shelf→shelves leaf→leaves wife→wives 예외: belief→beliefs proof→proofs roof→roofs |

● **불규칙**

| | |
|---|---|
| • 모음이 변한다. | tooth→teeth man→men woman→women foot→feet goose→geese mouse→mice |
| • 어미에 –(r)en을 붙인다. | child→children ox→oxen |
| • 단수, 복수가 같다. | fish→fish deer→deer sheep→sheep Japanese→Japanese Swiss→Swiss |

**2.** 항상 복수형으로 쓰는 명사가 있다. 복수형 앞에 a pair of를 쓰기도 한다.

glasses(안경)  jeans(청바지)  pants(바지)  pajamas(잠옷)  scissors(가위)  socks(양말)

Where are my **glasses**? 내 안경 어디 있지?
Your **pants** are really nice. 네 바지 정말 멋있다.
I need **a** new **pair of jeans**. 나는 새로운 청바지가 필요해.

# Unit Test

**1.** 다음 단어의 복수형을 쓰시오.

day -_____    week -_____    month -_____    year -_____

dish -_____    flower -_____    umbrella -_____    baby -_____

woman -_____    man -_____    knife -_____    dictionary -_____

party -_____    potato -_____    tomato -_____    box -_____

sheep -_____    fish -_____    tooth -_____    mouse -_____


**2.** 틀린 곳을 찾아 고쳐 쓰시오.

1. Sheeps eat grass.    → _____
2. There is a lot of fish in the pond.    → _____
3. Where is my pants?    → _____
4. I need a new pair of jean.    → _____
5. Your sunglass look good.    → _____
6. There aren't many woman here.    → _____
7. Man like sports.    → _____
8. I like tomatos.    → _____
9. Mr. Bin has four childs.    → _____
10. There are many benchs in the park.    → _____


**3.** 보기와 같이 괄호안의 단어를 이용하여 현재형문장을 완성하시오.

> 보기 |　There (be) a lot of fish here. → There <u>are</u> a lot of fish here.
> 　　　　Grapes (taste) good. → Grapes <u>taste</u> good.

1. Your jeans _____ (be) in the dryer.

2. Tomatoes _____ (taste) good.

3. There _____ (be) seven days in a week.

4. Your hands _____ (be) beautiful.

5. My teeth really _____ (hurt).

6. These pants _____ (be) too tight.

7. Your glasses _____ (look) good on you.

8. Apples _____ (be) good for health.

9. Mice _____ (be) smaller than dogs.

10. His pajamas _____ (be) in the closet.

# Writing Pattern Practice

**1.** 「There is + a 명사」→ 「There are + 명사s」

여기에 의자가 하나 있다. _____

여기에 의자들이 있다. _____

여기에 모자가 하나 있다. _____

어기에 모자들이 있다. _____


**2.** 「There is + a (−s, −x, −sh, −ch, −o)명사」→ 「There are + 명사es」

여기에 박스가 하나 있다. _____

여기에 박스들이 있다. _____

여기에 토마토가 하나 있다. _____

여기에 토마토들이 있다. _____


**3.** 「There is + a (자음+y)명사」→ 「There are + (자음+ies)명사」

여기에 한 아기가 있다. _____

여기에 아기들이 있다. _____

여기에 사전이 하나 있다. _____

여기에 사전들이 있다. _____


**4.** 「There is + (−f,−fe)명사」→ 「There are + (−ves)명사」

여기에 칼이 하나 있다. _____

여기에 칼들이 있다. _____

여기에 선반이 하나 있다. _____

여기에 선반들이 있다. _____


**5.** 「그 밖 불규칙 명사」

여기에 한 여자가 있다. _____

여기에 여자들이 있다. _____

어기에 한 남지가 있다. _____

여기에 남자들이 있다. _____

여기에 한 아이가 있다. _____

여기에 아이들이 있다. _____

여기에 물고기가 한 마리 있다. _____

여기에 물고기들이 있다. _____

# 05 | 부정관사

**Grammar in Practice**

A: Describe the picture you're holding.

B: It's a beautiful day.

A woman is waiting for a taxi.

She has a cell phone in her hand.

A boy is standing next to her.

He's wearing a hat.

**Grammar in Use**

**1.** 부정관사 a는 셀 수 있는 단수 명사와 함께 쓴다. 이때 명사가 모음(a,e,i,o,u)으로 시작하면 an 을 쓴다.

Do you want **an** apple or **a** pear? 너는 사과를 원하니 아니면 배를 원하니?

She bought **a** raincoat and **an** umbrella. 그녀는 우비와 우산을 샀다.

| 주의 | an hour, an honest person, a one way street, a European country, a university
└ h: 묵음 ┘          발음: 반자음[w]          └ 발음: 반모음[j] ┘

**2.** a/an은 다양한 의미로 쓴다.

● 불특정한 하나(특별히 해석할 필요 없다.)

Tom lives in **an** apartment. Tom은 아파트에 산다.

● 하나(=one)

I couldn't say **a** word. 나는 한마디도 할 수 없었다.

● ~마다(=per)

I work five days **a** week. 나는 일주일에 5일 일한다.

**3.** 대표명사를 나타낼 때 쓴다.

**A** rose is beautiful. (=Roses are beautiful.) 장미는 아름다워.

**An** apple tastes good. (=Apples taste good.) 사과는 맛이 좋다.

**4.** 무슨 종류인지 말하거나 직업명을 나타낼 때 쓴다.

Tennis is **a** sport. 테니스는 스포츠다.

A rose is **a** flower. 장미는 꽃이다.

"What do you do?" "I'm **a** teacher." 당신 직업이 뭐죠? 선생님이에요.

"What does Tom do?" "He's **a** firefighter." Tom은 직업이 뭐죠? 소방관이에요.

# Unit Test

**1.** 빈칸에 a 또는 an을 넣으시오.

1. _____ new car     2. _____ artist

3. _____ orange     4. _____ hour

5. _____ umbrella     6. _____ house

7. _____ old man     7. _____ woman

**2.** 보기에서 알맞은 말을 골라 1번과 같이 빈칸을 채우시오.

보기 | city   fruit   sport   vegetable   animal   planet   country   mountain

1. New York is <u>a city</u> in the United States.
2. A tiger is _____ .
3. An apple is _____ .
4. Everest is _____ .
5. The earth is _____ .
6. Canada is _____ .
7. An onion is _____ .
8. Basketball is _____ .

**3.** 보기와 같이 그림에 맞는 직업을 골라 쓰시오.

A: What does he do?
B: He is a doctor.

보기 |   sales clerk     firefighter     taxi driver     teacher

1.
A: What does he do?
B: He is _____

2.
A: What does he do?
B: He is _____

3.
A: What does she do?
B: She is _____

4.
A: What does she do?
B: She is _____

# Writing Pattern Practice

**1.** 「a + 자음으로 시작하는 명사」

그것은 배다. _____

그것은 말이다. _____

**2.** 「an + 모음으로 시작하는 명사」

그것은 사과다. _____

한 시간 걸린다.(take) _____

**3.** 「a(n) + 명사」 '불특정한 하나'

나는 아파트에 산다. _____

방에 전화가 있다.(There is~) _____

**4.** 「a(n)+명사」 '하나의~'

교실에 한명의 학생이 있다. _____

나는 여기에 일본인 친구가 한명 있다.(Japanese friend) _____

**5.** 「a(n) + 명사」 '~마다'

나는 일주일에 5일 일한다. _____

하루에 한번 나에게 전화줘.(once) _____

**6.** 「a(n) + 명사」 '대표명사'

장미는 아름다워. _____

사과는 맛이 좋아. _____

**7.** 「a(n) + 명사」 '종류'

테니스는 스포츠다. _____

장미는 꽃이다. _____

**8.** 「a(n) + 명사」 '직업명 앞에'

나는 선생님이야. _____

Tom은 소방관이야.(a firefighter) _____

# 06 | 정관사

A: What did you buy?
B: I bought a watch.
A: Was the watch made in Switzerland?
B: Yes, it was.

1. 정관사 the 는 '그'라는 뜻으로 서로 알고 있을 만한 명사 앞에 붙인다.

   ● 앞에 나온 명사를 되풀이해서 말할 때 쓴다.
   I bought a skirt. **The** skirt was very cheap, but also nice.
   치마를 샀는데, 그 치마는 매우 싸고 또한 좋았어.

   ● 어느 것을 가리키는지 알 수 있을 때 쓴다.
   I'll get **the** phone. 내가 전화 받을게.

   ● 명사가 수식어의 꾸밈을 받을 때 쓴다.
   **The** man in black is my teacher. 검정 옷을 입은 저 남자가 우리 선생님이야.
             수식어

   ● 형용사의 최상급, 서수, only, same 등이 명사를 꾸며줄 때 쓴다.
   Who is **the** best athlete on your team? 너희 팀에서 누가 제일 잘하니?
   I live on **the** fifth floor. 나는 5층에 살아.
   We have **the** same tastes. 우리는 취향이 같다.

   ● 세상에서 유일한 것이나 방위 앞에 쓴다.
   the sun, the moon, the world, the sky, the ground, the ocean, the north, the south, the west, the east 등
   **The** sun rises in the east. 해는 동쪽에서 뜬다.

   ● by 다음에 단위를 나타낼 때 쓴다.
   My father gets paid by **the** week. 아버지는 주급을 받으신다.

2. 운동경기, 식사명, 장소를 나타내는 고유명사 앞에는 the를 붙이지 않는다.
   Let's play soccer/ baseball/ basket ball. 축구/야구/농구 하자.
   * 악기명 앞에는 the를 붙인다. I played the piano.
   Let's have breakfast/ lunch/ dinner. 아침/점심/저녁 먹자.
   Let's go to France/ Burger King/ Asia 프랑스/버거킹/아시아에 가자.

3. next/last 다음에 week/month/year/winter/Monday/Christmas 등이 올 때는 앞에 the를 붙이지 않는다.
   I went to Europe **last Christmas**. 나는 지난 크리스마스에 유럽에 갔다.
   See you **next** Friday. 다음 금요일에 만나자.

4. 「the+형용사」는 '~한 사람들'을 뜻하며 복수 취급한다.
   **The** rich are not always happy. 부자라고 항상 행복한 것은 아니다.

# Unit Test

**1.** 다음 중 항상 the를 앞에 써야하는 명사에 동그라미 하시오.

| sun breakfast soccer earth country sky world same moon |

**2.** 빈칸을 채워 다음 그림을 묘사하시오.

1.
2.
3.

1. She is playing _____
2. Are these bags different? No, they are _____
3. _____ is going down.

**3.** 우리말과 일치하도록 괄호 안의 단어를 알맞게 배열하시오.

1. 가장 가까운 은행이 어디죠? (the/ where/ is/ nearest bank/ ?)

_____

2. 하늘이 파랗다. (sky/ the/ is/ blue)

_____

3. 해가 빛나고 있다. (sun/ the/ is/ shining)

_____

4. 축구하자. (play/ let's/ soccer)

_____

5. 저녁 먹자. (have/ let's/ dinner)

_____

6. 나는 피아노를 쳤어. (played/ I/ the piano)

_____

7. 달이 나왔다. (moon/ the/ came out)

_____

8. 나 다음 토요일에 일한다. (working/ I'm/ next/ Saturday)

_____

9. 우리는 바다에서 수영했다. (swam/ we/ in/ sea/ the)

_____

10. 저 별들을 봐. (at/ look/ stars/ the)

_____

# Writing Pattern Practice

**1.** 「the + 명사(앞에 나온 명사)」

그 영화는 지루했어.(boring) _____

그 치마는 매우 쌌어. _____


**2.** 「the + 명사(어느 것을 가리키는지 알 수 있을 때)」

내가 전화 받을게.(get) _____

문 닫아. _____


**3.** 「the + 명사 + 수식어(명사가 수식어의 꾸밈을 받을 때)」

책상위에 있는 책은 내거야. _____

검정 옷을 입은 그 남자가 우리 선생님이야.(in black) _____


**4.** 「the + 최상급/ 서수/ only/ same + 명사」

너는 5층에 살아.(fifth floor) _____

우리는 취향이 같아.(tastes) _____


**5.** 「the + 명사(세상에서 유일한 것이나 방위)」

해는 동쪽에서 뜬다. _____

달이 나왔다.(come out) _____

하늘이 파랗다. _____


**6.** 「by + the + 단위명사」

아버지는 주급을 받으셔.(get paid) _____

우리는 설탕을 pound당 살 수 있어. _____


**7.** 「the + 명사(운동경기/ 식사명/ 장소를 나타내는 고유명사)」

우리 축구하자. _____

우리 아침 먹자. _____

우리 프랑스에 가자. _____


**8.** 「the next/last + week/month/year/winter/Monday/Christmas 등」

나는 지난 크리스마스에 유럽에 갔었어. _____

다음 금요일에 만나. _____


**9.** 「the + 형용사」 '…한 사람들'

부자라고 항상 행복한 것은 아니야.(not always) _____

나는 가난한 사람을 도와주고 싶어.(want) _____

# Unit
# 07 | There+be동사+명사

**Grammar in Practice**

A: I'm so thirsty.
B: There is some juice on the table.
A: Isn't there any water?
B: There might be some water in the fridge.

---

**Grammar in Use**

**1.** 「There+be동사+명사」는 '~가 있다' 라는 뜻으로 이 때 There는 해석하지 않는다.

**There is** some Coke in the fridge. 냉장고에 콜라가 있다.
**There are** a lot of people in the park. 공원에 사람들이 많다.
I like Chicago. **There is** a beautiful lake in that city.
나는 시카고를 좋아한다. 그 도시에는 아름다운 호수가 있다.

**2.** 시제와 따라오는 명사의 수에 따라 be동사를 변형시킨다.

- 과거
  **There was** a party last night. 어젯밤 파티가 있었다.
  **There were** thousands of people at the concert. 콘서트에 수천 명이 있었다.

- 현재완료
  **There has been** a lot of snow here. 여기에 눈이 많이 왔었어.
  **There have been** a lot of car accidents here. 여기 차사고가 많이 났었어.

- 현재
  **There is** an apple in the basket. 바구니에 사과가 하나 있다.
  **There are** some oranges in the basket. 바구니에 오렌지가 좀 있다.

- 미래
  **There will be** a lot of snow this winter. 올 겨울에 눈이 많이 올 거야.
  **There is going to be** a meeting on Monday morning. 월요일 아침에 회의가 있을 예정이다.

**3.** 부정문은 be 동사 다음에 not을 쓴다.

**There isn't** any reason to get upset. 화를 낼 아무런 이유가 없다.
**There aren't** any grammatical errors in your essay. 네 작문에 문법적인 오류는 없어.

**4.** 의문문은 「Is/Are there~?」로 쓰고 대답은 「Yes, there is/are.」로 한다.

**Is there** an *ATM around here? 근처에 현금지급기가 있나요?
Yes, there is./No, there isn't.                    *ATM: Automated Teller Machine

**Are there** any movie theaters around here? 근처에 극장 있나요?
Yes, there are./No, there aren't.

# Unit Test

**1.** 빈칸에 is, are, was, were 중 가장 알맞은 것을 써 넣으시오.

    1. There _____ a train at 10 o'clock today.

    2. There _____ a great movie on TV last night.

    3. There _____ twelve months in a year.

    4. There _____ a lot of people at the party last Saturday.

    5. Excuse me. _____ there a bank near here?

**2.** 다음 그림을 보고 보기와 같이 구체적으로 설명하시오.

| 보기 | A Chinese restaurant | There is one Chinese restaurant. |
|---|---|---|
| | A university | There is no university. |

    1. A hospital

    2. A bakery

    3. A bus stop

    4. A movie theater

    5. A swimming pool

    6. A church

    7. A book store

**3.** There be를 이용하여 문장을 완성하시오.(현재시제)

    1. _____ any students in the classroom?

    2. _____ any water in the refrigerator?

    3. _____ any nice restaurants in this town?

    4. _____ any restaurant in this building?

    5. How many players _____ on your team?

# Writing Pattern Practice

**1.** 「There is/are + 명사」

냉장고에 콜라가 좀 있어.(fridge) _____

바구니에 사과가 하나 있어.(basket) _____

거기에는 아름다운 호수가 있어.(beautiful) _____

10시에 기차가 있어. _____

공원에 사람들이 많아.(a lot of) _____

일년은 열두 달이 있어.(in a year) _____

**2.** 「There isn't/aren't + 명사」

물이 많이 없어.(much) _____

화를 낼 아무런 이유가 없어.(get upset) _____

여기에 사람들이 전혀 없어.(any people) _____

**3.** 「Is/Are there + 명사?」

은행이 있나요? _____

아이스크림 좀 있니? _____

사람들이 많이 있니?(many) _____

**4.** 「There was/were+명사」

여기에 빵이 좀 있었어. _____

어젯밤 TV에서 멋진 영화가 있었어.(great) _____

콘서트에 수천 명이 있었어.(thousands of) _____

파티에 사람들이 많이 있었어.(a lot of) _____

**5.** 「There has been/have been + 명사」

여기에 눈이 많이 왔었어. (a lot of) _____

여기에 차사고가 많이 났었어. (a lot of car accidents) _____

**6.** 「There will be/ is going to be + 명사」

올겨울에 눈이 많이 올 거야.(will) _____

월요일 아침에 회의가 있을 예정이야.(be going to) _____

# REVIEW 1

**1.** 다음 우리말을 영어로 바꿔 쓰시오.

① 여자들의 옷      →
② 그 노래의 제목      →
③ 그 영화의 시작      →
④ 종이 한 장      →
⑤ 빵 두 덩어리      →

**2.** 다음 영어 문장을 우리말로 쓰시오.

① Jane lives in an apartment.      →
② I couldn't say a word.      →
③ Tennis is a sport.      →
④ I'll get the phone.      →
⑤ There is some Coke in the fridge      →

**3.** 다음 중 틀린 곳을 바르게 고치시오.

① Mr. McConnell is teacher.      →
② Come to John birthday party tonight. →
③ This is Tom computer.      →
④ This is my parents's car.      →
⑤ There are some flower here.      →
⑥ My brother car is a BMW.      →
⑦ We have three childs.      →
⑧ Sky is blue.      →
⑨ I need a umbrella.      →
⑩ Can I give some foods to the cats?      →

**4.** 둘 중에서 알맞은 것을 골라 동그라미 하시오.

① I've waited for you for (a/ an) hour.
② (A/ The) sun came up.
③ Let's have (the/ X) lunch.
④ A rose is (a/ the) flower.
⑤ I'm (a/ X) nurse.
⑥ Kevin is (a/ an) honest person.
⑦ Why don't we play (the/ X) soccer?
⑧ See you (the/ X) next Friday.
⑨ The rich (is/ are) not always happy.
⑩ There is an ATM on (the/ X) second floor.

# REVIEW 2

**1.** 명사가 문장 안에서 할 수 없는 역할을 고르시오.

① 주어
② 목적어
③ 보어
④ 전치사의 목적어
⑤ 서술어

**2.** 밑줄 친 명사 중 문장 안에서의 역할이 <u>다른</u> 하나를 고르시오.

① People like <u>movies</u>.
② Today is <u>Sunday</u>.
③ I love <u>Brad Pitt</u>.
④ We had <u>dinner</u>.
⑤ My friend bought a <u>coat</u>.

**3.** 어법상 맞는 문장을 고르시오.

① There are three bottle of Coke.
② Who is best athlete on your team?
③ What's the title of this song?
④ I drink a lot of waters every day.
⑤ Let's play the basketball.

**4.** 밑줄 친 부분이 <u>다르게</u> 쓰인 하나를 고르시오.

① <u>My father's</u> car is kind of expensive.
② We're having a party at <u>Cindy's</u> house.
③ <u>Janet's</u> sister is a nurse.
④ The bag is <u>Susan's</u>.
⑤ The boy is <u>Kate's</u> brother.

**5.** 명사의 복수형이 적절하지 <u>않게</u> 쓰여진 문장을 고르시오

① There are three apples in the basket.
② I took some photoes.
③ There are a lot of fish in the pond.
④ I bought some potatoes.
⑤ I saw some deer on my way here.

[6-7] 밑줄 친 부분에 들어갈 수 있는 말을 고르시오.

**6.** _____ are birds.

① A penguin
② The penguin
③ A penguins
④ Penguins
⑤ penguin

**7.** _____ in red is my teacher.

① The woman
② A woman
③ Woman
④ The women
⑤ Women

**8.** 다음 글을 읽고 빈칸에 들어갈 말로 알맞은 것을 고르시오.

① the - the
② a - the
③ X - X
④ the - X
⑤ a - X

 The Indians celebrated _____ first Thanksgiving a long time ago.

They prepared turkey, deer meat, corn, and bread to celebrate a good harvest. Today we also celebrate Thanksgiving. Many families get together and have _____ dinner. Thanksgiving always comes in November. It is a time to get together and talk with each other.

# *Chapter 2 | 대명사

# 08 | 인칭대명사와 지시대명사

Grammar
in
Practice

A: I'm going to Florida.
B: Wow, great! Florida is famous for its beaches.
A: Yes, it's a beautiful place.
B: I envy you.

Grammar
in
Use

**1.** 대명사는 명사를 대신해서 쓰는 말이다.
　　Cindy is a teacher. **She** teaches English. Cindy는 선생님이다. 그녀는 영어를 가르친다.
　　Eric is a student. **He**'s from Canada. Eric은 학생이다. 그는 캐나다 출신이다.

**2.** 대신하는 명사가 사람일 때 인칭대명사를 쓴다. 이 때 it은 동물이나 물건을 가리킨다.

| 인칭대명사의 변화 | | 주격 | 소유격 | 목적격 | 소유대명사 |
|---|---|---|---|---|---|
| | | ~은/는/이/가 | ~의 | ~을, 에게 | ~의 것 |
| 1인칭 | 나 | I | my | me | mine |
| | 우리 | we | our | us | ours |
| 2인칭 | 너 | you | your | you | yours |
| | 너희들 | you | your | you | yours |
| 3인칭 | 그 | he | his | him | his |
| | 그녀 | she | her | her | hers |
| | 그것 | it | its | it | x |
| | 그들 | they | their | them | theirs |

**3.** 지시대명사 이것(this)/이것들(these)은 물리적, 심리적으로 가까운 사람이나 사물을 가리킬 때 쓴다.
　　What's **this**? It's a rose. 이것은 무엇이니? 그것은 장미야.
　　What are **these**? They are lilies. 이것들은 무엇이니? 그것들은 백합들이야.

**4.** 저것(that)/저것들(those)은 물리적, 심리적으로 먼 사람이나 사물을 가리킬 때 쓴다.
　　Is **that** Mary? Yes, it is. 저 사람이 Mary니? 응, 그래.
　　Are **those** your parents? Yes, they are. 저분들이 너희 부모님이시니? 응, 그래.

**5.** this, these, that, those는 지시형용사로 쓰여 명사를 꾸며 주기도 한다.
　　I want **this** book. 나는 이 책을 원한다.
　　I want **these** books. 나는 이 책들을 원한다.
　　**That** girl is my daughter. 저 여자애가 내 딸이다.
　　**Those** girls are my daughters. 저 여자애들이 내 딸들이다.

# Unit Test

**1.** 문장의 괄호 안에서 가장 알맞은 것을 골라 동그라미 하시오.

1. I don't know his phone number. Do you know (it/ them)?
2. I bought some tomatoes. Do you want to eat (it/ them)?
3. Karen likes music. (She/ It) plays the piano very well.
4. Kevin never goes drinking. (He/ It) doesn't drink.
5. Who is that man? Do you know (him/ it)?
6. What's your name again? I forgot (it/ them).
7. I like (her/ hers) smile. It's so beautiful.
8. Do you know (his/ him) phone number?
9. These are (my/ mine) new shoes. Do you like (it/ them)?
10. I can't find my keys. Where are (they/ them)?

**2.** 빈칸에 this 또는 these를 쓰시오.

1. "Do you like _____ glasses?" "Yes, I like them."
2. "Is _____ your book?" "Yes, it's mine."
3. "Do you like _____ picture?" "Yes, I like it."
4. _____ flowers are for you.
5. _____ coat was very expensive, but it's very nice.

**3.** 빈칸에 that 또는 those를 쓰시오.

1. Who's _____ boy?
2. Look at _____ skirts. They are very nice.
3. _____ girl is Heather.
4. "Betty is a good singer." "Really? I didn't know _____."
5. _____ questions are pretty difficult.

**4.** 보기와 같이 빈칸을 채우시오.

> 보기 | Is this/that your pen? - Yes, it is.
> Are these/those your pens? - Yes, they are.

1. Is this your bag? - Yes, _____ is.
2. Is that your umbrella? - Yes, _____ is.
3. Are these shoes yours? - Yes, _____ are.
4. Are those your friends? - Yes, _____ are.

# Writing Pattern Practice

**1.** 「I/We/You/You/He/She/It/They + 동사~」 '나는/우리는/너는/너희는/그는/그녀는/그것은/그들은 …다'

나는 학생이야. _____

우리는 의사들이야. _____

너는 예쁘구나. _____

너희들은 길을 잃었구나.(lost) _____

그는 여기에 있어. _____

그녀는 영어공부를 열심히 해. _____

그것은 사실이야.(true) _____

그들은 서로 사랑해. _____

**2.** 「my/our/your/your/his/her/its/their + 명사」 '나의/우리의/너의/너희의/그의/그녀의/그것의/그들의 …'

나의 이름은 Sonia야. _____

나는 그의 전화번호를 몰라. _____

너의 이름은 뭐니? _____

너의 오빠는 학생이니? _____

나는 그녀의 미소가 좋아. _____

그것의 꼬리는 길어.(tail) _____

**3.** 「~ 동사+me/us/you/you/him/her/it/them」 '나를/우리를/너를/너희를/그를/그녀를/그것을/그들을 …한다'

우리 부모님은 나를 사랑하신다. _____

우리에게 돈 좀 줘. _____

나는 너희들을 그리워해.(miss) _____

Cindy가 그를 초대했어. _____

나는 그녀를 봤어. _____

나는 내 여자친구에게 그것을 받았어.(get) _____

나는 그것들을 어제 샀어. _____

**4.** 「my/our/your/your/his/her/its/their+명사」 = 「mine/ours/yours/yours/his/hers/theirs」
'나의 것/우리의 것/너의 것/너희들의 것/그의 것/그녀의 것/그것의 것/그들의 것'

그것은 내거야. _____

이 차는 우리 것이 아니야. _____

이 신발이 너의 것이니? _____

나의 집은 그의 것보다 크다. _____

그 생각은 그녀의 것이었다. (That idea~) _____

이 차는 그들의 것이니? _____


**5.** 「this/these/that/those」 '이것/이것들/저것/저것들'

이것은 뭐니? _____

이것을 봐.(look at) _____

이것늘는 무엇이니? _____

저것은 너의 우산이니? _____

저 사람이 Mary니? _____

저것들은 내 책들이야. _____

저분들이 너희 부모님이시니? _____


**6.** 「this/these/that/those + 명사」 '이것의/이것들의/저것의/저것들의…'

이 코트는 정말 비싸. _____

나는 이 책을 원한다. _____

나는 이 책들을 원한다. _____

이 안경 마음에 드니?(like, glasses) _____

이 꽃들은 너를 위한 거야. _____

저 여자애가 내 딸이야. _____

저 남자는 누구니? _____

저 치마들을 봐. _____

그 문제들은 꽤 어려워.(pretty) _____

# 09 | 부정대명사

A: Let's go to a Japanese restaurant. I feel like eating Sushi.

B: That sounds good. Let's go.

A: Let me take out some money first. Is there an ATM near here?

B: Yes, there's one on the corner.

*take out some money 돈을 찾다

---

**1.** 부정대명사는 특별히 정해지지 않은 사람이나 사물을 가리킬 때 쓴다.

one, some, any, -body, -one, -thing, all, none, both, either, neither 등이 이에 속한다.

● **one 하나** : 같은 종류의 사람이나 사물 *반면에 it은 앞에 정해진 명사, 즉 the+명사를 다시 받는다.

"Do you have a pen?" 너 펜 있니?

"Yes, I have **one**."(= a pen) 응, 하나 있어.

"These tangerines taste really good. Would you like **one**?"(= a tangerine)

이 귤 정말 맛있어. 하나 줄까?

"Yes, please." 응.

● **some, any 몇몇/ 약간** : some- 막연한 수량(약간)을 나타내고 주로 긍정문에 쓰임. any- 의문문에서 막연한 수량(약간)을 나타내고 부정문에서는 not과 함께 '전혀 ~않다' 라는 뜻으로 쓰임.

I didn't eat any cookies, but Liz ate **some**.(=some cookies)

나는 과자를 안 먹었지만 Liz는 좀 먹었다.

"Do you need any money?" "No, I don't need **any**." (=any money)

돈이 좀 필요해? 아니, 전혀 필요하지 않아.

● **-body, -one, -thing 누군가, 어떤 것**: 긍정문은 'some-'을 부정문과 의문문은 'any-' 를 쓰는데 상대방에게 권유할 때는 'some-'을 쓴다.

"**Somebody**(or **Someone**) wants to see you." 누군가 너를 보고 싶어하는데.

"I'm sorry, but I don't want to see **anybody**(or **anyone**) now."

미안하지만 지금은 아무도 보고 싶지 않아.

"Do you want **something** to drink?" 마실 거줄까?

"No, thank you. I don't want **anything**." 고맙지만 됐어. 아무 것도 원하지 않아.

- all, none 모두, 하나도~아님: 「all」 또는 「all+of+the+명사」 형태로 쓰기도 한다.

  **All** of them are happy. 그들 모두가 행복하다.

  I invited **all** of my friends to my birthday party. 나는 내 생일파티에 내 친구 모두를 초대했다.

  "How many people came to the party?" "**None**"

  파티에 몇 명이 왔니? 아무도 안 왔어.

- both, either, neither 둘 다, 둘 중 어느 것이나, 둘 중 어느 것도 아닌 것

  「both/either/neither」 또는 「both/either/neither+of+the+명사」 형태로 쓰기도 한다.

  I have two sisters. **Both** are in the United States.

  두 언니가 있는데 둘 다 미국에 살아요.

  Here or to go? You can choose **either**.

  여기서 드실래요, 포장해 가실래요? 둘 중하나 선택하실 수 있어요.

  **Neither** of my parents speaks English. 부모님 중 아무도 영어를 못하신다.


**2.** 부정대명사 some, any, all, both, either, neither 등은 형용사 역할을 하기도 한다.

  "Is there **any** milk in the fridge?" 냉장고에 우유 좀 있어?

  **All** children need love. 모든 아이들은 사랑을 필요로 한다.

  Come to my place on Monday or Tuesday. **Either** day is fine with me.

  우리 집에 월요일이나 화요일에 와. 나는 둘 중 아무 날이나 좋아.

# Unit Test

**1.** 문장의 괄호 안에서 알맞은 것을 골라 동그라미 하시오.

1. "Do you have a pencil?" "Yes, I have (one/ it)."
2. This cake tastes really good. Would you like (some/ one)?
3. I have a stomachache. I don't want to eat (something/ anything).
4. "Did you buy any bread?" "Yes, I bought (some/ any)."
5. All of them (is/ are) present at the meeting.

**2.** 빈칸에 something/ somebody/ anything/ anybody 중 하나를 써 넣으시오.

1. I didn't eat _____.
2. I'm bored. I want to do _____ fun.
3. Sally went shopping, but she didn't buy _____.
4. "What happened to him?" "_____ broke into his house and stole _____.
5. There is _____ to eat on the table.
6. I don't have _____ to talk to.
7. Are you doing _____ tonight?
8. I'm supposed to meet _____ in the afternoon.
9. Would you like _____ to drink?
10. There is _____ in the kitchen.

**3.** 우리말과 일치하도록 괄호 안의 단어를 알맞게 배열하시오.

1. 뭔가 나에게 말을 해봐.(something/ say/ to me)

_____

2. 나는 아무 말도 하지 않았어요. (I/ say/ didn't/ anything)

_____

3. 누군가 너한테 전화했었어. (called/ somebody/ you)

_____

4. 아무도 없어요. (isn't/ there/ anybody/ here)

_____

5. 두개다 비싸다. (are/ both/ expensive.)

_____

6. 너는 그것들 중 하나를 가져도 좋아. (can/ you/ either of them/ have)

_____

7. 우리 중 아무도 배고프지 않다. (of us/ neither/ hungry/ is)

_____

# Writing Pattern Practice

**1.** one 하나

"Do you have a pen?" "응, 하나 있어." _____

These apples taste really good. 하나 줄까? (Would you like~) _____

**2.** some, any 몇몇/ 약간

나는 과자를 전혀 안 먹었지만 Liz는 좀 먹었다.(any cookies) _____

"너 돈이 좀 필요해?" "아니, 전혀 필요하지 않아." _____

**3.** -body, -one, -thing 누군가, 어떤 것

누군가 너를 보고 싶어하는데.(-body) _____

여기에 누구 있어?(-body) _____

사람들 다 어디 있어?(-one) _____

나는 뭔가 따뜻한 게 필요해. _____

나는 뭔가 나쁜 짓을 했어. _____

나는 누군가 새로운 사람을 만나기를 원해.(-body new) _____

무슨 일인가 벌어났어.(happen) _____

**4.** all, none 모두, 하나도 …아님

그들 모두가 행복해. _____

나는 내 생일파티에 내 친구 모두를 초대했다.(all of my friends) _____

여기에 아무도 없어.(none : 보통 복수취급) _____

**5.** both, either, neither 둘 다, 둘 중 어느 것이나, 둘 중 어느 것도 아닌 것

둘 다 미국에 있지.(the United States) _____

당신은 둘 중하나 선택하실 수 있어요.(take) _____

부모님 중 아무도 영어를 못하셔.(Neither of~) _____

Grammar
in
Practice

A: Look at yourself in the mirror. You look terrible.
B: I fell down and hurt myself on the way here.
A: Oh, your knee is bleeding. I think you'd better see a doctor.
B: No, I'm going to put some *iodine on it. It'll be OK.

*iodine: 소독약

Grammar
in
Use

**1.** 재귀대명사란 '~자신'이라는 뜻으로 주어를 다시 목적어로 쓰거나 주어나 목적어를 강조할 때 쓴다.

| I – myself | | you(너) – yourself | |
|---|---|---|---|
| he – himself | she – herself | it – itself | |
| you(너희들) – yourselves | we – ourselves | they – themselves | |

**2.** 주어를 다시 목적어로 쓰는 경우에 사용한다.

I cut **myself**. 나는 베었다.

Cindy looked at **herself** in the mirror. (herself=Cindy)
그녀는 그녀 자신을 거울에 비춰보았다.

My friends and I had a great time at the party. We enjoyed **ourselves**.
(ourselves=my friends and I)
친구들과 나는 파티에서 즐거운 시간을 보냈다. 우리는 즐겼다.

**3.** 주어나 목적어를 강조하는 경우에 사용한다.

I want to do it **myself**. 나는 직접 그것을 하고 싶다.

The house **itself** was humble, but the garden was beautiful.
집 자체는 변변치 않았지만 정원은 아름다웠다.

**4.** 재귀대명사를 이용한 표현은 다음과 같다

by oneself 홀로
talk to oneself 혼잣말하다
in itself 본래
help oneself 마음껏 먹다
make oneself at home(=make oneself comfortable) 편히 있다

for(by) oneself 혼자 힘으로
of itself 저절로
enjoy oneself 즐기다

*of oneself와 for oneself는 현대영어에서는 잘 쓰이지 않는다.

46

# Unit Test

**1.** 알맞은 재귀대명사를 쓰시오.

I - _____     you(너) - _____     you(너희들) - _____
he - _____     she - _____     it - _____
we - _____     they - _____


**2.** 재귀대명사를 써서 빈칸을 채우시오.

1. Look at _____. (상대방이 한명일 때) You look great today.
2. Jane and Henry went on a picnic. They enjoyed _____.
3. Dinner is ready. Help _____. (상대방이 두 명 이상일 때)
4. She cut _____ with a knife.
5. Bill had a cold. He took some medicine and took are of _____.
6. Jennifer is not angry with us. She is angry with _____.
7. Mrs. Smith killed _____.
8. Please make _____ at home. (상대방이 한명일 때)
9. Please tell me something about _____. (상대방이 두 명 이상일 때)
10. My brother fell down the stairs, but he didn't hurt _____.


**3.** 보기에서 빈칸에 들어갈 말을 골라 인칭에 맞게 고쳐 쓰시오.

| 보기 | by oneself    for oneself    oneself |

1. 나는 혼자 산다.
   → I live _____ .

2. 너는 혼자 힘으로 모든 일을 해내야해.
   → You have to do everything _____ .

3. 오늘 네가 오늘 즐거운 시간보내길 바란다.
   → I hope you enjoy _____ today.

4. 편안히 계세요. (상대방이 한명일 때)
   → Make _____ comfortable

5. Mary는 가끔 혼잣말을 한다.
   → Mary sometimes talks to _____ .

# Writing Pattern Practice

**1.** 주어를 다시 목적어로 쓰는 경우
myself/ yourself/ himself/ herself/ itself/ yourselves/ ourselves/ themselves

너 자신을 봐. _____

나는 비었어. _____

나는 다쳤어. _____

내가 내 소개할게.(I'll~) _____

그녀는 그녀자신을 거울에 비춰보았다. _____

우리는 즐겼다. _____

**2.** 주어나 목적어를 강조하는 경우
myself/ yourself/ himself/ herself/ itself/ yourselves/ ourselves/ themselves

내가 직접 그것을 하고 싶어 _____

내가 직접 그것을 보고 싶어. _____

너는 숙제를 네가 직접 하는 게 좋아.('d better) _____

그는 직접 그 케익을 만들었다. _____

**3.** 재귀대명사를 이용한 표현
by oneself (홀로)/ say(talk) to oneself(혼잣말하다)/ in itself(본래)/ enjoy oneself(즐기다)
help oneself(마음껏 먹다)/ make oneself at home(=make oneself comfortable)(편히 있다)

나는 혼자 산다. _____

나는 혼자 힘으로 그것을 끝마쳤다.(finish, by oneself) _____

Mary는 가끔 혼잣말을 한다.(talk) _____

우리는 파티에서 즐거웠다.(enjoy) _____

마음껏 먹어.(yourself) _____

편안히 있어.(yourself) _____

# 11 | it의 특별한 쓰임

Grammar in Practice

A: **It**'s freezing.

B: Yes, it is. What time is it?

A: **It**'s ten to four. We've waited for David for about an hour.

B: We'd better go. I think he forgot our appointment.

A: OK. Here comes the bus. Let's just go.

Grammar in Use

**1.** 막연한 시간, 날씨, 요일, 날짜, 거리, 상황 등을 가리킬 때 it을 쓴다. 이 때 it은 해석하지 않는다.

● 시간

"What time is **it**?" "**It**'s a quarter to seven." 몇 시야? 6시 45분이야.

● 날씨

"How's the weather?" 날씨가 어때?

"**It**'s hot/ warm/ cool/ chilly(쌀쌀한)/ cold/ freezing(얼어붙는)/ dry/ humid(습기찬)/ sunny/ foggy(안개낀)/ windy/ cloudy" 등.

● 요일

"What day is **it** today?" "**It**'s Wednesday." 오늘이 무슨 요일이야? 수요일이야.

● 날짜

"What date is **it** today?" "**It**'s July 24th." 오늘이 며칠이야? 7월24일이야.

"What month is **it**?" "**It**'s February." 몇 월이야? 2월이야.

● 거리

"How far is **it**?" "**It**'s about ten kilometers from here." 얼마나 멀어? 여기서 10km 정도야.

● 상황

"How is **it** going?" "**It**'s going well." 어떻게 되어가? 잘되고 있어.

**2.** 가주어 it은 주어가 길 때 주어를 대신하며 진짜 주어는 뒤로 보낼 수 있다.

To get up early is difficult. (to get up early – 진짜주어)

→ **It**'s difficult to get up early. 일찍 일어나는 것은 어렵다.

# Unit Test

**1.** 보기와 같이 그림의 날씨를 묘사하시오.

> 보기 | It's snowing.

1. _____   2. _____   3. _____

**2.** 주어진 대답이 나올 수 있도록 질문을 쓰시오.

1. A: _____?
   B: It's Tuesday.
2. A: _____?
   B: It's December 24th.
3. A: _____?
   B: It's half past nine.
4. A: _____?
   B: It's a long way from here.
5. A: _____?
   B: It's hot and humid.

**3.** A와 B에서 적당한 말을 찾아 빈칸을 채우시오.

| | A | | B |
|---|---|---|---|
| It's | easy<br>impossible<br>nice<br>dangerous | to | finish it by then<br>meet you<br>travel by yourself<br>understand |

1. My name is David._____
2. I have to hand in the report by tomorrow, but _____
3. Don't go._____
4. Susan speaks English slowly, so _____

# Writing Pattern Practice

**1.** 시간 it

몇 시니?

6시 정각이야.

**2.** 날씨 it

더워.

따뜻해.

시원해.

쌀쌀해.(chilly)

추워.

몹시 추워.(freezing)

건조해.

후덥지근해.(hot and humid)

화창해.

안개 꼈어.

바람불어.

구름 꼈어.

**3.** 요일 it

수요일이야.

토요일이야.

일요일이야.

**4.** 날짜 it

2월이야.

1월 1일이야.

7월 24일이야.

**5.** 거리 it

은행까지 5마일이야.

여기서 10km 정도야.(from here)

**6.** 상황 it

어떻게 되어가고 있어?

잘되고 있어.

# REVIEW 1

**1.** 보기를 참고하여 밑줄 친 대명사가 가리키는 말에 동그라미 하시오.

> 보기 | This is my laptop computer. I bought it yesterday.

① I take a computer class. <u>It</u>'s really fun.

② Mary is my best friend. <u>She</u>'s from Australia.

③ I bought these shoes in Italy. <u>They</u> were very expensive.

④ Please come to my party. <u>It</u> begins at 8 o'clock.

⑤ Look at that beautiful girl. Is <u>she</u> Mike's girlfriend?

**2.** 다음 영어 문장을 우리말로 쓰시오.

① Somebody wants to see you.    → _____

② All of them are happy.    → _____

③ Do you want something to drink?    → _____

④ Both of us are 15 years old.    → _____

⑤ Neither of my parents speaks English.    → _____

**3.** 밑줄 친 곳을 바르게 고치시오.

① Mom and Dad really love <u>I</u>.    → _____

② David cleaned <u>him</u> room and went out.    → _____

③ All of them <u>is</u> happy.    → _____

④ <u>Jason and me</u> help each other.    → _____

⑤ <u>This is</u> my sisters.    → _____

⑥ Look at <u>that stars</u>. They are so beautiful.    → _____

⑦ "Are those your pens?" "Yes, <u>it is</u>."    → _____

⑧ "Do you have any money?" "No, I don't have <u>some</u>."    → _____

⑨ I think you hurt <u>you</u>.    → _____

⑩ I cut <u>me</u>.    → _____

**4.** 둘 중에서 알맞은 것을 골라 동그라미 하시오.

① "Do you have a laptop computer?" "Yes, I have (it/ one)."

② Susan has a toy car. (It's/ Its) door is broken.

③ What's that? (There/ It) is a rabbit.

④ All of my friends (live/ lives) in Canada.

⑤ Let me introduce (me/ myself).

[1-2] 밑줄 친 명사와 바꾸어 쓸 수 있는 단어를 고르시오.

**1.** <u>Tom and I</u> are friends.

① I     ② You
③ We    ④ They
⑤ It

**2.** <u>Janet and you</u> look very good today.

① I     ② You
③ We    ④ They
⑤ It

[3-6] 괄호 안에 들어갈 알맞은 대명사를 고르시오.

**3.** Cindy is a teacher. _____ teaches music.

① I     ② You
③ She    ④ We
⑤ They

**4.** "What are these?" "_____ are roses."

① I     ② You
③ She    ④ We
⑤ They

**5.** "Do you have a pen?"
   "Yes, I have _____ ."

① one     ② it
③ any     ④ both
⑤ either

**6.** "Is there any milk in the fridge?"
   "Yes, there is _____ ."

① one     ② it
③ some    ④ any
⑤ all

**7.** 밑줄 친 재귀대명사가 <u>다르게</u> 쓰인 하나를 고르시오.

① Look at <u>yourself</u>.
② Julian cut <u>himself</u>.
③ We enjoyed <u>ourselves</u>.
④ I did it <u>myself</u>.
⑤ I'll introduce <u>myself</u> to you.

**8.** 밑줄 친 it의 쓰임이 <u>다른</u> 하나를 고르시오.

① What time is <u>it</u>?
② <u>It</u>'s Tuesday.
③ <u>It</u>'s January.
④ <u>It</u>'s far from here.
⑤ <u>It</u>'s good to see you.

**9.** 다음 글을 읽고 밑줄친 them이 가리키는 것을 고르시오.

① Christmas trees
② lights
③ presents
④ stockings
⑤ ornaments

Christmas is celebrated in Korea and all over the world. It is on December 25th. During the Christmas season, people decorate their houses with lights and ornaments. Christmas trees are also decorated. Presents are put under <u>them</u>.

Christmas Eve is the day before Christmas. Some children hang stockings by a fire place and wish for presents from Santa. We all like Christmas very much.

*ornament 장식 *stocking 목이 긴 양말

# \*Chapter 3 | 형용사와 부사

# 12 | 형용사의 쓰임

Grammar in Practice

A: What a nice dress!
B: I wanted to wear something special today.
A: You look good in it.
B: Thank you.

Grammar in Use

**1.** 형용사는 사물이나 사람의 상태, 모양 등을 나타낸다.
- big(큰), kind(친절한), terrific(매우 좋은), messy(지저분한)
- British(영국의), American(미국의), French(프랑스의), Dutch(네덜란드의)
- interesting(흥미를 주는)/ interested(흥미를 느끼는), tiring(피곤하게 하는)/ tired(피곤함을 느끼는), boring(지루하게 하는)/ bored(지루함을 느끼는)

**2.** 형용사가 명사를 앞에서 수식한다. [형용사+명사]
You are a **nice** person. 당신은 멋진 사람이다.
She has a **beautiful** smile. 그녀는 아름다운 미소를 가졌다.

**3.** 명사가 something, anything, somebody, anybody, somewhere 등일 경우 형용사가 뒤에서 수식한다. [명사+형용사]
She did something **bad**. 그녀는 나쁜 무언가를 했다.
I met somebody **new**. 나는 새로운 누군가를 만났다.

**4.** 우리말로 '비싼 시계'를 '시계가 비싸다'라고도 하듯이 be동사 다음 형용사를 쓸 수도 있다. [be동사(am/are/is)+형용사]
My brother is **smart**. 내 남동생은 똑똑하다.
These flowers are so **beautiful**. 이 꽃들은 정말 아름답다.

**5.** 감각동사 다음에 와서 주어의 상태를 설명한다. [감각동사(look/feel/smell/taste/sound)+형용사]
You **look** tired. 너 피곤해 보인다.
It **feels** soft. 그것은 부드러운 느낌이다.
This fish **smells** bad. 이 생선은 냄새가 나쁘다(상했다).
Does it **taste** good? 그것은 맛이 좋아?
It **sounds** good. 그거 좋게 들리는데.

# Unit Test

**1.** 보기에서 알맞은 형용사를 골라 그림을 설명하시오.

> 보기 | Japanese   raining   surprised   boring   cold

1. That movie is _____   2. It's _____   3. It's _____ .

4. He was very _____   5. She likes _____ food.

**2.** 알맞은 말에 동그라미 하시오.

1. It sounds (interested/ interesting).

2. That movie is very (shocked/ shocking).

3. Do you feel (tired/ tiring)?

4. The classical music concert was (bored/ boring).

5. Is the story (excited/ exciting)?

**3.** 우리말과 일치하도록 괄호 안의 단어를 알맞게 배열하시오.

1. Laura는 갈색 눈을 가지고 있다. (has/ Laura/ eyes/ brown)

_____

2. 그들은 새 아파트에 산다. (new/ live/ they / a / apartment / in)

_____

3. 나 피곤해 보이니? (I/ do/ tired/ look/ ?)

_____

4. 나는 지루하지 않다. (I/ bored/ don't/ feel)

_____

5. 이 책은 흥미롭지 않다. (isn't/ this book/ interesting)

_____

# Writing Pattern Practice

**1.** 「형용사 + 명사」

당신은 멋진 사람이다.(nice) _____

그녀는 아름다운 미소를 가졌다. _____

David은 멋진 차를 가지고 있다.(great) _____

그것은 흥미로운 책이다. _____

Jason은 지루한 사람이다. _____

**2.** 「명사(something, anything, somebody, anybody, somewhere) + 형용사」

나는 뭔가 새로운 것이 필요하다. _____

그녀는 좋은 무언가를 했다.(something) _____

우리는 나쁜 어떤 짓도 하지 않았다. _____

나는 새로운 누군가를 만났다. _____

**3.** 「be동사(am/are/is) + 형용사」

나는 피곤하다. _____

나는 두렵다.(afraid) _____

너는 매력적이다.(attractive) _____

너는 말랐다.(skinny) _____

내 남동생은 똑똑하다. _____

인생은 짧다. _____

이 꽃들은 정말 아름답다.(so) _____

이 가방들은 작다. _____

**4.** 「look/feel/smell/taste/sound + 형용사」

너 피곤해 보인다. _____

그들은 지루해 보인다. _____

그것은 부드러운 느낌이다. _____

나는 아픈 느낌이다. _____

이 생선은 냄새가 나쁘다. _____

뭔가 좋은 냄새가 난다.(good) _____

그것은 맛이 좋아?(good) _____

이 수프는 맛이 정말 좋다.(terrific) _____

그것 좋게 들린다.(good) _____

그 음악은 환상적으로 들린다.(fantastic) _____

# 13 | 수량형용사

**Grammar in Practice**

A: Where will we have our meeting?
B: On the second floor.
A: Are there a lot of people up there?
B: There are some, but not many. I think you'd better hurry up.

**Grammar in Use**

**1.** 수와 양을 표시하는 형용사는 셀 수 있는 명사의 셀 수 없는 명사 앞에서 구분하여 쓴다.

| 셀 수 있는 명사 | 셀 수 없는 명사 |
| --- | --- |
| many(많은), a few(약간의), few(거의 없는) | much(많은), a little (약간의), little(거의 없는) |
| 공통으로 사용 a lot of/ lots of(많은), some/any(약간의) | |

| **MORE** TIPS | some은 긍정문과 권유의 의문문에, any는 부정문과 의문문에 쓴다.
I have some cake. 나는 케익을 좀 가지고 있다.    Would you like some cake? 케익 좀 먹을래?
There isn't any juice. 주스가 전혀 없어.    Do you have any juice? 주스 좀 있니?

**2.** 숫자를 나타내는 수사는 기본적인 수를 나타내는 기수와 순서나 서열을 나타내는 서수가 있다.

| | 기수 | 서수 | | 기수 | 서수 |
| --- | --- | --- | --- | --- | --- |
| 1 | one | first(1st) | 18 | eighteen | eighteenth(18th) |
| 2 | two | second(2nd) | 19 | nineteen | nineteenth(19th) |
| 3 | three | third(3rd) | 20 | twenty | twentieth(20th) |
| 4 | four | fourth(4th) | 21 | twenty-one | twenty-first(21st) |
| 5 | five | fifth(5th) | 30 | thirty | thirtieth(30th) |
| 6 | six | sixth(6th) | 40 | forty | fortieth(40th) |
| 7 | seven | seventh(7th) | 50 | fifty | fiftieth(50th) |
| 8 | eight | eighth(8th) | 60 | sixty | sixtieth(60th) |
| 9 | nine | ninth(9th) | 70 | seventy | seventieth(70th) |
| 10 | ten | tenth(10th) | 80 | eighty | eightieth(80th) |
| 11 | eleven | eleventh(11th) | 90 | ninety | ninetieth(90th) |
| 12 | twelve | twelfth(12th) | 100 | one hundred | one hundredth(100th) |
| 13 | thirteen | thirteenth(13th) | 200 | two hundred | two hundredth(200th) |
| 14 | fourteen | fourteenth(14th) | 1000 | one thousand | one thousandth(1,000th) |
| 15 | fifteen | fifteenth(15th) | 만 | ten thousand | ten thousandth(10,000th) |
| 16 | sixteen | sixteenth(16th) | 백만 | million | millionth |
| 17 | seventeen | seventeenth(17th) | 십억 | billion | billionth |

# Unit Test

**1.** 기수와 서수를 서로 바꾸어 쓰시오.

one - _____    second - _____    third - _____    five - _____    eight - _____

nine - _____    twelve - _____    twenty - _____    fortieth - _____


**2.** 둘 중 알맞은 말에 동그라미 하시오.

1. They don't have (many/ much) snow in Tokyo.
2. Did you buy (many/ much) apples?
3. We don't have (many/ much) luggage.
4. There wasn't (many/ much) food in the fridge.
5. Were there (many/ much) people in the restaurant?


**3.** 보기 중 가장 알맞은 말을 골라 빈칸에 써 넣으시오.

| 보기 | a few    few    a little    little |
| --- | --- |

1. I'll be there in _____ minutes.
2. There was _____ traffic, so we got there 10 minutes early.
3. I have _____ friends. I feel lonely all the time.
4. May I ask you _____ questions?
5. There was _____ snow last winter, so I hope there will be snow this winter.
6. Be careful! There were _____ accidents right here.
7. "Are there any good movies playing?" "Yes, _____ "
8. "When did Sarah leave?" " _____ hours ago"
9. "Do you need any boxes?" "Yes, _____ "
10. "Would you like some more water?" "Yes, _____ "


**4.** 우리말과 일치하도록 괄호 안의 단어를 알맞게 배열하시오.

1. 나는 약간의 물을 마셨다. (a little/ I/ drank/ water)

_____

2. Jack은 돈이 거의 없다. (little/ has/ Jack/ money)

_____

3. 여기 사람들이 거의 없습니다. (people/ few/ there/ are/ here)

_____

4. 나는 일본어 몇 마디를 안다. (a few/ know/ I/ words of Japanese)

_____

5. Sally는 실수를 거의 안한다. (makes/ few/ Sally/ mistakes)

_____

# Writing Pattern Practice

**1.** many/ much '많은'

사람들이 많이 있니? _____

사람들이 많이 없어. _____

동경에는 눈이 많이 있니?(Is there~) _____

동경에는 눈이 많이 없어. _____

너는 많은 돈을 가지고 있니? _____

나는 많은 돈을 가지고 있지 않아. _____


**2.** a few/ a little '약간의'

나는 일본어 몇 마디를 안다.(words of Japanese) _____

내가 몇 분 후에 거기에 도착할거야.(be there in~) _____

나는 약간의 물을 마셨어. _____

나는 약간의 과일을 샀어.(fruit) _____


**3.** few/ little '거의 없는'

Sally는 실수를 거의 안 해.(make, mistakes) _____

여기 사람들이 거의 없어. _____

Jack은 돈이 거의 없어. _____

난은 돈이 거의 없어.(There's + 비) _____


**4.** a lot of(=lots of) '많은'

나는 많은 친구가 있어. _____

Bob은 많은 돈을 번다.(make) _____


**5.** some/any '약간의'

우리 우유 좀 사자. _____

토요일에는 수업이 없어.(classes) _____

너는 커피를 좀 먹을래?(Would you like~) _____


**6.** one, two, three~ '하나, 둘, 셋…'

사과 하나가 있어. _____

배 두개가 있어. _____


**7.** first, second, third~ '첫 번째, 두 번째, 세 번째…'

나는 1층에 있어.(floor) _____

이것이 내 두 번째 시도야.(second) _____

# 14 부사의 쓰임

**Grammar in Practice**

A: How's the weather out there?
B: It's raining heavily.
A: Really? It was sunny this morning.
B: It started to rain suddenly. I think it'll *let up soon.

*let up 안개나 비등이 그치다, 잦아들다

---

**Grammar in Use**

**1.** 부사는 동사, 형용사, 다른 부사, 또는 문장 전체를 수식한다.

● 동사수식　My family <u>lives</u> **here.** 나의 가족은 여기에 산다.

● 형용사수식　You are **so** <u>beautiful</u>. 너는 정말 아름답다.

● 다른 부사수식　I walked **very** <u>carefully</u>. 나는 매우 조심스럽게 걸었다.

● 문장 전체수식　**Happily,** <u>he got all As</u>. 기쁘게도 그는 전부 A를 받았다.

**| MORE TIPS |** 일반적으로 부사의 어순은 동사는 뒤에서 수식하고 형용사, 부사, 구, 절은 앞에서 수식한다.

**2.** 대부분의 부사는 형용사에 '-ly'를 붙여서 쓴다.

happy → happily(행복한-행복하게),　easy → easily(쉬운-쉽게),
gentle → gently(부드러운-부드럽게),　extreme → extremely(극도의-극도로),
terrible → terribly(끔찍한-끔찍하게),　sudden → suddenly(갑작스러운-갑자기)

**| MORE TIPS |** -ly로 끝나는 형용사가 있음을 주의한다.
friendly(정다운), lovely(사랑스러운), curly(곱슬의), ugly(못생긴,추한), silly(어리석은) 등

**3.** 형용사와 부사의 형태가 같은 단어가 있다.

John's job is very **hard.** (형) John의 일은 정말 힘들다.
John works very **hard.** (부) John은 정말 열심히 일한다.
People like **fast** food. (형) 사람들은 패스트푸드를 좋아한다.
People eat **fast** in Korea. (부) 한국에서 사람들은 빨리 먹는다.
My father was **late** for work. (형) 아버지가 회사에 늦으셨다.
My father came back home **late.** (부) 아버지가 집에 늦게 돌아오셨다.
Karen is an **early** riser. (형) Karen은 일찍 일어나는 사람이다.
Karen gets up **early.** (부) Karen은 일찍 일어난다.
She has **straight** hair. (형) 그녀는 곧은 머리야.
Go **straight** for two blocks. (부) 두 블럭을 쭉 가.

**4.** 형용사에 -ly를 붙여 뜻이 달라지는 경우도 있다.

hard(어려운) →hardly(거의~않다), late(늦은)→lately(최근에), high(높은)→highly(아주)

# Unit Test

**1.** 그림을 참고하여 보기 중 알맞은 말을 골라 빈칸에 써 넣으시오.

1.
2.
3.

| 보기 | heavily      early      well |
| --- | --- |

1. She gets up _____ .
2. He speaks English very _____ .
3. It's snowing _____ .

**2.** 다음 문장에서 부사에 동그라미 하시오.

1. Her silk scarf was very expensive.
2. Listen carefully and repeat after me.
3. He came here by bus.
4. Are you going back to the United States?
5. It's really freezing.

**3.** 둘 중 알맞은 것에 동그라미 하시오.

1. I'll go there (quick/ quickly).
2. Be (careful/ carefully).
3. They lived (happy/ happily) ever after.
4. He speaks too (fast/ fastly). I can hardly understand him.
5. She's studying (hard/ hardly) for her final exams.
6. Something smells really (nice/ nicely).
7. I'm sleepy. I went to bed (late/ lately) last night.
8. I feel (nervous/ nervously) when I'm in front of a lot of people.

**4.** 밑줄 친 부사가 수식하는 말에 동그라미 하시오.

1. I'll be <u>right</u> there.
2. Thank you <u>very</u> much.
3. <u>Luckily</u>, he won the first prize.
4. He studies <u>only</u> at night.
5. You speak English <u>quite</u> well.

# Writing Pattern Practice

**1.** **부사가 동사를 수식**

나의 가족은 여기에 산다.

한국에서 사람들은 빨리 먹는다.

아버지가 집에 늦게 돌아오셨다.

Karen은 일찍 일어난다.

두 블럭을 쭉 가.(straight)

Nina는 요리를 잘한다.

기차가 5분 늦게 도착했다.(five minutes late)

나는 최근에 흥미로운 책을 읽었다.(I've~, interesting, lately)


**2.** **부사가 형용사를 수식**

너는 정말 아름답다.(so)

John은 정말 열심히 일한다.(very)

그녀의 실크 스카프는 매우 비쌌다.(very)

오늘밤 정말 춥다.(really freezing)

저 영화는 정말 충격적이었어.(really shocking)


**3.** **부사가 다른 부사를 수식**

나는 매우 조심스럽게 걸었다.(very)

그녀는 영어를 매우 잘한다.(very)

거북이들은 매우 늦게 걷는다.(very)

나 곧바로 거기에 갈께.(be, right)

너 영어 꽤 잘하는구나.(speak, quite)


**4.** **부사가 문장 전체를 수식**

기쁘게도 그는 전부 A를 받았다.(get, all As)

다행히도 그녀는 시험에 합격했다.(Fortunately~ )

확실히 그녀는 그 직장을 얻을 것이다.(Certainly~)

# 15 부사의 종류

Grammar in Practice

A: Do you ever play tennis?
B: Yes, very often. I usually play tennis after work.
A: Are you a good player?
B: No, not really.

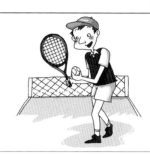

Grammar in Use

**1.** 시간부사 before, after, now, then

My brother came home 10 minutes **ago**. 남동생이 10분 전에 집에 왔다.
I've never been to Hawaii **before**. 나는 전에 하와이에 가본 적이 없다.
We're taking a break **now**. 우리는 지금 쉬고 있다.
Things will be different <u>then</u>. 그때는 상황이 달라질 거야.
현재, 미래 모두 쓰임

**2.** 장소부사 here, there, near

I've lived **here** since 2004. 나는 2004년 이래로 여기에 살아왔다.
I'll walk you **there**. 내가 거기에 너를 데려다 줄게.
Do you live **near** here? 여기 근처에 사니?

**3.** 빈도부사 always, usually, often, sometimes, rarely, hardly, never의 위치는 일반동사의 앞
이나 be동사 또는 조동사 다음에 온다.

I must **always** get up early. 나는 항상 일찍 일어나야한다.
I **usually** have breakfast. 나는 보통 아침을 먹는다.
I **often** play basketball with my friends. 나는 친구들과 자주 농구를 한다.
I **sometimes** eat Chinese food. 나는 가끔 중국 음식을 먹는다.
My father **rarely** gets angry. 아버지는 좀처럼 화를 내지 않으신다.
I'm **hardly** ever late for school. 나는 학교에 거의 늦지 않는다.
I **never** cheat. 나는 사기/커닝을 하지 않는다.

**4.** 의문부사 where, when, how, why

**Where** do you live? 너는 어디에 사니?
**When** do you study English? 너는 언제 공부하니?
**How** does your father get to work? 너의 아버지는 어떻게 회사 다니시니?
**Why** do you go to bed late every night? 너는 왜 매일 밤 잠자리에 늦게 드니?

**5.** 정도부사 so, very, much, a little, too, enough

You're **so** beautiful. 당신 정말 아름다워요.
You speak **too** fast to understand. 너는 너무 빨리 말해서 이해할 수 없다.
Your English is good **enough**. 네 영어는 충분히 훌륭해.
* 부사 enough와 형용사의 위치는 「형용사+enough」이다.

# Unit Test

**1.** 괄호 안의 단어를 알맞은 곳에 넣어서 다시 쓰시오.

1. He comes home late. (always) _____

2. My mother is busy. (usually) _____ _____

3. I can believe it. (hardly) _____

4. John calls me at night. (sometimes) _____

5. Kim is late. (often) _____

6. I eat too much. (never) _____

7. My grandfather brushes his teeth. (rarely) _____

**2.** 빈칸에 where, when, why, how 중 알맞은 것을 쓰시오.

1. "_____ do you live?" "I live in Malaysia."

2. "_____ do you exercise?" "I exercise every morning."

3. "_____ did you lose weight?" "I have been exercising."

4. "_____ didn't you do your homework?" "I was busy taking care of my brother."

**3.** 빈칸에 too 또는 enough를 써 넣으시오.

1. There is _____ much sugar in this coffee.

2. That hat isn't big _____ . You'd better try on a bigger one.

3. You're very skinny. I think you don't eat _____ .

4. I'm _____ tired to go dancing.

5. You speak _____ fast to understand.

**4.** 우리말과 일치하도록 괄호 안의 단어를 알맞게 배열하시오.

1. 나는 이탈리아 음식을 무척 많이 좋아한다.(much/ like/ very/ I/ Italian food)

_____

2. 그는 이틀 전에 떠났다. (two days/ left/ he/ ago)

_____

3. 내가 너를 거기에 차로 데려다 줄게. (drive/ I/ will/ you/ there)

_____

4. 나는 항상 너를 기억할 거야. (always/ will/ I/ remember/ you)

_____

5. 너는 보통 학교에 걸어가니? (to school/ walk/ you/ usually/ do/ ?)

_____

6. 이 집은 충분히 크지 않다. (big/ house/ this/ isn't/ enough)

_____

# Writing Pattern Practice

**1.** 시간부사 ago, before, after, now, then

남동생이 10분전에 집에 왔다.

나는 전에 하와이에 가본 적이 없다.(I've never~)

우리는 지금 쉬고 있다. (take a break)

그때는 상황이 달라질 거야.(Things, different)


**2.** 장소부사 here, there, near

나는 1999년 이래로 여기에 살아왔다.(since)

내가 거기에 너를 데려다 줄께.(walk you)

너는 여기 근처에 사니?


**3.** 빈도부사 always, usually, often, sometimes, rarely, hardly, never

나는 항상 일찍 일어나야한다.(must)

나는 보통 아침을 먹는다.

나는 친구들과 자주 농구를 한다.

나는 가끔 중국 음식을 먹는다.

아버지는 좀처럼 화를 내지 않으신다.(rarely get)

나는 학교에 거의 늦지 않는다.(hardly)

나는 사기/커닝을 절대 하지 않는다.(cheat)


**4.** 의문부사 where, when, how, why

너는 어디 사니?

너는 언제 영어 공부하니?

너의 아버지는 어떻게 회사 다니시니?(get to work)

너는 왜 매일 밤 잠자리에 늦게 드니?


**5.** 정도부사 so, very, much, little, enough

당신 정말 아름다워요.(so)

나는 매우 잘 지내고 있어요.(get along)

나는 그 콘서트에서 매우 지루했다.(much)

네 영어는 충분히 훌륭해.(good)

**1.** 다음 우리말을 영어로 바꿔 쓰시오.

① 흥미를 주는(excite)　　　　　→ _____
② 흥미를 느끼는(excite)　　　　→ _____
③ 피곤하게 하는(tire)　　　　　→ _____
④ 피곤함을 느끼는(tire)　　　　→ _____
⑤ 지루하게 하는(bore)　　　　　→ _____
⑥ 지루함을 느끼는(bore)　　　　→ _____

**2.** 다음 영어 문장을 우리말로 쓰시오.

① I met somebody new.　　　　→ _____
② She did something bad.　　　→ _____
③ Something smells bad.　　　　→ _____
④ It feels soft.　　　　　　　　→ _____
⑤ Does it taste good?　　　　　→ _____

**3.** 다음 중 틀린 곳을 바르게 고치시오.

① There aren't much people.　　　　　　　　　　→ _____
② I don't have some money.　　　　　　　　　　→ _____
③ Dave has little friends.　　　　　　　　　　　→ _____
④ I don't have much CDs.　　　　　　　　　　　→ _____
⑤ I have few time to waste.　　　　　　　　　　→ _____
⑥ There are a few book on the shelf.　　　　　　→ _____
⑦ I want to buy any new clothes.　　　　　　　　→ _____
⑧ Sarah left a little hours ago.　　　　　　　　　→ _____
⑨ There wasn't many food in the fridge.　　　　→ _____
⑩ There aren't much students in the classroom. → _____

**4.** 둘 중에서 알맞은 것을 골라 동그라미 하시오.

① I walked very (careful/ carefully).
② My father came back home (late/ lately) today.
③ You're (probable/ probably) right.
④ (Happy/ Happily), he got all As.
⑤ Sue has (curl/ curly) hair.
⑥ You're a (love/ lovely) person.
⑦ I'm (terrible/ terribly) sorry.
⑧ You speak English very (good/ well).
⑨ I was (bored very/ very bored) at the concert.
⑩ Your English is (enough good/ good enough).

**1.** 부사의 수식을 받을 수 있는 것을 고르시오.(4개)

① 명사
② 형용사
③ 동사
④ 부사
⑤ 문장전체

**2.** 형용사 – 부사가 알맞게 짝지어진 것은?

① happy(행복한) – happily(행복하게)
② hard(힘든) – hardly(힘들게)
③ late(늦은) – lately(늦게)
④ high(높은) – highly(높기)
⑤ fast(빠른) – fastly(빠르게)

**3.** 다음 중 부사의 위치가 <u>틀린</u> 것은?

① I always get up early.
② I usually have breakfast.
③ Ross often plays basketball.
④ Susan hardly is ever late for school.
⑤ We never cheat.

**4.** 다음 중 부사가 <u>아닌</u> 것은?

① gently
② easily
③ suddenly
④ friendly
⑤ terribly

**5.** 밑줄 친 서수가 알맞게 쓰인 것은?

① I'm on the <u>forth</u> floor.
② Jane is in the <u>fiveth</u> grade.
③ I got the <u>second</u> prize.
④ Liz couldn't answer the <u>nineth</u> question.
⑤ Her <u>twelveth</u> book came out.

[6–7] 빈 칸에 들어갈 수 없는 말을 고르시오.

**6.** The movie was _____ interesting.

① so
② very
③ really
④ highly
⑤ good

**7.** I have _____ homework.

① a lot of
② lots of
③ some
④ many
⑤ a little

**8.** There are _____ apples in the basket.

① a lot of
② lots of
③ some
④ many
⑤ a little

**9.** 다음 글을 읽고 밑줄 친 단어 중 품사가 <u>다른</u> 하나를 고르시오.

Look at the sky ①<u>during</u> the day.
You will ②<u>probably</u> see the sun. The sun is ③ <u>actually</u> one of the stars.
It gives us light and heat.
However, you can't see the moon or any stars during the day because the sun shines so ④<u>brightly</u>.
At night the sun shines on the other side of the earth, so we can see the moon ⑤<u>then</u>. At night you can also see other stars. Each star has its own name. Look at the sky right now. What do you see?

# *Chapter 4 | 비교

## Unit 16 형용사와 부사의 비교급

**Grammar in Practice**

A: This camera is too expensive. I need a less expensive one.
B: OK. I'll show you another. How about this one?
A: How much is that?
B: It is $20 cheaper than that one.

**Grammar in Use**

**1.** 비교급이란 형용사, 부사의 성질, 상태의 차이를 나타내기 위해 어미를 변화시키는 것이다.

[ 비교급 만드는 법 ]

- 단음절어: 원급 + -(e)r

  old → older    slow → slower    cheap → cheaper    nice → nicer    late → later

- 단모음+단자음으로 끝나는 단어: 마지막자음 + -er

  big → bigger    thin → thinner

- y로 끝나는 2음절어: -y → -ier

  easy → easier    heavy → heavier    early → earlier

- 대부분의 2음절어, 3음절어, -ed -ing로 끝나는 단어: more+원급

  careful → more careful    polite → more polite    beautiful → more beautiful
  expensive → more expensive    tired → more tired    tiring → more tiring
  interested → more interested    interesting → more interesting

- 불규칙변화

  good – better    bad – worse    far – farther    many/much – more
  little – less    old – older/elder    well – better

**2.** 두 사람, 사물을 비교하는 경우 「형용사/부사의 비교급+than」의 형태를 쓴다.
I'm **taller than** my brother is. 나는 내 동생보다 크다.
Athens is **older than** Rome is. 아테네가 로마보다 오래되었다.
Karen speaks English **better than** I do. Karen은 나보다 영어를 잘한다.

**3.** 일상영어(informal English)에서는 'than I am/do/can~'을 'than me' 라고 쓰기도 한다.
My mother is a better cook **than I am.** = My mother is a better cook **than me.**
I can swim better **than he can.** = I can swim better **than him.**

**| MORE TIPS |** "Your bag is more expensive than mine" 처럼 비교대상에 따라 「than+소유대명사」를 쓰기도 한다.

**4.** 비교급에서 than 이하는 생략할 수 있다.
My father wants a **bigger** car. 아버지는 더 큰 차를 원하신다.
This skirt is good, but I want a **less** expensive one. 이 스커트도 좋은데 난 덜 비싼 걸 원해.

72

# Unit Test

**1.** 보기와 같이 그림을 비교하여 말하시오.

보기 |  $200    $300
expensive    more expensive

1.

big _____

2

far _____

3.

fat _____

4.

comfortable _____

**2.** 단어의 비교급을 쓰시오.

| | | |
|---|---|---|
| old → _____ | strong → _____ | happy → _____ |
| important → _____ | good → _____ | well → _____ |
| bad → _____ | large → _____ | serious → _____ |
| pretty → _____ | beautiful → _____ | crowded → _____ |
| tired → _____ | embarrassing → _____ | thin → _____ |
| early → _____ | | |

**3.** 비교급을 이용하여 다음 문장을 완성하시오.

1. My father's car isn't very big. He wants a _____ one.
2. I'm not very tall. My sister is _____ .
3. This book isn't very interesting. I want to see a _____ one.
4. His idea isn't very good. Your idea is _____ .
5. This cake doesn't taste good. The other one tastes _____ .

# Writing Pattern Practice

**1.** 「주어 + 동사 + 비교급(형용사/부사+er)」

나는 기분이 더 좋다.

나는 기분이 더 나쁘다.

더 조심해라.(Be~)

너 점점 더 예뻐진다.(get)

아버지는 더 큰 차를 원하신다.

Carol이 더 빨리 달린다.

난 덜 비싼 걸 원해.(one)

이 케익이 더 맛있는데.(taste)

너의 아이디어가 나은데.


**2.** 「주어 + 동사 + 비교급(형용사/부사+er) than ~」

나는 내 남동생보다 크다.

아테네가 로마보다 오래되었다.(Athens)

Karen은 나보다 영어를 잘 말한다.

그녀는 나보다 더 일찍 일어난다.

한 시간보다 덜 걸려요. (take)

나는 그보다 더 수영을 잘할 수 있다.

나는 여기에 Sue보다 일찍 왔다.

Sarah는 전보다 더 건강하다.


**3.** 「주어 + 동사 + 비교급 (more+형용사/부사)」

이 책이 저거보다 더 흥미로워.(that one)

좀더 느리게 말해줄래요?(Can~)

이 의자가 저거보다 더 편안해.(comfortable)

이 노래가 저거보다 더 유명해.


**4.** 「주어 + 동사 + 비교급 (more+형용사/부사) than ~」

네가 Susan보다 더 아름답다.

이 시계가 저것보다 더 비싸다.(that one)

이 영화가 그것보다 더 감동적이다.(touching, that one)


너 전보다 더 피곤해 보인다.

# Unit 17 | 비교급을 이용한 표현

Grammar in Practice

A: How do you feel today?
B: I feel much better than yesterday.
A: Good for you.
   You should rest as much as possible.
B: OK. I'll try.

Grammar in Use

**1.** 비교급을 강조하기 위해 much, a lot, even, far 등을 앞에 쓴다.
The United Kingdom is **much** older than the United States.
영국은 미국보다 훨씬 오래 됐다.

The Hyatt Hotel is **a lot** more expensive than the Holiday Inn.
Hyatt호텔은 Holiday Inn 보나 훨씬 비싸나.

**2.** 「비교급 and 비교급」은 '점점 더 … 하다' 라는 비교급을 강조하는 표현이다.
It's getting **hotter and hotter**. 점점 더 더워진다.
You're getting **more and more beautiful**. 너는 점점 더 아름다워지는구나.

**3.** 「as 형용사/부사 as」는 '~만큼 … 하다' 라는 뜻이다.
I am **as tall as** my mother. 나는 엄마만큼 키가 크다.
I can swim **as well as** you. 나는 너만큼 수영을 할 수 있다.
Jessie weighs twice **as much as** me. Jessie의 몸무게는 나의 두 배야.

**4.** 「not as(so) 형용사/부사 as」는 '~만큼 … 하지 않다' 라는 뜻으로 「비교급 than」과 바꿔 쓸 수 있다.
Jeju Island **isn't as big as** Hawaii. 제주도는 하와이만큼 크지 않다.
= Hawaii is **bigger than** Jeju Island. 하와이가 제주도 보다 크다.

I **don't eat as much as** you. 나는 너만큼 많이 먹지 않는다.
= You eat **more than** me. 네가 나보다 더 많이 먹는다.

**5.** 「as~as one can」은 '가능한 …하게' 라는 뜻으로 「as ~ as possible」괴 비꿔 쓸 수 있다.
I'll call you back **as soon as I can**. 가능한 빨리 다시 전화 드릴게요.
=I'll call you back **as soon as possible**.

**6.** 비교급의 형태를 사용하면서 최상급의 의미를 가질 수 있다.
Nothing is **more important than** health. 건강보다 중요한 건 없다.

Health is **more important than any other thing in the world**.
= Health is **the most important thing** in life.
세상에 어떤 것 보다 건강이 더 중요하다.

# Unit Test

**1.** 다음은 Susan과 Susan의 여동생에 관한 내용이다. 보기와 같이 비교하시오.

**Susan**

1. She's 16 years old.
2. She doesn't speak English very well.
3. She's not very tall.
4. She dances well.
5. She isn't very diligent.
6. She doesn't get up early.
7. She's not very pretty.

**Susan's sister**

She's 14 years old.
She speaks English very well.
She's tall.
She doesn't dance very well.
She's diligent.
She gets up early.
She's pretty.

| 보기 | 1. She's older than her sister. |
| --- | --- |
| | 2. Her sister speaks English better than her. |

3. _____

4. _____

5. _____

6. _____

7. _____

**2.** 다음 문장을 'as ~ as'가 들어간 문장으로 바꾸시오.

1. Your English is better than mine. →My English isn't _____
2. My bag is bigger than yours. →Your bag isn't _____
3. I run faster than you. →Yon don't run _____
4. Jane got here earlier than you. →You didn't get here _____
5. This car is more expensive than his. →His car isn't _____

**3.** 우리말과 일치하도록 괄호 안의 단어를 알맞게 배열하시오.

1. 점점 추워지는구나. (colder/ and/ getting/ it's/ colder)

_____

2. 나는 너만큼 많이 자지 않아. (as/ sleep/ don't/ I/ much/ as/ you)

_____

3. 너는 나보다 TV를 더 많이 본다. (than/ watch TV/ you/ more/ me)

_____

4. 호주가 뉴질랜드 보다 훨씬 더 크다 (is/ Australia/ New Zealand/ bigger/ than/ much)

_____

5. 제가 가능한 빨리 거기에 갈게요. (as/ be/ there/ as/ I'll/ soon/ possible)

_____

# Writing Pattern Practice

**1.** 「much, a lot, even, far + 비교급」 '훨씬 더 … 하다'

너는 훨씬 더 피곤해 보인다.(even) _____

영국은 미국보다 훨씬 오래 됐다.(The United Kingdom, much) _____

Hyatt호텔은 Holiday Inn 보다 훨씬 비싸다.(a lot) _____


**2.** 「비교급 and 비교급」 '점점 더 … 하다'

점점 더 더워지고 있다.(It's getting~) _____

점점 더 어두워지고 있다. _____

점점 더 흥미로워 지는데. _____

너는 점점 더 아름다워지는구나. _____


**3.** 「as 형용사/부사 as」 '~만큼 …하다'

나는 엄마만큼 키가 크다. _____

나는 너만큼 수영을 잘 할 수 있다.(can) _____

Jessy의 몸무게는 나의 두 배야.(weigh twice) _____


**4.** 「not as(so) 형용사/부사 as」 '~만큼 … 하지 않다'

제주도는 하와이만큼 크지 않다. _____

한국에서 농구는 축구만큼 인기 있지 않다.(popular) _____

나는 너만큼 많이 먹지 않는다. _____


**5.** 「as~as one can(=possible)」 '가능한 …하게'

가능한 빨리 나에게 전화해.(one can) _____

내가 너에게 가능한 빨리 이메일 보낼게.(e-mail) _____

나는 항상 가능한 열심히 공부한다.(I always ~) _____

가능한 영어를 느리게 말해 주세요. _____


**6.** 비교급 문장 = 최상급의 의미

건강보다 중요한건 없다.(Nothing is ~) _____

세상에 어떤 것 보다 건강이 더 중요하다.(Health is ~) _____

# 18 | 형용사와 부사의 최상급

A: What is the best movie you've ever seen?
B: I think *Harry Potter* is the best movie of all.

**1.** 최상급은 셋 이상을 비교하면서 '가장 ~한' 이라는 뜻으로 보통 앞에 the를 붙인다.

[ 최상급 만드는 법 ]

● 단음절어: 원급 + ‒(e)st

old ‒ oldest      slow ‒ slowest      cheap ‒ cheapest
nice ‒ nicest      late ‒ latest

● 단모음+단자음으로 끝나는 단어: 마지막자음 + ‒est

big ‒ biggest      thin ‒ thinnest

● y로 끝나는 2음절어: ‒y → ‒iest

easy ‒easiest      heavy ‒ heaviest      early ‒ earliest

● 대부분의 2음절어, 3음절어, ‒ed ‒ing로 끝나는 단어: most + 원급

beautiful ‒ most beautiful      polite ‒ most polite   careful ‒ most careful
expensive ‒ most expensive   tired ‒ most tired      tiring ‒ most tiring
interested ‒ most interested   interesting ‒ most interesting

● 불규칙변화

good ‒ best      bad ‒ worst      far ‒ farthest      many/much ‒ most
little ‒ least      old ‒ oldest/eldest      ill ‒ worst      well ‒ best

**2.** 최상급 앞에 the가 붙지 않는 경우도 있다.

**Heather is my best friend.** Heather는 나의 가장 친한 친구이다.
[최상급 앞에 소유격이 올 때]

**Most women like shopping.** 대부분의 여자들은 쇼핑을 좋아한다.
[most가 대부분의 뜻으로 쓰일 때]

| MORE TIPS | 부사의 최상급은 경우에 따라 the를 생략하기도 한다.

**3.** '~중에서' 라는 비교 대상을 나타낼 때 〈of+복수명사〉 또는 〈in+장소명사〉를 주로 쓴다.

**Carol runs the fastest of us all.** 우리 모두 중에서 Carol이 가장 빨리 뛴다.
**Winter is the coldest of the four seasons.** 겨울이 사계절 중 가장 춥다.
**It's the oldest building in this city.** 그것은 이 도시에서 가장 오래된 건물이다.
**Seoul is the biggest city in Korea.** 서울이 한국에서 가장 큰 도시이다.

# Unit Test

**1.** 단어의 최상급을 쓰시오.

old → _____     strong → _____     happy → _____

good → _____     well → _____     bad → _____

serious → _____     pretty → _____     beautiful → _____

tired → _____     embarrassing → _____     thin → _____

**2.** 그림을 보고 다음 단어를 이용하여 최상급 문장을 만드시오.

A    B    C

1. (young/old)

A is _____

C is _____

A    B    C

$10    $50    $100

2. (cheap/expensive)

A is _____

C is _____

A    B    C

3. (short/tall)

C is _____

A is _____

**3.** 보기 안의 단어를 이용하여 최상급 문장을 완성하시오.

| 보기 | big    long    short    boring    important |
|---|---|

1. I think good health is _____ thing in life.
2. The Nile River is _____ river in the world.
3. Jon is _____ person I've ever met.
4. February is _____ month of the year.
5. Alaska is _____ state in the United Sates.

**4.** 다음 질문에 각자 대답해 보자.

1. A: Who's the best singer in Korea?

   B: I think _____

2. A: What's the worst movie you've ever seen?

   B: I think _____

3. A: What's the most important thing in your life?

   B: I think _____

# Writing Pattern Practice

**1.** 「the + 최상급」

Carol이 가장 어린 사람이다. _____

Jason이 가장 똑똑한 사람이다.(smart) _____

Monopoly가 가장 신나는 게임이다.(exciting) _____

문법이 학습할 가장 중요한 것이다.(Grammar~) _____

Paris는 가장 아름다운 도시다. _____

Peter가 가장 잘생긴 사람이다.(good-looking) _____

가장 가까운 은행이 어디죠? _____

내가 영어를 가장 잘한다. _____

Sally가 가장 빨리 뛴다. _____

이 것이 가장 맛있는 음식이다. _____

Richard가 가장 열심히 일한다. _____

King Sejong은 최고로 훌륭한 지도자셨다.(great) _____

봤던 것 중에 무엇이 최악의 영화예요?(~you've ever seen) _____

**2.** 「the + 최상급」

Heather는 나의 가장 친한 친구이다.(best) _____

대부분의 여자들은 쇼핑을 좋아한다. _____

**3.** 「최상급 + of + 복수명사」

우리 모두 중에서 Carol이 가장 빨리 뛴다. _____

겨울이 사계절 중 가장 춥다. _____

우리 아버지가 그들 중 키가 가장 작으시다. _____

David이 그들 모두 중 가장 키가 크다. _____

**4.** 「최상급 + in + 장소명사」

서울이 한국에서 가장 큰 도시다. _____

나일 강이 세계에서 가장 긴 강이다. _____

Bill Gates가 세상에서 가장 부유한 남자다. _____

그것은 이 도시에서 가장 오래된 건물이다. _____

# REVIEW 1

**1.** 다음 우리말을 영어로 바꿔 쓰시오.

① 더 나이든 → _____

② 더 어려운 → _____

③ 더 나쁜 → _____

④ 가장 싼 → the _____

⑤ 가장 중요한 → the _____

**2.** 다음 영어 문장을 우리말로 쓰시오.

① You are a better swimmer than Dave. → _____

② You're eating less than before. → _____

③ I don't watch movies as often as you. → _____

④ Kevin is the shortest of us all. → _____

⑤ Health is the most important thing in life. → _____

**3.** 다음 중 틀린 곳을 바르게 고치시오.

① She gets up more early than me. → _____

② The skirt is very good, but I want a more cheaper one. → _____

③ You speak English more better than me. → _____

④ This movie is interestinger than that one. → _____

⑤ I'm as taller as my mother. → _____

⑥ Who's pretty, you or your sister? → _____

⑦ February is the most shortest month of the year. → _____

⑧ What is the most large country in the world? → _____

⑨ Heather is the my best friend. → _____

⑩ Sears Tower was the most tall building. → _____

**4.** 둘 중에서 알맞은 것을 골라 동그라미 하시오.

① Your car is more expensive than (Tom/ Tom's).

② You look (very/ much) prettier than before.

③ The Nile is (long/ longer) than the Amazon.

④ You swim (very/ much) better than Laura.

⑤ Call me as (soon/ sooner) as possible.

⑥ Europe isn't as (large/ larger) as Asia.

⑦ What is the (most large/ largest) country in the world?

⑧ This coat is the (expensivest/ most expensive) one of them all.

⑨ I'll get back to you as (quick/ quickly) as I can.

⑩ Your English is as good as (her/ hers)

# REVIEW 2

**1.** 비교급을 만들 때 more가 필요한 형용사를 고르시오.

① wise      ② crazy
③ tall      ④ pretty
⑤ bored

**2.** 최상급 만들 때 most가 필요한 형용사를 고르시오.

① big      ② easy
③ thin      ④ tiring
⑤ bad

**3.** 어법상 가장 맞는 문장을 고르시오.

① What is better movie you've ever seen?
② You aren't as taller as Ariel.
③ The Amazon is the second longest river in the world.
④ I love sports the most than anything else.
⑤ The American Mall is biggest one in the United States.

**4.** 빈칸에 공통으로 들어갈 말은?

I don't exercise as much _____ Mike.
Please come as soon _____ possible.

① than      ② in
③ as      ④ most
⑤ so

**5.** 밑줄 친 부분과 바꿔 쓸 수 있는 것을 고르시오.

I ate as much as possible.

① as much as could
② as much as me
③ as much as I can
④ as much as I could
⑤ as much as I should

**6.** 밑줄 친 형용사의 원급을 고르시오.

I need a less expensive one.

① good      ② bad
③ many      ④ much
⑤ little

**[7-8]** 괄호 안에 들어갈 수 있는 말을 고르시오.

**7.** Which is _____, New York or Chicago?

① bigger than      ② bigger
③ as big      ④ as big as
⑤ the biggest

**8.** Who can sing _____ all the girls?

① better in      ② better of
③ as well as      ④ the best in
⑤ the best of

**9.** 다음 글을 읽고 빈칸에 들어갈 말이 알맞게 짝지어진 것을 고르시오.

 The Pacific Ocean is the _____ of the world's five oceans (followed by the Atlantic Ocean, Indian Ocean, Southern Ocean, and Arctic Ocean). The total surface area of the Pacific is about 170,000,000 square km. It's twice as _____ as the Atlantic and cover almost one third of the earth's surface.

*the Pacific 태평양 *the Atlantic *the Indian 인도양
*the Southern 남극해 *the Arctic 북극해

① large-larger      ② larger-large
③ largest-larger      ④ largest-large
⑤ large-large

# ✲ Chapter 5 | 접속사

# 19 | 접속사 and/ but/ or/ so

A: You look sick.
B: I have a cold, but I feel OK.
A: Call me after class. I'll pick you up.
B: Thanks, mom.

---

**1.** 단어와 단어, 구와 구, 문장과 문장을 이어주는 것을 접속사라고 한다.
It's <u>hot</u> **and** <u>humid</u>. 덥고 습기 차다.
     단어        단어

You can go there <u>by bus</u> **or** <u>by subway</u>. 너는 버스 또는 지하철을 타고 거기에 갈 수 있어.
          구         구

<u>Jack is young</u>, **but** <u>he is very smart</u>. Jack은 어리지만 매우 영특하다.
     절             절

**2.** and는 서로 비슷한 내용을 이어준다.
My father loves fishing **and** hiking. 아버지는 낚시와 등산을 좋아하신다.
I like Coke, **and** my sister does, too. 나는 콜라를 좋아하는데 여동생도 그렇다.

**3.** but은 서로 반대되는 내용을 이어준다.
I like watching movies, **but** Paul doesn't. 나는 영화 보는 걸 좋아하지만 Paul은 그렇지 않다.
Maria is rich, **but** she isn't happy. Maria는 부자지만 행복하지 않다.

**4.** or은 둘 중 하나를 선택할 때 쓴다.
She may become a model **or** an actress. 그녀는 아마 모델이나 배우가 될거야.
Do you want to stay **or** go? 너는 있고 싶은 거야, 가고 싶은 거야?

**5.** so는 원인과 결과를 말할 때 쓰고 so 뒤에 결과가 온다.
I stayed up all night, **so** I am very tired. 잠을 못자서 정말 피곤하다.

**6.** both A and B A와 B 둘 다        – 복수 취급한다.
    either A or B A와 B 둘 중 하나     – 동사는 B에 일치시킨다.
    neither A nor B A 와 B 둘 다 아닌   – 동사는 B에 일치시킨다.
**Both** she **and** I are from Canada. 그녀와 나 모두 캐나다 출신이다.
**Either** Jane **or** I am going to attend the meeting. Jane이나 내가 회의에 참석할 예정이다.
They can speak **neither** English **nor** Korean. 그들은 영어와 한국말 모두 못한다.

# Unit Test

**1.** 빈칸에 and/ but 중 가장 알맞은 접속사를 써 넣으시오.

1. I bought some apples, _____ I didn't eat them.
2. My sister is married, _____ she lives in Japan.
3. I usually eat breakfast, _____ I skipped it today.
4. Bill promised to be on time, _____ he was late.
5. It's a nice house, _____ it has only two bedrooms.

**2.** 빈칸에 or/ so 중 가장 알맞은 접속사를 써 넣으시오.

1. Do you want to pay with cash _____ check?
2. I didn't have anything to do, _____ I went out for a walk.
3. It was very cold, _____ I closed the window.
4. It started to rain, _____ I went home.
5. "For here _____ to go?" "For here, please."

**3.** 보기를 참고하여 밑줄 친 접속사가 무엇과 무엇을 이어주는지 동그라미 치시오.

> 보기 | I like apples and oranges.

1. Which city is bigger, Seoul <u>or</u> New York?
2. I bought a pair of jeans <u>and</u> a skirt.
3. Is it Wednesday <u>or</u> Thursday today?
4. Sue <u>and</u> I are friends.
5. Jason is young <u>but</u> rich.
6. It rained heavily, <u>so</u> they didn't go outside.
7. I helped her, <u>but</u> she didn't thank me.
8. Do you like tennis <u>or</u> badminton?
9. It was very hot, <u>so</u> I took off my jacket.
10. Would you like coffee <u>or</u> tea?

**4.** 둘 중 알맞은 말에 동그라미 하시오.

1. Is that a yes (and/ or) a no?
2. Both she and I (am/ are) living in Seoul.
3. Neither Janet nor Tom (is/ are) angry with you.
4. Either he or you (has/ have) to finish it.
5. You must be sick. Go home (and/ but) get some sleep.

# Writing Pattern Practice

**1.** and '…와'

덥고 습기 차다.(humid)

Sue와 나는 친구다.

아버지는 낚시와 등산을 좋아하신다.(love)

나는 콜라를 좋아하는데 여동생도 그렇다.

**2.** but '…하지만'

나는 영화 보는 것을 좋아하지만 Paul은 그렇지 않다.(watch movies)

Maria는 부자다 하지만 그녀는 행복하지 않다.

나는 그녀를 도왔다. 하지만 그녀는 나에게 고마워하지 않았다.(thank)

**3.** or '…또는'

그녀는 아마 모델이나 배우가 될거야.(may)

너는 있고 싶은 거야, 가고 싶은 거야?(stay)

어느 도시가 더 큰가요, 서울이요, 뉴욕이요?

오늘이 수요일이니, 목요일이니?

**4.** so '…해서'

나는 잠을 못자서 정말 피곤하다.(stay up all night)

비가 많이 와서 그들은 나가지 않았다.

너무 더워서 나는 재킷을 벗었다.(take off)

**5.** both A and B 'A와 B 둘 다'

그녀와 나 모두 캐나다 출신이다.(be from)

Jane과 Susan 모두 서울에 살고 있다.

**6.** either A or B 'A와 B 둘 중 하나'

Jane이나 내가 회의에 참석할 예정이다.(be going to)

그 사람이나 네가 그것을 끝마쳐야해.(have to)

**7.** neither A nor B 'A 와 B 둘 다 아닌'

그들은 영어와 한국말 모두 못한다.

86

# 20 명사절을 이끄는 접속사
## that/if/whether/who/where/what/how/why/when

**Grammar in Practice**

A: I'm going on a trip with my dad.
B: Where are you going?
A: I'm not sure. My dad said that he wants to drive
   here and there.

**Grammar in Use**

**1.** 절(주어, 동사를 포함한 문장)이 하나의 그룹을 이루어 명사역할을 할 수 있다. that은 '…라는 것'의 의미로 명사절을 이끈다.

- **주어역할** – that 명사절이 주어자리에 오는 경우는 거의 없다. 이때는 가주어 it을 사용한다.
  It is true **that he passed the test**. 그가 시험에 합격한 것은 사실이다.

- **목적어역할** – that을 생략할 수 있다.
  I think **(that) he is a liar**. 나는 그가 거짓말쟁이라고 생각한다.

- **보어역할** – that을 생략하지 않는다.
  The problem is **that I have no money**. 문제는 내가 돈이 없다라는 것이다.

**2.** if와 whether가 '…인지, 아닌지'라는 의미로 명사절을 이끈다. 이 때 if 명사절 경우 주어역할은 하지 않는다.

- **주어역할**
  **Whether** you like me or not isn't important.
  네가 나를 좋아하는지 그렇지 않은지는 중요하지 않다.

- **목적어역할**
  Do you know **whether**(or if) Mary won the game or not?
  너는 Mary가 게임에 이겼는지 아닌지 아니?

- **보어역할**
  The question is **whether**(or if) Tom got fired or not.
  문제는 Tom이 해고당했는지 그렇지 않은 지다.

**3.** 의문사(what, where, when, how, why, who)가 간접의문문의 형식으로 명사절을 이끌기도 한다.

- **주어역할**
  **How** you study English is important. 네가 어떻게 영어를 공부하느냐가 중요하다.
  **Where** he lives shows that he is very rich. 그가 어디에서 사느냐는 그가 매우 부자라는 것을 보여준다.

- **목적어역할**
  Do you know **what** it means? 그것이 무엇을 의미하는지 아세요?
  I don't know **when** he came back last night. 나는 그가 어젯밤 언제 돌아왔는지 모른다.

- **보어역할**
  The question is **why** he stole it. 문제는 그가 왜 그것을 훔쳤냐 이다.

# Unit Test

**1.** 다음 문장에서 명사절을 이끄는 접속사 that을 쓸 곳에 ✓표 하시오.

1. The problem is you don't have enough money.
2. I hope you like this present.
3. I'm glad I could meet you here.
4. Are you sure he's not single?
5. Jane told me she wanted to come to your party.
6. I didn't know Beth and you got married.
7. The point is he can't do such a thing.

**2.** 밑줄 친 명사절이 주어로 쓰였으면 '주', 목적어로 쓰였으면 '목', 보어로 쓰였으면 '보'를 써 넣으시오.

1. I don't know <u>what I should do</u>. (      )
2. <u>Whether it's true or not</u> is hard to tell. (      )
3. The question is <u>why he didn't show up at the meeting</u>. (      )
4. I'd like to know <u>if you like me or not</u>. (      )
5. It is certain <u>that he will be absent</u>. (      )

**3.** 다음 두 문장을 보기와 같이 한 문장으로 만드시오.

> 보기 | I know + he has a girlfriend. → I know that he has a girlfriend.
> Tell me + how much is it? → Tell me how much it is.

1. I wonder + how far is it?          → _____
2. I'd like to know + what is his name?   → _____
3. Please tell me + how did you lose weight?

   → _____
4. Does he think + she is beautiful?    → _____
5. I think + the prices are going up.    → _____
6. Do you know + who lives there?      → _____
7. I wonder +how did she make it?      → _____
8. I'm sure + she'll be here on time.     → _____
9. Could you tell me + where do you exercise?

   → _____
10. Nobody told me + why did we lose the game?

    → _____

# Writing Pattern Practice

**1.** 「that+수어+동사」'~하는 것'

**주어 역할**

그가 시험에 합격한 것은 사실이다.(It is true that~)

_____

**목적어 역할**

나는 그가 거짓말쟁이라고 생각한다.(a liar)

_____

**보어 역할**

문제는 내가 돈이 없다라는 것이다.

_____


**2.** 「if/ whether+주어+동사」'~인지 아닌지'

**주어 역할**

네가 나를 좋아하는지 그렇지 않은지는 중유하지 않다.

_____

**목적어 역할**

너는 Mary가 게임에 이겼는지 아닌지 아니?

_____

**보이 역할**

문제는 Tom이 해고당했는지 아닌지이다.(The question is~) _____


**3.** 「의문사(what, where, when, how, why, who)+(주어)+동사」'무엇이(무엇을)/어디에서/언제/어떻게/왜/누가(누구를) ~하는 것'

**주어 역할**

네가 어떻게 영어를 공부하느냐가 중요하다.

_____

그가 어디에서 사느냐는 그가 매우 부자라는 것을 보여준다.

_____

**목적어 역할**

너는 그것이 무엇을 의미하는지 아니?

_____

나는 그가 어젯밤 언제 돌아왔는지 모른다.

_____

**보어 역할**

문제는 그가 왜 그것을 훔쳤냐 이다.

_____

중요한 것은 그녀가 누구를 사랑하느냐이다.

_____

# 21 | 부사절을 이끄는 접속사
### when/before/after/because/although/if

**Grammar in Practice**

A: I'm broke.
B: If you need money, I'll lend you some.
A: Really? I can't thank you enough.
B: No problem. What are friends for?

---

**Grammar in Use**

1. 절(주어, 동사를 포함한 문장)이 하나의 그룹을 이루어 부사역할을 할 수 있다. 이 때 접속사를 포함한 절이 앞이나 뒤에 모두 올 수 있다.

   **Because** it was very hot, we opened a window. 매우 더워서 우리는 창문을 열었다.
   (= We opened a window because it was very hot.)

   **When** you cross the street, look out for cars. 길 건널 때 차 조심해라.
   (= Look out for cars when you cross the street.)

   **If** it rains, what will we do? 비가 오면 우리 뭐하지?
   (= What will we do if it rains?)

2. 시간 접속사: when, while, before, after, until
   **When** I went out, it was cold. 밖에 나갔을 때 추웠다.
   **While** you were sleeping, Kate called. 네가 잠들어 있는 동안 Kate가 전화했다.
   Brush your teeth **before** you go to bed. 자러가기 전에 이 닦아라.
   **After** I got home, I had dinner. 집에 도착한 후 저녁을 먹었다.
   I'll be here **until** you come back. 네가 돌아올 때까지 여기 있을게.

3. 원인, 이유 접속사: because, since, as 등이며 이때 as와 since는 이미 알만한 이유를 나타내며 because는 듣는 사람이 잘 알지 못하는 이유를 나타낼 때 주로 쓴다.
   **As** Ted is underage, he can't drink at bars.
   Ted는 미성년자이므로 그는 술집에서 술을 마실 수 없다.

   **Since** I had a big lunch, I don't feel hungry. 나는 점심을 거하게 먹어서 배고프지 않다.

   **Because** Susie was sick, she couldn't sing well.
   Susie가 아팠기 때문에 그녀는 노래를 잘 부를 수 없었다.

4. 조건, 양보 접속사: if, although
   **If** we take the bus, it will be cheaper. 만약 우리가 버스를 탄다면 더 저렴할 거야.
   **Although** my brother is young, he is wise. 내 동생은 젊지만 현명하다.

   | **MORE** TIPS | 시간과 조건을 나타내는 부사절에서는 현재가 미래를 대신한다.

   **When** you <u>come</u> back, I'll be at home. 네가 돌아 올 때 나는 집에 있을 거야.
   **If** it <u>rains</u>, we won't go on a picnic. 비가 오면 우리는 피크닉 안 갈 거야.

# Unit Test

**1.** A와 B에서 한 문장씩 골라 Because로 시작하는 문장을 완성하시오.

| 1. I didn't sleep well | I opened the window |
|---|---|
| 2. I was sick | I'm hungry |
| 3. It was very hot | I went to see a doctor |
| 4. I didn't eat anything today | I feel sleepy |
| 5. I got all As | My mother is very happy |

1. Because _____ , _____

2. Because _____ , _____

3. Because _____ , _____

4. Because _____ , _____

5. Because _____ , _____

**2.** 빈칸에 적당한 말을 보기에서 골라 써 넣으시오.

보기 | after you go out    although he's very old    while I was walking down the street
after we had a fight  when you're sleepy    if you don't hurry

1. You'll miss the train _____

2. Lock the door _____

3. It began to snow _____

4. Don't drive _____

5. She never said hello to me _____

6. He's quite strong _____

**3.** 둘 중 알맞은 것을 골라 동그라미 하시오.

1. I'll go to bed when (I finish/ I will finish) my work.

2. If it (rains/ will rain) I won't go out to eat.

3. I'll wait inside until the rain (stops/ will stop)

4. I'll be at my uncle's while I (am/ will be) in Japan.

5. Lisa (is/ will be) in Hawaii when I get there tomorrow.

6. Happy birthday to you! Make a wish before you (blow/ will blow) out the candles.

7. Tom (gives/ will give) you a call when he gets there tomorrow.

# Writing Pattern Practice

**1.** 「시간 접속사: when, while, before, after, until+주어+동사」
  '~할 때/~하는 동안/~하기 전에/~한 후에/~할 때 까지'

내가 밖에 나갔을 때 추웠다.(When~) _____

당신이 돌아 올 때 나는 집에 일을 거예요.(When~) _____

너 잠들어 있는 동안 Kate가 전화했다.(While you were~) _____

내가 샤워하는 동안 남동생이 집에 왔다.(While I was~) _____

너 자러가기 전에 이 닦아라.(Before~) _____

너 나가기 전에 불 꺼라.(Before~, turn off the lights.) _____

나는 집에 도착한 후 저녁을 먹었다.(After~) _____

나는 저녁을 먹고 TV를 봤다.(After~) _____

네가 돌아올 때까지 나는 여기 있을게.(I'll~) _____

**2.** 「원인, 이유 접속사: because, since, as+주어+동사」 '~ 때문에/이라서'

매우 더워서 우리는 창문을 열었다.(Because~) _____

Susie가 아팠기 때문에 그녀는 노래를 잘 부를 수 없었다.(Because~) _____

Ted는 미성년자이므로 그는 술집에서 술을 마실 수 없다.(As~) _____

나는 점심을 거하게 먹어서 배고프지 않다.(Since~) _____

**3.** 「조건, 양보 접속사: if, although+주어+동사」 '~에도 불구하고'

만약 우리가 버스를 탄다면 더 저렴할 거야.(If~) _____

만약 비가 오면 우리는 피크닉 안 가요.(If~) _____

만약 비가 오면 우리 어떻게 해야 하지?(If~) _____

만약 네가 여기에 오면, 나는 행복할 거야.(If~) _____

내 동생은 젊지만 현명하다.(Although~) _____

그는 겨우 15살이지만 5개 국어를 말 할 수 있다.(Although~)

# REVIEW 1

**1.** 다음 우리말을 영어문장으로 바꿔 쓰시오.

① 나는 사과와 배를 좋아한다.  →_____

② 나는 영화를 좋아하지만 Paul은 그렇지 않다.  →_____

③ Mary는 부자지만 그녀는 행복하지 않다.  →_____

④ 너는 머물고 싶니 아니면 가고 싶니?  →_____

⑤ 매우 추워서 나는 창문을 닫았다.  →_____


**2.** 다음 영어 문장을 우리말로 쓰시오.

① Both she and I are from Korea.  →_____

② Either Jim or I will go there.  →_____

③ They can speak neither English nor Korean.  →_____

④ Do you know if Mary won the game?  →_____

⑤ Whether you go or not isn't important.  →_____


**3.** 다음 중 틀린 곳을 바르게 고치시오.

① My friends and me did our homework together.  →_____

② I like both tennis or badminton.  →_____

③ Brad has neither a house or a car.  →_____

④ If you like me or not isn't important.  →_____

⑤ How do you study English is important.  →_____

⑥ Do you know what does it mean?  →_____

⑦ The questions is why did he steal it.  →_____

⑧ When you will come back, I'll be at home.  →_____

⑨ I'll be here until the train will arrive here.  →_____

⑩ If we'll take the bus, it will be cheaper.  →_____


**4.** 둘 중에서 알맞은 것을 골라 동그라미 하시오.

① Sally felt better, (so/ but) she went out.

② I bought a coat (and/ but) a skirt.

③ I'm going to buy either a motorbike (or/ nor) a bike.

④ Alice was very sick, (so/ but) she was absent.

⑤ Who is older, Kate (and/ or) Tess?

⑥ Charlie fell down (and/ but) broke his leg.

⑦ (Because/ Although) It rained a lot, we stayed at home.

⑧ (Because/ Although) I didn't have breakfast, I feel OK now.

⑨ If it (is/ will be) sunny, we'll go on a picnic.

⑩ Brush your teeth before you (X/ will) go to bed.

# REVIEW 2

[1–7] 빈칸에 들어갈 가장 알맞은 말을 고르시오.

**1.** I always eat dinner, ____ I skipped it today.

① and      ② but
③ so      ④ or
⑤ how

**2.** It was very cold, ____ I put on my jacket.

① for      ② but
③ so      ④ or
⑤ how

**3.** Do you like watching movies, ____ watching TV?

① for      ② but
③ so      ④ or
⑤ how

**4.** Do you think ____ Susan is a genius?

① that      ② but
③ if      ④ where
⑤ when

**5.** I want to know ____ Tom loves.

① and      ② but
③ or      ④ who
⑤ so

**6.** ____ it was very hot inside, we opened a window.

① Although      ② If
③ That      ④ Whether
⑤ Because

**7.** Wash your hands ____ you get home.

① although      ② while
③ that      ④ after
⑤ because

[8–9] 빈칸에 공통으로 들어갈 알맞은 말을 고르시오.

**8.** I haven't seen _____ Kate or her sister.
You can pay _____ by cash or check.

① both      ② if
③ either      ④ neither
⑤ whether

**9.** It is true _____ he passed the test.
The problem is _____ he doesn't have enough money.

① and      ② if
③ because      ④ that
⑤ as

**10.** 다음 글을 읽고 빈칸에 공통으로 들어갈 알맞은 접속사를 고르시오.

① That      ② How
③ Where      ④ When
⑤ Why

What do you want to be in the future?
Some of you might want to be a fire fighter.
Fire fighters have a dangerous job. _____ a fire breaks out, the fire fighters rush there to put it out.
Fire fighters wear special clothes that protect them from heat and water, and a special hat, too.

_____ a fire fighter is on duty, he must always be ready for fires. He might save many lives.

*a fire breaks out 화재가 발생하다
*put out (불을)끄다

94

✻ **Chapter 6** | **전치사(구)**

# 22 | 시간전치사 1 at/ in/ on

Grammar in Practice

A: When is the concert?
B: It is on December 31st.
A: What time?
B: It starts at 7:30.

Grammar in Use

**1.** 시간 전치사 at 은 비교적 짧은 시간 앞에 쓴다.
   **at** 8 o'clock 8시에
   **at** dawn/ noon/ night/ midnight 새벽에/ 정오에/ 밤에/ 자정에

**2.** in은 비교적 긴 시간 앞에 쓴다.
   **in** the morning/afternoon/evening/middle of the night 아침에/오후에/저녁에/한밤중에
   **in** April/ June 4월/ 6월에
   **in** (the) spring/ summer/ fall/ winter 봄/ 여름/ 가을/ 겨울에
   **in** 2006 2006년에

**3.** on은 특정한 날이나 특정한 날의 일부분 앞에 쓴다.
   ● 요일: **on** Sunday(s)/ Monday(s) 일요일(마다)에/ 월요일(마다)에
   ● 요일의 일부분: **on** Sunday morning/ Friday night 일요일 오전에/ 금요일 밤에
   ● 날짜: **on** July 24th/ December 29th 7월 24일에/ 12월 29일에
   ● 특정한 날: **on** Christmas Day/ Valentine's Day 크리스마스 날에/ 밸런타인데이에

**4.** next, last, this, every, all 등이 시간을 나타내는 명사 앞에 쓰이면 전치사를 생략한다.
   See you next week. 다음 주에 보자.
   I was in Europe last Christmas. 나는 지난 크리스마스에 유럽에 갔다.
   Jack will be here this Friday. Jack이 이번 금요일에 여기에 올 거야.
   I go to church every Sunday. 나는 일요일마다 교회에 다닌다.
   The baby slept all afternoon. 그 아기는 오후 내내 잤다.
   Janet stayed up all night. Janet은 밤을 새웠다.

# Unit Test

**1.** 빈칸에 at, in, on 중 알맞은 전치사를 쓰시오.

_____ January       _____ the morning       _____ midnight

_____ 6 o'clock       _____ Christmas day       _____ Friday night

_____ December 1st       _____ the fall       _____ 12:40

_____ the middle of the night       _____ the weekend       _____ Wednesday

_____ 1972       _____ noon       _____ Halloween

**2.** 문장이 맞으면 T(True), 틀린 곳이 있으면 F(False)에 동그라미 하시오.

1. I go to the gym at every night.  (T/ F)

2. Do you study at school on Sundays?  (T/ F)

3. Central Park is beautiful in the fall.  (T/ F)

4. I'm going to Europe in next month.  (T/ F)

5. Laura always gets up late at the morning.  (T/ F)

6. Katie is going to have a baby in August.  (T/ F)

7 What are you going to do at this weekend?  (T/ F)

8. I couldn't sleep well last night.  (T/ F)

9. We don't often eat at night.  (T/ F)

10. Are you leaving at January 9th?  (T/ F)

**3.** 우리말과 일치하도록 괄호 안의 단어를 알맞게 배열하시오.

1. 나는 Jack을 지난 크리스마스에 만났다. (I/ Jack/ met/ Christmas/ last)

_____

2. 너는 토요일에 일하니? (Saturdays/ work/ do/ on/ you/ ?)

_____

3. Lisa는 너를 금요일 밤에 봤다. (on/ saw/ you/ Lisa/ Friday night)

_____

4. 나는 그를 토요일 저녁에 못 만나. (meet/ on/ I/ him/ can't/ Saturday evening)

_____

5. Paul은 9월 22일에 떠나. (is/ on/ Paul/ leaving/ September 22nd)

_____

6. 그 영화는 3시 반에 시작해. (starts/ the movie/ 3:30/ at)

_____

7. 나는 하루 종일 너의 전화를 기다려왔다. (I've/ day/ your call/ all/ waited for)

_____

# Writing Pattern Practice

**1.** 「at + 비교적 짧은 시간 명사」

8시에

새벽에

정오에

밤에

자정에

**2.** 「in + 비교적 긴 시간 명사」

아침에

오후에

저녁에

한밤중에

4월에

봄에

2006년에

**3.** 「on + 특정한 날/특정한 날의 일부분 명사」

수요일에

일요일마다

금요일 밤에

1월 5일에

크리스마스 날에

내 생일에

**4.** 「전치사 next, last, this, every, all + 시간 명사」

다음 주에

지난 크리스마스에

이번 금요일에

일요일마다

하루 종일

아침 내내

오후 내내

밤새

# 23 | 시간전치사 2 for/ during/ by/ until/ in/ within/ from/ since

Grammar
in
Practice

A: What will you do during the summer vacation?
B: I'll go to Paris.
A: How long will you be there?
B: For a couple of weeks.

Grammar
in
Use

**1.** 시간 전치사 for는 '···동안에' 라는 뜻으로 구체적인 기간 앞에 쓴다.
I'll stay in Japan **for** a month. 나는 일본에 한 달 동안 머무를 거야.

**2.** during은 '···중에' 라는 뜻으로 for와 비슷한 뜻이지만 for는 주로 뒤에 「숫자+명사」가 오고 during은 「the+특정기간을 나타내는 명사」가 온다.
I went to Malaysia **during** the vacation. 나는 방학동안에 말레이시아에 갔다.

**3.** by는 '···까지' 라는 뜻으로 동작의 완료를 의미한다.
I have to go home **by** 10 p.m. 나는 10시까지 집에 돌아가야 해.

**4.** until (or till)은 : by와 같이 '···까지' 라는 뜻이지만 동작이 ···까지 계속 진행됨을 의미한다.
"How long will you be here?" "**Until** Friday." "여기에 얼마나 오래 있을 거야?" "금요일까지"

**5.** in은 주로 미래문장에 쓰여서 '···후에, 만에' 라는 의미를 가진다.
I'll be there **in** an hour. 1시간 후에 거기 갈게.

**6.** within은 '···이내에' 라는 뜻이다.
You have to finish this exam **within** 30 minutes. 너 30분 안에 시험을 끝내야해.

**7.** from은 '···부터' 라는 뜻으로 완료형을 제외한 모든 시제에 쓸 수 있다.
Jack works **from** nine to five. Jack은 9시에서 5시까지 일한다.

**8.** since는 '···이래로' 라는 뜻으로 주로 완료시제와 함께 쓴다.
I've lived in Seoul **since** 1990. 나는 1990년 이래로 서울에 살아왔다.

# Unit Test

**1.** 빈칸에 for 또는 during을 써 넣으시오.

1. I'm tired. I'm going to lie down _____ a few minutes.
2. Jack didn't say anything _____ the meal.
3. I felt sleepy _____ the class.
4. Jane will be away _____ a week.
5. We played badminton _____ three hours.

**2.** 빈칸에 by 또는 until을 써 넣으시오.

1. I have to finish the report _____ tomorrow.
2. I'll stay here _____ tomorrow.
3. Beth has to get home _____ 11 o'clock.
4. You have to hand in your homework _____ Friday.
5. I stayed in bed _____ noon.

**3.** 빈칸에 from 또는 since를 써 넣으시오.

1. I work _____ nine to five.
2. John's been here _____ yesterday.
3. I've lived in Seoul _____ 1990.
4. We lived in Thailand _____ 1999 to 2005
5. Jane's been working here _____ last year.

**4.** 우리말과 일치하도록 괄호 안의 단어를 알맞게 배열하시오.

1. 일주일동안 비가 내렸다. (rained/ for/ it's/ a week)

_____

2. Beth는 수업 중에 졸렸다. (Beth/ sleepy/ the class/ during/ felt)

_____

3. 결과는 내일까지 나올 거야. (will/ by/ the results/ come out/ tomorrow)

_____

4. 나는 한 시간 후에 거기에 도착할 거야. (I/ be/ in/ will/ there/ an hour).

_____

5. 그는 두 시간 안에 돌아올 거야. (He/ will/ within/ back/ be/ two hours)

_____

6. 너는 월요일부터 금요일까지 일하니? (you/ from Monday/ do/ to/ work/ Friday/ ?)

_____

7. 내가 그때까지 여기에 있을게. (here/ I/ be/ then/ will/ until)

_____

# Writing Pattern Practice

**1.** for '…동안에'

나는 일본에 한 달 동안 머무를 거야.

일주일동안 비가 내렸다.(It has~)

우리는 배드민턴을 세 시간 동안 쳤다.

**2.** during은 '…중에'

나는 방학동안에 말레이시아에 갔다.

Jack은 식사 중에 아무 말도 안했다.

Beth는 수업 중에 졸렸다.(feel sleepy)

**3.** by '…까지'

나는 10시까지 집에 돌아가야 해.

Jane은 11시까지 집에 도착해야 한다.(have to)

나는 내일까지 리포트를 끝마쳐야해.

너는 네 숙제를 금요일까지 제출해야해. (hand in)

**4.** until (or till) '…까지 (계속)'

나는 여기에 금요일까지 머무를 거야.

나는 정오까지 침대에 있었다.(stay in bed)

**5.** in '…후에, 만에'

내가 1시간 후에 거기 갈께.(be)

Jason이 여기에 30분 후에 도착할 거야.(get)

**6.** within '…이내에'

내가 1시간 안에 거기 갈게.(be)

너 30분 안에 시험을 끝내야해.(have to)

**7.** from '…부터'

Jack은 9시에서 5시까지 일한다.

너는 월요일부터 금요일까지 일하니?

**8.** since '…이래로'

나는 1990년 이래로 서울에 살아왔다.

# 장소전치사 at/ in/ above/ over/ on/ under/ below/ in front of/ behind/ next to

**Grammar in Practice**

A: Where is my coat?
B: It's in the closet.
A: Where are my glasses?
B: They might be on the desk.

---

**Grammar in Use**

**1.** 장소전치사 in은 '~안에' 또는 '~(비교적 넓은)공간 및 장소에'라는 뜻으로 쓴다.

There are some books **in** the box. 박스에 책이 좀 있어요.

"Where is David?" "He's **in** his room." David은 어디 있어요? 방에 있어요.

I've lived **in** Seoul since I was born. 나는 태어나면서부터 서울에 살아왔다.

**I MORE TIPS I** 집안의 공간은 보통 in+명사를 쓴다. in the room, in the kitchen, in the garage 등

**2.** at은 장소를 한 지점으로 말할 때 '(비교적 좁은) 장소나 같은 목적을 가지고 모인 장소에'라는 뜻으로 쓴다.

Somebody is **at** the door. 누가 문에 왔어요.

Sally's talking on the phone **at** her desk. Sally는 책상에서 전화통화하고있다.

Jack needs to use English **at** work. Jack은 직장에서 영어가 필요하다.

I had a great time **at** the party. 나는 파티에서 좋은 시간을 보냈다.

My friends and I did our homework **at** Jane's (place). 친구들과 난 Jane집에서 숙제를 했다.

**3.** 그밖에 방향과 위치를 나타내는 전치사는 다음과 같다.

- above: 막연한 위에
  The plane flew **above** the clouds. 비행기가 구름 위로 날아가 버렸다.

- over: 면이 닿지 않은 위에
  Be careful. There is a bee **over** your head. 조심해라. 네 머리 위에 벌이 있어.

- on: 표면에 접촉해서
  Your cell phone is **on** the table. 네 핸드폰은 탁자 위에 있어.

- under: 아래에
  I lay down **under** the tree. 나는 나무 아래에 누웠다.

- below: 막연한 아래에
  The sun dipped **below** the horizon. 태양이 지평선 아래로 졌다.

- in front of: ~앞에
  Who parked **in front of** the entrance? 누가 입구에 주차했어?

- behind: ~뒤에
  He's standing **behind** the chair. 그는 의자 뒤에 서있다.

- next to: ~옆에 (=by, beside)
  Can I sit **next to** you? 네 옆에 앉아도 될까?

# Unit Test

**1.** 그림을 보고 다음 질문에 보기와 같이 답하시오. (전치사 in 또는 at을 이용)

 보기     1.      2.      3.

> 보기 | Where is she? She's <u>at the airport</u>.

1. Where are they? They're _____
2. Where is he? He's _____
3. Where are we? We're _____

**2.** 빈칸에 알맞은 전치사를 적으시오.

1. "Where were you last night?" "_____ my sister's "
2. I live _____ New Zealand.
3. "Were you at home?" "No, I was _____ school."
4. Did you have a good time _____ the party?
5. "Where is your brother?" "He's _____ his room."
6. People are swimming __ the pool
7. This bookstore is the biggest _____ this city.

**3.** 그림을 보고 빈칸에 알맞은 전치사를 넣으시오.

1. John is _____ the bed.
2. The telephone is _____ the computer.
3. The calendar is _____ the wall.
4. The dog is _____ the desk.
5. The cat is _____ the curtain.

# Writing Pattern Practice _ 장소 전치사

**1.** in '~안에' '~(비교적 넓은)공간 및 장소에'

박스에 책이 좀 있어요. _____

그는 자기 방에 있어요. _____

나는 태어나면서부터 서울에 살아왔다.(I've) _____

사람들이 수영장에서 수영하고 있다 _____

나는 공원에서 개를 산책시켰다.(walk) _____

이 빌딩이 이 도시에서 가장 높다. _____

**2.** at '~에' 장소를 한 지점으로 말할 때, (비교적 좁은) 장소, 같은 목적을 가지고 모인 장소

나는 집에 있다. _____

누가 문에 왔어요.(Somebody is~) _____

Sally는 책상에서 전화 통화하고 있다. _____

나는 파티에서 좋은 시간을 보냈다.(have a great time) _____

친구들과 나는 Jane 집에서 숙제를 했다.(Jane's) _____

나는 버스정류장에서 버스를 기다리고 있다.(at the bus stop) _____

**3.** above '막연한 위에'

비행기가 구름 위로 날아가 버렸다.(fly) _____

**4.** over '면이 닿지 않은 위에'

너 머리위에 벌이 있어. _____

**5.** on '표면에 접촉해서'

너의 핸드폰은 테이블 위에 있어. _____

**6.** under '아래에'

나는 나무 아래에 누웠다. _____

**7.** below '막연한 아래에'

태양이 지평선 아래로 졌다.(dip, horizon) _____

**8.** in front of '~앞에'

누가 입구에 주차했어?(entrance) _____

**9.** behind '~뒤에'

그는 의자 뒤에 서있다. _____

**10.** next to '~옆에'

내가 너 옆에 앉아도 될까?(Can I~) _____

# 25 | 그 밖의 주요전치사

A: Have you ever traveled on the KTX?

B: No, not yet.

A: Those trains are very fast. They can travel **at** 300 kilometers an hour.

B: Wow, *terrific!

*terrific 굉장한

---

**1.** 방향전치사

- into '···안으로'
  It's too hot. Let's jump **into** the water. 너무 덥다. 물속으로 들어가자.

- out of '···으로부터'
  He went **out of** the room. 그는 방 밖으로 나갔다.

- up '···위쪽으로'
  We went **up** the hill. 우리는 언덕을 올라갔다.

- down '···아래쪽으로'
  We came **down** the hill. 우리는 언덕을 내려왔다.

**2.** 가격, 속도 표시 전치사

- for '··· (얼마)에'
  I bought the CDs **for** $20. 나는 그 CD를 모두해서 20달러에 샀다.

- at '··· (속도)로'
  Slow down. You're driving **at** 110 km an hour. 속도를 줄여. 너 시속 100킬로로 달리고 있어.

**3.** 도구, 수단 전치사

- by ···로, ···를 타고
  I'll pay **by** check. 수표로 지불할게요.
  Karen goes to school **by** bus. Karen은 학교에 버스타고 다닌다.

**4.** 그 외 전치사

- with +사람: ···와 함께
  I live **with** my parents. 나는 부모님과 함께 살아요.
  I need someone to talk **with**. 나는 얘기 나눌 누군가가 필요해.

- with +사물: ···를 가지고
  Eat that fish **with** your chopsticks. 생선을 젓가락으로 먹어라.
  I need something to write **with**. 나는 쓸 것(필기도구)이 필요해요.

- between: 둘의 '···사이'
  I sat **between** John and Mary. 나는 John과 Mary 사이에 앉았다.

- among: 셋 이상의 '···사이'
  There is a cottage **among** the trees. 나무에 둘러싸인 오두막집이 있다.

# Unit Test

**1.** 빈칸에 들어갈 알맞은 전치사를 보기에서 고르시오.

| 보기 | into | with | by | between |

1. Let's jump _____ the water.
2. Emily is standing _____ Bob and Ed.
3. Fred always goes to school _____ bus.
4. Anne is eating fish _____ her chopsticks.


**2.** 빈칸에 알맞은 전치사를 보기에서 골라 넣으시오.

| 보기 | into | for | by | with |
| | by | at | out of | |

1. 나는 이 시계를 20달러에 샀다. - I bought this watch _____ 20 dollars.
2. 제가 수표로 내도될까요? - Can I pay _____ check?
3. Jimmy는 부모님과 함께 산다. - Jimmy lives _____ his parents.
4. Adam은 직장에 지하철 타고 다닌다. - Adam goes to work _____ subway.
5. 나는 100 킬로로 운전했다. - I drove _____ 100 km an hour.
6. 방에서 나오세요. - Come _____ the room.
7. 뭔가 눈 속에 들어갔다. Something got _____ my eye.


**3.** 다음 해석을 참고하여 어법상 맞지 않은 부분을 찾아 고치시오.

1. 나는 그 가방을 20달러에 샀다.
   - I bought the bag to $20.                    → _____
2. 그는 현금으로 지불했다.
   - He paid for cash.                            → _____
3. 나는 할아버지 할머니와 함께 산다.
   - I live for my grandparents.                  → _____
4. 피자헛은 버거킹과 KFC 사이에 있다.
   - Pizza Hut is among Burger King and KFC.      → _____

# Writing Pattern Practice

**1.** into '···안으로'

물속으로 들어가자.(jump) _____

뭔가 내 눈 속에 들어갔다.(get) _____

**2.** out of '···으로부터'

차에서 내려.(get) _____

그는 방 밖으로 나갔다.(go) _____

**3.** up '···위쪽으로'

우리는 언덕을 올라갔다. _____

**4.** down '···아래쪽으로'

우리는 언덕을 내려왔다 _____

**5.** for '···(얼마)에'

나는 그 CD들을 20달러에 샀다. _____

**6.** by '···로,' '···를 타고'

나는 수표로 지불할게요. _____

Karen은 학교에 버스타고 다닌다 _____

**7.** with +사람: ···와 함께

나는 부모님과 함께 살아요. _____

나는 얘기 나눌 누군가가 필요해.(someone) _____

**8.** with +사물: ···를 가지고

생선을 젓가락으로 먹어라.(the chopsticks) _____

나는 쓸 것(필기도구)이 필요해.(to write with) _____

**9.** between: 둘의 '···사이'

나는 John과 Mary 사이에 앉았다. _____

**10.** among: 셋 이상의 '···사이'

나무들에 둘러싸인 오두막집이 있다.(a cottage) _____

# WRAP-UP | 전치사를 이용한 주요표현

## 1. 형용사 + 전치사

- **be good at** …에 소질이 있다
  I'm good at math. 나는 수학에 소질이 있다.

- **be afraid of** …를 두려워하다
  Tom is afraid of being alone in the dark.
  Tom은 어두운데 홀로 있는 것을 두려워한다.

- **be mad at** …에게 화나다
  Why are you mad at me? 너 왜 나한테 화났어?

- **be full of** …로 가득차다
  The room was full of children. 방은 아이들로 가득
  차 있었다.

- **be proud of** …를 자랑스럽게 여기다
  I feel proud of my son. 나는 아들을 자랑스럽게 생각
  한다.

- **be ashamed of** …를 창피하게 여기다
  I've done something bad. I'm ashamed of
  myself. 나는 나쁜 짓을 했어. 내 자신이 창피해.

- **be interested in** …에 흥미있다
  "What activities are you interested in?" "너는 무
  슨 활동에 관심있니?"
  "I'm interested in sports." "나는 스포츠에 관심있
  어."

- **be satisfied with** …에 만족하다
  We were satisfied with the result. 우리는 결과에
  만족했다.

- **be married to** …와 결혼하다
  Cindy is married to a doctor. Cindy는 의사와 결혼
  했다.

- **be sorry about** …에 대해 미안하다
  I'm extremely sorry about this mess.
  이렇게 지저분하게 해서 정말 죄송해요.

## 2. 동사+전치사

- **listen to** …를 듣다
  Listen to me. This is very important. 내말 들어봐.
  이거 정말 중요한 거야.

- **look at** …를 보다
  Look at that baby. He's so cute. 저 아기봐. 정말
  귀엽다.

- **look for** …를 찾다
  "What are you looking for?" 뭐 찾고 있어?
  "I'm looking for my glasses." 안경을 찾고 있어.

- **get over** …를 극복하다
  I got over my cold. 나 감기 나았어.

- **talk to** …와 얘기 나누다
  Can I talk to you for a minute? 잠깐 얘기할 수 있
  을까?

- **talk about** …에 대해 얘기하다
  Let's not talk about it right now. 지금은 그것에 대
  해서 얘기하지 말자.

- **think about** …에 대해 생각하다
  I'm thinking about studying abroad. 나 유학 갈까
  생각 중이야.

- **wait for** …를 기다리다
  Wait for me to finish my homework. 숙제 끝낼 때
  까지 기다려줘.

- **depend on** …에 달려있다
  "Do you enjoy watching TV?" 너 TV 보는 거 좋아
  하니?
  "It depends on the program." 프로그램에 따라 다
  르지.

- **worry about** …를 걱정하다
  I worry about your health. 나는 네 건강이 걱정이야.

# REVIEW 1

**1.** 다음 우리말을 영어로 바꿔 쓰시오.

① 아침에 → _____
② 4월에 → _____
③ 여름에 → _____
④ 2000년에 → _____
⑤ 일요일 오전에 → _____
⑥ 1월 31일에 → _____
⑦ 일요일에 → _____
⑧ 크리스마스 날에 → _____
⑨ 다음 주에 → _____
⑩ 지난 금요일에 → _____

**2.** 다음 영어 문장을 우리말로 쓰시오.

① Jane will be away for a week. → _____
② I went to Japan during my vacation. → _____
③ I'll stay in New York until tomorrow. → _____
④ You have to finish it within 30 minutes. → _____
⑤ He'll be here in an hour. → _____

**3.** 다음 중 틀린 곳을 바르게 고치시오.

① I slept during five hours. → _____
② Everybody felt sleepy for the class. → _____
③ You have to hand in the report until tomorrow. → _____
④ I'll wait for you by 11 o'clock. → _____
⑤ Jack works since 9 to 5. → _____
⑥ I've studied English from 1995. → _____
⑦ "Where are you?" "I'm in the bus stop." → _____
⑧ Is John on the party? → _____
⑨ I first met Kate of the meeting. → _____
⑩ Is your father still in work? → _____

**4.** 둘 중에서 알맞은 것을 골라 동그라미 하시오.

① Someone is (in/ at) the door.
② My grandparents live (in/ at) Busan.
③ Sally is talking on the phone (in/ at) her desk.
④ "Where is David?" "He's (in/ at) his room.
⑤ Did you have a good time (in/ at) the party?
⑥ I need to use English (in/ at) work.
⑦ My friends and I studied (in/ at) Jane's.

# REVIEW 2

**1.** 다음 중 빈칸에 들어갈 수 없는 것은?

You can sit _____ me.

① in front of      ② behind
③ next to      ④ by
⑤ among

**2.** 밑줄 친 전치사 중 성격이 다른 하나를 고르시오.

① My school starts <u>at</u> 8 o'clock.
② I was born <u>in</u> 1989.
③ See you <u>on</u> Christmas Day.
④ What do you have <u>in</u> your bag?
⑤ I'll call you <u>on</u> Monday morning.

[3–7] 빈칸에 들어갈 알맞은 전치사를 고르시오.

**3.** There is a bank in front _____ Burger King.

① of      ② to
③ in      ④ off
⑤ with

**4.** An old lady sat next _____ me.

① of      ② to
③ in      ④ off
⑤ with

**5.** Eat fish _____ your chopsticks.

① of      ② to
③ in      ④ off
⑤ with

**6.** There is a cottage _____ the trees.

① about      ② for
③ of      ④ above
⑤ among

**7.** Slow down. You're driving _____ 110 km an hour.

① at      ② of
③ in      ④ for
⑤ with

[8–10] 빈칸에 공통으로 들어갈 알맞은 전치사를 고르시오.

**8.** See you _____ September 16th.
We live _____ the second floor.

① at      ② of
③ in      ④ on
⑤ with

**9.** I get up _____ 7 o'clock.
I was having fun _____ the party.

① at      ② of
③ in      ④ on
⑤ with

**10.** 다음 글을 읽고 빈 칸에 공통으로 들어갈 전치사를 찾으시오.

① in      ② at
③ on      ④ for
⑤ with

People ___ North America and Europe change their clocks on certain days. ____ March or April, they set their clocks one hour forward. ____ October, they set their clocks one hour back. This helps people be more efficient. First, they can work more during daylights hours. Second, they use less energy for lights.

*efficient 효율적인

110

# *Chapter 7 | 관계사(구)

# 26 관계대명사 who

Grammar in Practice

A: What kind of a girl do you like?
B: I like a girl who smiles a lot.
I like a girl whose hair is long.
I also like a girl whom I can trust.

---

Grammar in Use

**1.** 관계대명사는 명사를 꾸미는 절(형용사절)을 이끄는 말이다. 두 문장을 연결하는 접속사와 대명사 역할을 동시에 한다.

Yuki is my friend. + He lives next door. (2문장) Yuki는 내 친구다. + 그는 옆집에 산다.
→ Yuki is <u>my friend</u> <u>who</u> lives next door. (1문장) Yuki는 옆집에 사는 내 친구다.
　　　　　명사(선행사)　관계대명사
　　　　　　　　　　　　형용사절

**2.** 관계대명사의 종류

| 선행사 | 주격 | 소유격 | 목적격 |
|---|---|---|---|
| 사람 | who | whose | who(m) |
| | I know a boy <u>who</u> can sing well. | I know a girl <u>whose</u> father is an actor. | The man <u>who(m)</u> I like is John. |
| 사물, 동물 | which | whose/of which | which |
| | A plane is a machine <u>which</u> flies. | I have a dog <u>whose</u> name is Mary. | This is the shoes <u>which</u> I bought yesterday. |
| 사람, 사물, 동물 | that | – | that |
| | This is the person <u>that</u> I like. | – | This is the book <u>that</u> I read. |

**3.** 관계대명사 who: 꾸미는 명사(선행사)가 사람일 때 사용한다.

〈주격〉 Janet is <u>my friend</u>. + <u>She</u> can dance well.
　　→ Janet is my friend **who** can dance well. Janet은 춤을 잘 추는 내 친구다.

〈소유격〉 Janet is <u>my friend</u>. + <u>Her</u> father teaches art.
　　→ Janet is my friend **whose** father teaches art. Janet은 아버지가 미술을 가르치시는 내 친구다.

〈목적격〉 Janet is <u>my friend</u>. + I like <u>her</u> a lot.
　　→ Janet is my friend **who(m)** I like a lot. Janet은 매우 좋아하는 내 친구다.

**| MORE TIPS |** 목적격 관계대명사는 who 또는 whom을 모두 쓸 수 있지만, 일상생활에서 whom을 사용할 경우, 딱딱하게 들릴 수 있다.

# Unit Test

**1.** 다음 빈칸에 who, whose, who(m) 중 알맞은 관계대명사를 써 넣으시오.

1. Jane is my friend. I can trust her.

   Jane is my friend _____ I can trust.

2. I know a person. His wife is a Canadian.

   I know a person _____ wife is a Canadian.

3. John is a boy. He has a beautiful smile.

   John is a boy _____ has a beautiful smile.


**2.** 다음 문장의 괄호 안에서 알맞은 것을 고르시오.

1. I know some people (who, whose, who(m)) could help you.
2. Do you have a close friend (who, whose, who(m)) you like?
3. This is a person (who, whose, who(m)) I can trust.
4. Heather has a dog (who, whose, who(m)) tail is very long.
5. I have a friend (who, whose, who(m)) collects tops.          *top 팽이


**3.** 관계대명사를 이용하여 두 문장을 한 문장으로 적으시오. 보기를 참고하시오.

> 보기 | Where is that nurse? I saw her last time.
> → Where is that nurse who(m) I saw last time?

1. That is the man. I wanted to see him.

   → _____

2. I know a man. He cooks very well.

   → _____

3. That is a girl. Her father is a pilot.

   → _____

# Writing Pattern Practice

**1.** 「선행사 + who + 동사 ~」

나는 노래를 잘 할 수 있는 소년을 안다.(can sing) _____

나는 춤을 잘 출 수 있는 사람을 좋아한다.(people, can dance)

_____

나는 당신을 도와줄 수 있는 사람들을 알고 있다.(~some people, could help)

_____

나는 친절한 이웃이 좋다.(neighbors) _____

중국에 사는 사람들은 중국말을 한다.(The people~, Chinese)

_____


**2.** 「선행사 + whose+명사 ~」

머리가 갈색인 그 여자아이는 내 친구이다.(The girl~ )

_____

Janet은 그녀의 아버지가 미술을 가르치는 내 친구다.(Janet is my friend~)

_____


**3.** 「선행사 + who(m)+주어 ~」

Janet은 내가 좋아하는 소녀이다. _____

나는 내가 믿을 수 있는 친구가 필요하다.(I need ~, trust)

_____

내가 좋아하는 소녀는 Mary이다.(The girl~) _____

이효리는 우리가 매우 잘 아는 가수다. (Hyo Ree Lee is ~ very well.)

_____

# 27 | 관계대명사 which, that

**Grammar in Practice**

A: Where do you live?
B: I live in a house which has a beautiful garden.
   Where do you live?
A: I live in an apartment that has a great view.

**Grammar in Use**

1. 관계대명사 which: 꾸미는 명사(선행사)가 사물, 동물일 때 사용한다.

〈주격〉 This is <u>the house</u>. + <u>It</u> has 6 bedrooms.
   → This is the house **which** has 6 bedrooms. 이것은 침실이 6개 있는 집이다.

〈소유격〉 This is <u>the dog</u>. + <u>Its</u> ears are big.
   → This is the dog **whose** ears are big. 이것은 귀가 큰 개다.

〈목적격〉 This is <u>the car</u>. + My father bought <u>it</u> last week.
   → This is the car **which** my father bought last week. 이것은 아버지가 지난주에 구입하신 차다.

2. 관계대명사 that: 관계대명사 who나 which를 대신한다. 즉, 꾸미는 명사(선행사)가 사람, 사물, 동물일 때 사용하고 소유격은 없다.

〈주격〉 This is <u>the boy</u>. + <u>He</u> won the race.
   → This is the boy **that** won the race. 이 사람은 경주에서 이긴 소년이다.

〈목적격〉 I lost <u>the book</u>. + I borrowed <u>it</u> yesterday.
   → I lost the book **that** I borrowed yesterday. 나는 어제 빌린 책을 잃어 버렸다.

3. 관계대명사 that의 특별 용법: 다음과 같은 경우는 that을 쓰는데, 선행사가 사람인 경우 who를 사용하기도 한다.

1. 선행사가 –thing으로 끝나는 명사일 때
   → Tell me something **that** you know. 네가 알고 있는 것을 내게 말 해.

2. 선행사에 최상급, 서수, the very, the only, all, every 등이 포함된 경우
   → This is the best movie **that** I have ever seen. 이것은 내가 본 것 중 최고의 영화다.
   → He is the only person **that** I respect. 그는 내가 존경하는 유일한 사람이다.

# Unit Test

**1.** 다음 문장의 괄호 안에서 가장 알맞은 것을 고르시오.

1. This is a bus (who, which, whose) goes to the city hall.
2. I found the book (who, that, whose) I wanted.
3. This is the boy (whom, that, whose) has a nice bike.
4. This is the house (who, that, whose) has three bathrooms.
5. This is the room (who, that, whose) wall is purple.
6. The picture (which, of which, who) is on the wall is nice.
7. Tell me something (who, that, which) you know.
8. This is the worst movie (who, that, which) I have ever seen.
9. I have a dog (who, whose, which) name is Happy.
10. This is (the girl, the doctor, the key) which I was looking for.
11. That bag (who, which, whose) I carried was heavy.
12. A woman (that, which, whose) I know speaks 5 languages.
13. A barber is a person (who, which, whose) cuts men's hair.

**2.** 보기를 참고하여 두 문장을 한 문장으로 적으시오. (괄호 안의 관계대명사를 이용하시오.)

> 보기 | She gave me the book+I wanted it. (which)
> → She gave me the book which I wanted.

1. This is the book. + I read it 5 times. (that)

→ _____

2. This is a book. + Its cover is red. (whose)

→ _____

3. You can eat anything. + It is on the table. (that)

→ _____

4. This is the only pencil. + I have it. (that)

→ _____

# Writing Pattern Practice

**1.** 「선행사 + **which** + 주어 ~」

이것은 어제 내가 산 시계이다. (This is~, watch) _____

이 것은 멋진 경치를 가진 집이다.(This is~, a great view)

_____

너는 좋은 커피를 파는 가게를 아니?(a shop, good coffee)

_____

이 것은 큰 귀를 가진 개이다.(This is~, whose) _____


**2.** 「선행사 + **that** + 주어 ~」

이 시람이 니가 네게 말헸딘 사림이야. (This is~, told you)

_____

이 것이 내가 가진 것 전부다. (This is all ~) _____

이 것은 내가 본 영화다.(This is ~) _____

나는 어제 빌린 책을 잃어 버렸다. (I lost~, borrow)

_____

그는 내가 존경하는 유일한 사람이다.(person, respect)

_____

# 28 관계대명사의 생략

A: Why are you so mad?

B: I'm mad at my brother (who is) playing
over there. He lost the ball (which) my father
bought me yesterday.

**1.** 목적격 관계대명사는 생략할 수 있다.

Do you remember the man **(who(m))** we met in L.A.?

우리가 L.A.에서 만난 그 남자를 기억하니?

I lost the watch **(which)** you gave me.

나는 네가 준 손목시계를 잃어버렸어.

This is everything **(that)** I've got.

이 것은 내가 가진 모든 것이다.

I have a lot of friends **(who(m))** I play with.

나는 같이 놀 친구들이 많다.

| MORE TIPS | 「전치사+목적격 관계대명사」의 형태로 쓰인 경우 목적격 관계대명사를 생략할 수 없다.
I need a friend **on (who(m))** I can rely. (X)
I need a friend **(who(m))** I can rely **on**. (O) 전치사를 형용사절 끝으로 보내고 생략한다.
나는 의지할 친구가 필요하다.

**2.** 주격관계대명사와 be동사 다음 분사나 형용사가 오는 경우 「주격관계대명사+be동사」를 생략할 수
있다.

The woman **(who is)** wearing sunglasses is my mother.

선글라스를 끼고 있는 저 여자 분은 내 엄마다.

The dog **(which is)** wagging its tail is my dog.

꼬리를 흔들고 있는 저 개는 내 개이다.

# Unit Test

**1.** 생략할 수 있는 것을 고르고, 생략할 수 있는 것이 없으면 그대로 두시오.

1. This is a car which is made in Korea.
   ①      ②    ③          ④

2. I want to have a room that has a large window.
   ①          ②    ③       ④

3. This is the picture which I drew.
   ①      ②    ③    ④

4. Look at the boy who is standing over there.
          ①    ②     ③     ④

5. The man that is smiling over there is my dad.
   ①    ②    ③        ④

6. That is my sister who has short hair.
   ①     ②    ③  ④

7. May I use the ruler that you have?
   ①       ②    ③    ④

8. The man whom I met yesterday is my boss.
   ①    ②    ③          ④

9. I want to live near neighbors who have children.
   ①  ②      ③     ④

10. The girl who is smiling there is my sister.
    ①    ②    ③       ④

11. I want to have a jacket which has pockets.
   ①       ②    ③    ④

12. A woman that I know lost 15 kg.
   ①      ②    ③    ④

**2.** 다음 우리말을 영작하시오. '관계대명사' 또는 '관계대명사+be동사' 는 생략하시오.

1. 저기에서 자고 있는 소녀가 내 여동생이야.
→ _____

2. 이것은 어제 내가 빌린 책이야.(borrow)
→ _____

3. 내게 네가 들은 것을 말해줘.(everything)
→ _____

# Writing Pattern Practice

**1.** 목적격 관계대명사 생략

이것은 내가 어제 산 가방이다.

_____

이 사람은 내가 정말 좋아하는 사람이다.(~a lot)

_____

너는 우리가 뉴욕에서 만난 남자를 기억하니?

_____

내가 산 선풍기가 부서졌다.(fan, buy, break)

_____

나는 네가 준 손목시계를 잃어버렸어.

_____

이 것은 내가 가진 모든 것이다.(everything, have)

_____

나는 같이 놀 친구들이 많다.(a lot of)

_____

이 것은 내가 쓴 책이다.

_____

**2.** 「관계대명사 + be동사」 생략

축구를 하고 있는 소년은 내 남동생이다. (The boy~)

_____

이 것은 일본에서 만들어진 차이다.

_____

선글라스를 끼고 있는 저 여자 분은 내 엄마다.(The woman, wear, sunglasses)

_____

꼬리를 흔들고 있는 저 개는 내 개이다.(The dog, wag)

_____

**1.** 다음 보기를 참고하여 우리말을 영어로 바꿔 쓰시오. 관계대명사는 who, whose, who(m), which 중 골라 쓰시오.

> 보기 | 내가 어제 만난 그 남자
> → the man who(m) I met yesterday

① 옆집에 사는 그 여자 (next door)

→ _____

② 내가 사기를 원했던 그 컴퓨터 (want to)

→ _____

③ 3시에 떠나는 그 기차 (leave)

→ _____

④ 그녀가 입었던 그 드레스 (wear)

→ _____

⑤ 아버지가 소방관인 그 소년 (a fire fighter)

→ _____


**2.** 다음 중 틀린 곳을 밑줄치고 바르게 고치시오.

① This is the girl whose I like.

→ _____

② Disneyland is an amusement park whose I want to go to.

→ _____

③ Italy is a country who has a lot of interesting things.

→ _____

④ A thief is a person whom steals things.

→ _____

⑤ A rose is a flower who has thorns.

→ _____

⑥ Japan is a country whose is next to Korea.

→ _____

⑦ I know someone whom father is a famous actor.

→ _____

# REVIEW 2

[1-2] 다음 두 문장을 한 문장으로 연결할 때, 빈칸에 들어갈 알맞은 것을 고르시오.

**1.**

> I met a girl. + Her father is an artist.
> → I met a girl _____ father is an artist.

① who　　　　　② which
③ whom　　　　④ what
⑤ whose

**2.**

> Do you remember the boy + We met him in New York.
> → Do you remember the boy _____ we met in New York?

① that　　　　　② which
③ of which　　　④ what
⑤ whose

**3.** 다음 중 어법상 알맞지 <u>않는</u> 것은?

① We know the boys who are playing soccer.
② Look at the man dances on the stage.
③ The fan which I bought broke.
④ That's the woman whose dog bit me.
⑤ You're the one who I like.

[4-5] 빈칸에 알맞은 것을 고르시오.

**4.** The people _____ live next door have five children.

① who　　　　　② what
③ whose　　　　④ whom
⑤ of which

**5.** The mountain _____ top is covered with snow is Mt. Fuji.

① who　　　　　② what
③ whose　　　　④ whom
⑤ that

[6-7] 다음 밑줄 친 부분이 생략 가능한 것은?

**6.** ① I can't lend you the book <u>that</u> you want.
② The man <u>who</u> is playing the guitar is my uncle.
③ Do you know a shop <u>which</u> sells a good dress?
④ This is the dog <u>whose</u> ears are big.
⑤ This is the boy <u>that</u> won the race.

**7.** ① Look at that castle <u>which</u> stands on the hill.
② The man <u>who</u> is wearing a hat is John.
③ The river <u>which</u> flows through London is the Thames.
④ She is a teacher <u>who</u> teaches us English.
⑤ The dog <u>which is</u> wagging its tail is my dog.

**8.** 다음 빈칸에 들어갈 관계대명사가 순서대로 짝지어진 것은?

① who - that　　　② whose - that
③ that - whom　　④ whose - who
⑤ which - whom

Pirates are criminals _____ steal what ships carry. Years ago, pirates worked for governments and attacked enemy ships. Later, they attacked all ships, and most were killed or put in jail. A few pirates remained free and became rich. These days, pirates use modern boats and guns and computers. Some companies pay millions of dollars to return ships _____ were stolen.

*pirate 해적 *criminal 범인, 범죄자 *government 정부
*attack 공격하다 *jail 감옥

# *Chapter 8 | 가정법

## Unit 29 | 가정법 과거, 과거완료

**Grammar in Practice**

A: If David were here, I would be happier.
B: If you hadn't made him angry,
   he would have come here.

---

**Grammar in Use**

**1.** 단순조건문과 가정법

- 단순 조건문: 어떤 조건이 주어졌을 때 앞으로 일어날 일을 말할 때 쓴다.
  If it **rains** tomorrow, I **will stay** home. 내일 비 오면 집에 있을 거야.

- 가정법: 실제 상황과 다른 불가능한 일을 상상하거나 소망할 때 사용한다.
  If I **were** rich, I **could buy** that car. 내가 부자라면 그 차를 살 수 있을 텐데.

**2.** 가정법 과거

「If+주어+동사과거형, 주어+조동사과거형+동사원형」형태로 '(만일 지금) ~라면 … 할 텐데' 로 해석한다. 현재사실과 반대되거나 일어날 것 같지 않은 일을 가정할 때 쓴다.

If I **had** an umbrella, I **could go** out now. 내가 우산이 있다면 지금 밖에 나갈 수 있을 텐데.
(→ As I don't have an umbrella, I can't go out now.)
If I **were** you, I **would not say** so. 내가 너라면 그렇게 말하지 않을 텐데.
If he **became** a doctor, he **could help** many people. 그가 의사가 되었다면 많은 사람들을 도울 수 있을 텐데.

> **| MORE TIPS |** 가정법 과거에서 if절에 be동사가 쓰일 경우 주어와 상관없이 were를 쓴다. 주어가 3인칭 단수일 경우 was를 쓰는 경우도 있다.
> If John **were**(=**was**) here with me, I **would be** happy. John이 여기에 나와 있다면 나는 행복할 텐데.
> If I **were** you, I **would forgive** him. 내가 너라면 그를 용서해 줄 텐데.

**3.** 가정법 과거완료

「If+주어+had+과거분사, 주어+조동사과거형+have+과거분사」형태로 '(만일 과거에) ~했다면 … 했었을 텐데' 로 해석한다. 과거사실과 반대되거나 일어날 것 같지 않던 일을 가정할 때 쓴다.

If I **had studied** hard, I **would have passed** the exam. 내가 열심히 공부했더라면 시험에 합격할 수 있었을 텐데.
(→ As I didn't study hard, I didn't pass the exam.)
If you **had not been** late, you **could have seen** that movie. 네가 늦지 않았더라면 그 영화를 볼 수 있었을 텐데.
If I **had taken** a subway, I **would have arrived** here on time. 내가 지하철을 탔더라면 제시간에 올 수 있었을 텐데.

# Unit Test

**1.** 둘 중 알맞은 것을 고르시오.

1. If I (were, am) not sick, I could play with you.

2. If it were not rainy, I (can, could) go out and play basketball.

3. If Neil (had played, played) well, the team would have won.

4. If I (miss, missed) the bus, I will be late.

5. If I (has, had) a million dollars, I would buy that building.

6. If I (had studied, studied) harder, I would have passed the exam.

7. If he (has, had) money, he would buy a house.

8. If I had a cell phone, I (can, could) call my mother.

9. If Sarah (has, had) enough money, she could go to Europe.

10. If Susan were here, we (would, will) be happy.

11. If I had lived 50 years ago, I (wouldn't have had, wouldn't have) a cell phone.

12. If I (hadn't missed, didn't miss) the bus, I wouldn't have been late for school.


**2.** 우리말과 일치하도록 빈칸에 알맞은 말을 써 넣으시오.

1. 내가 너라면 그렇게 말하지 않을 텐데.
   If I _____ you, I _____ say so.

2. 내가 의사선생님이라면, 너를 도와줄 수 있을 텐데.
   If I _____ a doctor, I _____ help you.

3. 그가 덜 먹는다면, 몸무게를 줄일 수 있을 텐데.
   If he _____ less, he _____ lose his weight.

4. 네가 편지를 일찍 부쳤더라면, 그것은 시간 안에 도착했을 텐데.
   If you _____ the letter earlier, it _____ arrived in time.

5. 네가 늦지 않았더라면 그 영화를 볼 수 있었을 텐데.
   If you _____ late, you _____ seen that movie.

# Writing Pattern Practice

**1.** **가정법 과거「If + 주어 + 동사과거형, 주어 + 조동사과거형 + 동사원형」**

내가 너라면 거기에 안갈 거야.(would)

_____

내가 의사선생님이라면 너를 도와줄 수 있을 텐데.(could)

_____

그가 여기에 있다면 나는 행복할 거야.

_____

비가 오지 않는다면 우리는 나갈 수 있을 텐데.(could)

_____

내가 돈이 있다면 그것을 살 수 있을 거야.(could)

_____

그가 담배를 끊는다면 건강할 텐데.(quit smoking, would, healthy)

_____

만약 일요일이라면 우리는 피크닉 갈 텐데.(go on a picnic)

_____


**2.** **가정법 과거완료「If + 주어 + had + 과거분사, 주어 + 조동사과거형 + have + 과거분사」**

내가 숙제를 끝마쳤더라면, 거기에 갈 수 있었을 텐데.(finish, could)

_____

그가 서둘렀으면 제시간에 여기에 도착 할 수 있었을 텐데.(hurry, arrive, on time)

_____

만약에 Neil이 잘 뛰었다면 팀이 우승했을 거야.(play well, win)

_____

# 30 | I wish 가정법, as if 가정법

Grammar
in
Practice

A: I wish he weren't here. Who invited him?

B: I don't know. I don't like him, either.

He talks as if he knew everything.

Grammar
in
Use

**1.** I wish+가정법

- 「I wish+가정법 과거(주어+동사과거형)」
  현재 사실과 다른 상황을 소원할 때 사용하며, 뜻은 '~하면 좋을 텐데'이다.
  **I wish I were** pretty. 내가 예쁘다면 좋을 텐데.
  **I wish I had** a baby brother. 아기 남동생이 있으면 좋을 텐데.

- 「I wish + 가정법 과거완료(주어 + had + 과거분사)」
  과거 사실과 다른 상황을 소원할 때 사용하며, 뜻은 '~했다면 좋을 텐데'이다.
  **I wish I had got up** early. 일찍 일어났더라면 좋을 텐데.
  **I wish** you **had finished** your homework. 네가 숙제를 끝마쳤더라면 좋을 텐데.

**2.** as if + 가정법

- 「as if+가정법과거(주어+동사과거형)」
  현재 사실과 다른 상황을 가정할 때 사용하며, 뜻은 '마치 ~인 것처럼'이다.
  He talks **as if** he **were** rich. 그는 마치 부자인 것처럼 말한다.

- 「as if+가정법과거완료(주어+had+과거분사)」
  과거 사실과 다른 상황을 가정할 때 사용하며, 뜻은 '마치 ~였던 것처럼'이다.
  He acts **as if** he **had been** sick. 그는 마치 아팠던 것처럼 행동한다.

# Unit Test

**1.** 보기와 같이 두 문장이 같은 뜻이 되도록 알맞은 말을 써넣으시오.

> 보기 | I'm sorry that I don't have a brother.
> → I wish I had a brother.
>
> I'm sorry that Ben didn't come to my birthday party.
> → I wish Ben had come to my birthday party.

1. I'm sorry that I can't speak Chinese.

→ I wish _____

2. I'm sorry that I'm not handsome.

→ I wish _____

3. He's sorry that he's not tall.

→ He wishes _____

4. I'm sorry that I'm not skinny like a model.

→ I wish _____

5. I'm sorry that I didn't study hard.

→ I wish _____

6. I'm sorry that I wasn't there.

→ I wish _____

7. I'm sorry that I didn't know the answer.

→ I wish _____

**2.** 우리말과 일치하도록 빈칸에 알맞은 말을 써 넣으시오.

1. 그녀는 마치 자기가 공주님인 것처럼 행동한다.

She acts as if she _____ a princess. (=In fact, she isn't a princess.)

2. 그녀는 마치 내가 아기인 것처럼 취급한다.

She treats me _____ . (=In fact, I'm not a baby.)

3. 그는 마치 그가 영화를 본 것처럼 말한다.

He talks as if he _____ that movie. (=In fact, he didn't see that movie.)

4. 그는 마치 숙제를 끝마친 것처럼 말한다.

He talks _____ . (=In fact, he didn't finish his homework.)

# Writing Pattern Practice

**1.** 「I wish + 가정법 과거(주어 + 동사과거형)」

내가 너라면 좋을 텐데. _____

내가 키가 크다면 좋을 텐데. _____

내가 핸드폰 있다면 좋을 텐데.(a cell phone) _____

내가 애완동물이 있다면 좋을 텐데.(a pet) _____

내가 영어를 잘 말할 수 있다면 좋을 텐데.(speak) _____


**2.** 「I wish + 가정법 과거완료(주어 + had + 과거분사)」

내가 숙제를 끝마쳤더라면 좋을 텐데.(finish, my homework)

_____

내가 답을 알았다면 좋을 텐데.(know) _____

내가 지하철을 탔더라면 좋을 텐데.(take a subway) _____


**3.** 「as if + 가정법과거(주어 + 동사과거형)」

그녀는 마치 자기가 공주님인 것처럼 행동한다. _____

그는 모든 것을 알고 있는 것처럼 행동한다. _____


**4.** 「as if + 가정법과거완료(주어 + had + 과거분사)」

그녀는 마치 숙제를 끝마친 것처럼 말한다. _____

그는 마치 유령을 본 것처럼 말한다.(talk, a ghost) _____

# REVIEW 1

**1.** 밑줄친 문장이 어법상 올바르면 O표, 올바르지 않으면 X표 하고 틀린 곳을 알맞게 고치시오.

① It's raining outside. <u>If it is fine, we could go on a picnic.</u>

→ _____

② I want to be alone. <u>I wish I didn't live with my parents.</u>

→ _____

③ He doesn't know much about it. <u>But he looks as if he knows everything.</u>

→ _____

④ I have no money. <u>I wish I have a lot of money.</u>

→ _____

⑤ I was sick yesterday. <u>If I hadn't been sick, I could have attended the meeting.</u>

→ _____

⑥ I don't know anything about it. <u>If I know something, I would tell you all.</u>

→ _____

⑦ I'm not you. <u>But if I am you, I wouldn't lend him the money.</u>

→ _____

⑧ I'm not a bird. <u>If I have wings, I would fly through the air.</u>

→ _____

⑨ I drove here. <u>If I had taken a subway, I wouldn't have been late.</u>

→ _____

⑩ I didn't finish my homework. <u>I wish I finished my homework.</u>

→ _____

**2.** 다음 문장을 우리말로 해석하시오.

① If I were you, I wouldn't tell a lie.

→ _____

② If you had asked me, I would have told you.

→ _____

③ I wish I had a baby brother.

→ _____

④ I wish I had done my work.

→ _____

⑤ She acts as if she were a model.

→ _____

⑥ He talks as if he had been honest.

→ _____

[1-2] 빈칸에 들어갈 가장 알맞은 말은?

**1.** If I were tall, I _____ play basketball well.

① can
② will
③ could
④ am able to
⑤ would have

**2.** He treats me as if I _____ a baby.

① am
② was
③ will be
④ were
⑤ should be

**3.** 다음을 가정법 문장으로 바꿀 때, 빈칸에 들어갈 알맞은 말을 고르시오.

In fact, something important happened. But everybody behaves as if nothing _____.

① happens
② happened
③ will happen
④ had happened
⑤ is happening

**4.** 다음 중 앞뒤 문장의 연결이 <u>어색한</u> 것을 고르시오.

① I don't have enough money. I wish I were rich.
② I don't play the piano well. I wish I were a good player.
③ I didn't study hard. I wish I had studied harder.
④ I couldn't sleep well. I wish I could have slept well.
⑤ I didn't walk here. I wish I wouldn't have walked here.

**5.** 우리말과 같은 뜻이 되도록 빈칸에 들어갈 알맞은 말을 고르시오.

그녀는 마치 자신이 모든 것을 아는 것같이 말한다.
She talks as if she _____ everything.

① knows
② knew
③ had known
④ will know
⑤ should know

**6.** 다음 중 어법상 어색한 것은?

① If David were here, everybody would be happy
② If I were you, I wouldn't say so.
③ I wish you were here with us.
④ If he had asked me out, I would have said yes.
⑤ She behaves as if she is a witch.

*witch 마녀

**7.** 다음 빈칸에 들어갈 말로 가장 알맞은 것을 고르시오.

① go
② can go
③ could go
④ could have gone
⑤ will go

My house has a big lake next to it. Every spring and fall, many ducks gather on the lake. They only stay a few days. Usually they make a lot of noise. They are either going south or coming north, depending on the season. In the winter when the snow comes, I envy the ducks. I wish I _____ south for warmer weather too.

# *Chapter 9 │ 일치와 특수구문

# 31 수의 일치

**Grammar in Practice**

A: Is Jack your friend?
B: Yes, he and I are very close friends.
Not only Jack but also Eric is one of
my best friends.

**Grammar in Use**

1. '수의 일치'란 주어가 단수인지 복수인지에 따라 동사의 수를 일치시키는 것을 말한다.
   ex. **She and I** <u>are</u> sisters. 그녀와 나는 자매다.

2. 단수 취급 하는 경우
   - 학과명, 병명, 나라이름
     **Physics** <u>is</u> my favorite subject. 물리학은 내가 좋아하는 과목이다.
     **Measles** <u>gives</u> us a high fever. 홍역은 높은 열이 난다.
   - (일정한 정도 · 양을 나타내는) 시간, 거리, 금액
     **Five dollars** <u>is</u> all I have. 5달러가 내가 가진 전부다.
     **Ten miles** <u>is</u> a long distance to walk. 10마일은 걷기에 먼 거리이다.
   - 주어가 every나 each로 시작할 때
     **Every student** <u>is</u> in the classroom. 모든 학생은 교실에 있다.

3. 복수 취급 하는 경우
   - A and B
     두 가지 이상을 and를 써서 나열하는 경우, 보통 복수형 동사를 쓴다.
     **Andy and David** <u>are</u> close friends. Andy와 David은 가까운 친구이다.
   - a number of +복수명사
     **A number of people** <u>are</u> jogging in the park. 많은 사람들이 공원에서 조깅하고 있다.

4. 상관접속사의 수의 일치
   B에 동사의 수를 일치시킨다.
   - Both A and B 'A와 B 모두'
     **Both Jack and I** <u>come</u> from China. Jack과 나는 모두 중국출신이다.
   - Either A or B 'A 또는 B'
     **Either you or Julie** <u>has</u> to go there. 너 또는 Julie가 거기에 가야한다.
   - Neither A nor B 'A도 아니고 B도 아닌'
     **Neither my parents nor my brother** <u>is</u> here. 부모님도 남동생도 여기에 없다.
   - not only A but also B (=B as well as A) 'A뿐만 아니라 B(도)'
     **Not only Jane but also I** <u>am</u> satisfied. Jane 뿐만 아니라 나도 만족한다.

# Unit Test

**1.** 둘 중 알맞은 것을 고르시오.

1. Two hours (is/ are) a long time to wait.
2. Every student (is/ are) in the classroom.
3. Mathematics (is/ are) my favorite subject.
4. You as well as he (is/ are) kind to us.
5. Ten dollars (is/ are) not much money for an adult.  *adult 어른
6. Andy and David (is/ are) close friends.
7. Either you or he (is/ are) right.
8. Not only he but also I (am/ is) satisfied.  *satisfied 만족한
9. Neither Peter nor his friends (was/ were) present at the meeting.
10. Both Sally and I (come/ comes) from the United States.


**2.** 우리말과 일치하도록 괄호 안에 알맞은 말을 써 넣으시오.(괄호 안의 말을 고쳐 쓰시오.)

1. 너 뿐만 아니라 James도 나를 이해한다.
   Not only you but also James ＿＿＿＿＿＿ me.(understand)

2. 내 남동생과 나는 둘 다 같은 학교에 다닌다.
   Both my brother and I ＿＿＿＿＿＿ to the same school.(go)

3. 너 또는 내가 이 것에 책임이 있다.
   Either you or I ＿＿＿＿＿＿ responsible for this.(be)

4. 수학은 쉬운 공부가 아니다.
   Mathematics ＿＿＿＿＿＿ not an easy study.(be)

5. 두 시간은 기다리기에 오랜 시간이다.
   Two hours ＿＿＿＿＿＿ a long time to wait.(be)

6. 모든 국가는 국기를 가지고 있다.
   Every country ＿＿＿＿＿＿ a national flag.(have)

7. 100 달러는 선물에 쓰기 너무 많다.
   100 dollars ＿＿＿＿＿＿ a lot to spend on a gift.(be)

# Writing Pattern Practice

**1.** 「주어+단수형동사」
단수취급

5달러가 내가 가진 전부다.(all I have) _____

두 시간은 기다리기에 오랜 시간이다.(a long time, wait)

_____

홍역은 높은 열이 난다.(Measles, give us, fever) _____

물리학은 내가 좋아하는 과목이다.(Physics~) _____

모든 학생은 교실에 있다.(Every~) _____


**2.** 「주어+복수형동사」
복수취급

Yuki와 David은 가까운 친구이다. _____

많은 학생들이 뛰고 있다.(A number of~) _____


**3.** 상관접속사의 수의일치

너 또는 네 언니가 거기에 가야한다.(Either~or) _____

부모님도 여동생도 여기에 없다.(Neither~nor) _____

Jane 뿐만 아니라 나도 만족한다.(Not only~but also)

_____

# 32 | 시제의 일치

**Grammar in Practice**

A: Neil, You came on time. I thought you would be late.

B: Jenny gave me a ride here, so I was able to come early.

**Grammar in Use**

**1.** '시제의 일치'란 주절의 시제에 따라 종속절의 시제를 맞추어 쓰는 것을 말한다. 주절의 동사가 현재일 경우, 종속절에는 '모든' 시제가 올 수 있다.

**I know** that Romeo <u>loves</u> Juliet. 나는 Romeo가 Juliet을 사랑하는 것을 알고 있다.
<u>현재</u>

**I know** that Romeo <u>loved</u> Juliet. 나는 Romeo가 Juliet을 사랑했던 것을 알고 있다.
<u>과거</u>

**I know** that Romeo <u>will love</u> Juliet. 나는 Romeo가 Juliet를 사랑할 것을 알고 있다.
<u>미래</u>

**2.** 주절의 동사가 과거일 경우, 종속절의 동사는 다음과 같이 변한다.

**I knew** that Romeo <u>loved</u> Juliet. 나는 Romeo가 Juliet을 사랑하는 것을 알고 있었다.
**I knew** that Romeo <u>had loved</u> Juliet. 나는 Romeo가 Juliet을 사랑했던 것을 알고 있었다.
**I knew** that Romeo <u>would love</u> Juliet. 나는 Romeo가 Juliet을 사랑할 것을 알고 있었다.

**3.** 시제일치의 예외

● 종속절이 일반적 진리, 사실을 나타낼 때, 주절의 시제와 상관없이 '현재'를 쓴다.
**We learned that water boils at 100°C** 우리는 물은 100°C에서 끓는다고 배웠다.

● 종속절이 역사적 사실을 나타낼 때, 주절의 시제와 상관없이 '과거'를 쓴다.
**My teacher says. "King Sejong made Hangeul in 1443."** 선생님이 말씀하시길 세종대왕이 1443년에 한글을 만드셨다고 하신다.

● 시간과 조건을 나타내는 부사절에서는 현재시제가 미래시제를 대신한다.
**If you go, I'll go.** 네가 가면 나도 갈게.

# Unit Test

**1.** 둘 중 알맞은 것을 고르시오.

1. I thought that she (looks/ looked) tired.

2. We learned that water (boils/ boiled) at 100°C

3. Everybody knows that the Korean war (breaks out/ broke out) in 1950.

4. He didn't know that I (am/ was) at work.

5. I knew that he (will/ would) come early.

**2.** 다음 문장을 과거 문장으로 바꿀 때 빈 칸에 알맞은 말을 써 넣으시오. 보기를 참고하시오.

> 보기 ｜  I know that she will give up.
>   → I knew that she would give up.

1. You tell me that you will be absent.

→ _____

2. She says that she has a cold.

→ _____

3. They think that they are happy together.

→ _____

**3.** 다음 밑줄 친 부분 중 어법상 틀린 부분을 골라 고치시오.

1. I <u>thought</u> that you <u>will</u> <u>leave</u> <u>on</u> Friday.
      ①          ②  ③  ④

2. <u>Everybody</u> <u>knows</u> that <u>the earth</u> <u>was</u> round.
     ①     ②       ③    ④

3. She <u>says</u> <u>that</u> Columbus <u>discovers</u> <u>the Americas</u>.
      ①  ②        ③      ④

# Writing Pattern Practice

**1.** 주절 + 종속절
현재  모든 시제

나는 그녀가 감기에 걸린 것을 안다.(have, a cold)

_____

나는 그가 숙제를 마쳤다고 생각한다.(finish, his homework)

_____

그녀는 체중을 줄일 거라고 말한다.(say, lose her weight)

_____

**2.** 주절 + 종속절
과거  과거, 과거완료

나는 그가 나를 도와줄 거라고 생각 했다.  _____

나는 그녀가 일본에 가본 것을 알고 있었다.(have been to) _____

그녀는 결석할 거라고 말했다.(say, absent)  _____

**3.** 주절 + 종속절
항상 현재시제: 일반적 진리 사실

우리는 지구가 둥글다는 것을 안다.(know, the Earth, round)

_____

그녀는 매일 조깅을 한다고 말했다.(say, jog)

_____

**4.** 주절 + 종속절
항상 과거시제: 역사적 사실

선생님께서 한국전쟁이 1950년에 일어났다고 말씀하셨다.(My teacher said, the Korean war, break out)

_____

우리는 콜럼버스가 미국을 발견한 것을 안다. (discover, the Americas)

_____

# 33 | 강조구문과 부정구문

A: Do you love Bob?

B: Yes, I do. I do love him.

A: When did you first met him?

B: It was last Christmas that I first met him.

**1.** do (does/did) 동사를 이용하여 동사의 의미를 강조할 수 있는데 '정말 ~하다'로 해석한다. do에 강세를 넣어 말한다.

I love you. → I **do** love you. 나는 정말 너를 사랑해.

He likes math. → He **does** like math. 그는 정말 수학을 좋아해.

I got the first prize. → I **did** get the first prize. 나는 정말 일등상을 탔어.

**2.** 「It is (was) ~ that」의 that 앞에 강조하고 싶은 말(문장의 주어, 목적어, 부사(구) 등)을 쓴다.

강조하고 싶은 문장: I met <u>Jane</u> <u>at a cafe</u> <u>yesterday</u>.
ⓐ      ⓑ      ⓒ        ⓓ

ⓐ 주어강조

**It was** <u>I</u> **that (=who)** met Jane at a cafe yesterday. 어제 카페에서 Jane은 만난 사람은 나였다.

ⓑ 목적어강조

**It was** <u>Jane</u> **that(=who(m))** I met at a cafe yesterday. 어제 카페에서 내가 만난 사람은 Jane이었다.

ⓒ 장소부사(구)강조

**It was** <u>at a cafe</u> **that(=where)** I met Jane yesterday. 어제 내가 Jane을 만난 곳은 카페였다.

ⓓ 시간부사강조

**It was** <u>yesterday</u> **that(=when)** I met Jane yesterday. 내가 카페에서 Jane을 만난 것은 어제였다.

**3.** 부정구문은 전체부정과 부분부정으로 나눌 수 있다.

● 전체부정

부정어 no, neither, none 등을 이용해 '어떤 ~도 …않다'라는 의미로 쓰인다.

**No** one likes him. 아무도 그를 좋아하지 않는다.

**Neither** of them came here. 그들 중 아무도 여기에 오지 않았다.

● 부분부정

부정어 not이 always, all 등과 함께 쓰여 '모두(항상) ~한 것은 아니다'라는 의미로 쓰인다.

You **cannot** be **always** right. 네가 항상 옳을 수는 없다.

**Not all** cats dislike dogs. 모든 고양이가 개를 싫어하지는 않는다.

# Unit Test

**1.** 다음 밑줄친 동사를 보기와 같이 강조해 쓰시오.

> 보기 | I love you
> → I do love you.

1. I love my parents.
→ _____

2. She likes movies.
→ _____

3. I finished my homework.
→ _____

**2.** 'It~that'을 사용하여 다음 밑줄 친 부분을 강조할 때 빈칸에 알맞은 말을 써넣으시오.

1. <u>Jane</u> met Tom at a cafe yesterday.
_____ that met Tom at a cafe yesterday.

2. Jane met <u>Tom</u> at a cafe yesterday.
_____ that Jane met at cafe yesterday.

3. I met Tom <u>at a cafe</u> yesterday.
_____ that I met Tom.

4. I met Tom at a cafe <u>yesterday</u>.
_____ that I met Tom at a cafe.

**3.** 우리말과 일치하도록 빈칸에 알맞은 말을 써 넣으시오.

1. 부자들이 항상 행복한 것은 아니다.
The rich are _____ happy.

2. 네가 항상 옳을 수는 없다.
You _____ right.

3. 아무도 그녀를 좋아하지 않는다.
_____ one likes him.

# Writing Pattern Practice

**1.** 「do/does/did+동사원형」

나는 정말 너를 사랑해. _____

그녀는 스포츠를 정말 싫어해. _____

나는 정말 숙제를 마쳤어. _____

**2.** 「It+is/was+강조할 단어/구+that」

내가 좋아하는 사람은 너다. _____

내가 작년에 Chicago에서 만난 사람은 Jane이였다.(It was~, meet, in) _____

내가 작년에 Jane을 만난 건 Chicago였다. _____

내가 공원에서 본 사람은 Tom이 아니었다.(It wasn't~) _____

내가 Tom을 본 곳은 공원에서가 아니었다.(It wasn't ~, in the park) _____

**3.** 전체부정/부분부정

아무도 상처받지 않았다.(be hurt) _____

가난한 사람들이 항상 불행하지는 않다.(The poor~, unhappy) _____

# 34 | 생략과 도치

Grammar in Practice

A: **Uh-oh!** There comes Katie.

B: **Oh, I'd better go. I don't really like her.**

A: Neither do I.

---

Grammar in Use

**1.** 반복되거나 문맥상 알 수 있는 어구는 '생략' 가능하다.

- 중복을 피하기 위한 생략

  I washed my face and **(I)** brushed my teeth. 나는 세수를 하고 이를 닦았다.

  Anny is a student and also her sister **(is a student)**. Anny는 학생이고, 동생도 학생 이다.

- 부사절에서 「주어+동사」 생략

  When **(I was)** young, I lived in Canada. 내가 젊었을 때 캐나다에서 살았다.

  If **(it is)** necessary, I'll give you that book. 필요하다면 네게 그책을 줄게.

- 관용적 생략

  **No smoking!**(=No smoking is allowed.) 금연입니다.

  **No swimming!**(=No swimming is allowed.) 수영금지입니다

  **Not for sale!**(=This is not for sale.) 이것은 비매품이다.

**2.** 원래 있던 위치를 뒤바꾸는 것은 '도치' 라고 하며, 특정어를 강조하기 위해서나 관용적인 표현에 서 쓴다.

- 부사(구) 강조를 위한 도치

  「부사(구)+동사+주어」

  Your book is on the desk. → **On the desk is your book.**

  Your boyfriend comes here. → **Here comes your boyfriend.**

- 부정어 강조를 위한 도치

  「부정어+조동사/do+주어+동사」

  I never saw him again. → **Never did I see him again.**

- 관용적 도치

  「So/Neither+동사+주어」

  앞에서 한 말에 대해 '~도 역시 그렇다' 는 의미로 긍정문 뒤에는 「So+동사+주어」를 부정문 뒤에는 「Neither+동사+주어」를 쓴다.

| So+동사+주어 | Neither+동사+주어 |
|---|---|
| A: I'm hungry.    B: **So am I.** | A: I'm not hungry.    B: **Neither am I.** |
| A: I like English.    B: **So do I.** | A: I don't like English.    B: **Neither do I.** |
| A: I ate lunch.    B: **So did I.** | A: I didn't eat lunch.    B: **Neither did I.** |

# Unit Test

1. 보기와 같이 문장에서 생략할 수 있는 부분에 괄호( ) 하시오.

> 보기ㅣ I lived in Seoul when (I was) young.

  1. I came back home and I had dinner.

  2. No parking is allowed here.

  3. This is not for sale.


2. 다음 문장을 과거 문장으로 바꿀 때 빈 칸에 알맞은 말을 써 넣으시오. 보기를 참고하시오.

  1. I never heard about it.

  → Never (did I/ I did) hear about it.

  2. Your bag is under the desk.

  → Under the desk (your bag is/ is your bag).

  3. She likes seeing a movie, and I like seeing a move, too.

  → She likes seeing a movie, and (so I do/ so do I/ so am I).

  4. She didn't do her homework, and I didn't do my homework, either.

  → She didn't do her homework, and (neither did I/ neither do I).


3. 보기와 같이 내가(I) 상대방 말에 동의하는 말을 써 넣으시오.

> 보기ㅣ A: I like soccer.
> 
>       B: So do I.

  1. A: I'm thirsty.

     B: _____

  2. A: I finished my report.

     B: _____

  3. A: I don't want to buy that.

     B: _____

  4. A: I didn't write a diary.

     B: _____

# Writing Pattern Practice

**1.** 반복 피하기 위한 생략

나는 세수를 하고 이를 닦았다.(←나는 세수를 하고 나는 이를 닦았다.)

그녀는 영어와 일본어를 말한다.(←그녀는 영어를 말하고 일본어를 말한다.)

**2.** 부사절에서 「주어+be동사」생략

젊었을 때 그녀는 날씬했었다.(When~, slim)

가능하면 나는 너를 보고 싶어. (want to, possible)

**3.** 관용적 생략

수영 금지

주차 금지

비매품

**4.** 부사(구)/부정어 강조를 위한 도치

책상위에 네 책이 있다.

나무 아래에 잘생긴 남자가 서 있었다.(Under~, stand)

그 소식을 전혀 믿을 수 없다. (Never can~, the news)

**5.** 관용적 도치

A: I'm tired.    B: 나도 그래.

A: I was hungry.    B: 나도 그랬어.

A: He doesn't get up early.    B: 그녀도 그래.

A: He didn't come to the meeting.    B: 그녀도 그랬어.

**1.** 둘 중 알맞은 것을 골라 동그라미 하시오.

① Mathematics (is/ are) my favorite subject.
② Both she and her sister (is/ are) very pretty.
③ Not only children but also my father (is/ are) interested in playing computer games.
④ Five dollars (is/ are) enough money for me.
⑤ A number of soldiers (was/ were) wounded in the war.
⑥ Everybody knows the sun (rises/ rose) in the east.
⑦ If it (rains/ will rain) tomorrow, I won't go out.
⑧ My teacher says that the Korean war (breaks out/ broke out) in 1950.

**2.** 다음 밑줄 친 부분의 시제를 과거로 바꿔 문장을 다시 쓰시오.

① He says that <u>he is in trouble</u>.
→ He said that _____

② He tells me that <u>he is going to be absent</u>.
→ He told me that _____

[3-4] 다음 우리말과 같은 의미가 되도록 할 때 빈칸에 들어갈 말로 알맞은 것은?

**3.**
> 모든 남자가 용감한 것은 아니다.
> → _____ all men are brave.

**4.**
> A: I'm not interested in sports.
> B: 나도 그래. → _____ am I.

**5.** 다음 문장의 어법상 잘못된 곳을 골라 고쳐 쓰시오.

> Under the tree a strange-looking man stood.

[1-2] 다음 밑줄 친 부분 대신 쓸 수 있는 말을 고르시오.

**1.**

> It is Jane <u>that</u> can speak 5 languages.

① who
② whom
③ which
④ when
⑤ where

**2.**

> A: I like seeing a movie.
> B: <u>I like seeing a movie, too.</u>

① So am I.
② So do I.
③ So was I.
④ So did I.
⑤ So will I.

**3.** 다음 우리말과 같은 의미가 되도록 빈칸에 들어갈 말로 알맞은 것은?

> Anny의 오빠는 항상 컴퓨터를 하지만 Anny는 그렇지 않다.
> → Anny's brother always plays computer games but Anny _____.

① don't
② doesn't
③ didn't
④ isn't
⑤ wasn't

**4.** 다음 보기의 밑줄 친 do와 용법이 같은 것은?

> 보기 | A: Do you like learning English?
> B: Yes, I <u>do</u> love learning English.

① Please <u>do</u> me a favor.
② I didn't <u>do</u> my homework.
③ Can you help me <u>do</u> the dishes?
④ We <u>do</u> exercise everyday.
⑤ Jane doesn't like math and neither <u>do</u> I.

**5.** 다음 중 어법상 알맞지 <u>않는</u> 것은?

① It was in 1592 that the war broke out.
② I did told you that.
③ No one likes heavy rain.
④ The poor are not always unhappy.
⑤ It was Jane that I ran into yesterday.

**6.** 다음 빈칸에 공통으로 들어갈 알맞은 말은?

> a. Not only you but also I _____ responsible for this.
> b. Either Heather or I _____ going to attend the meeting tomorrow.

① am
② are
③ is
④ was
⑤ were

**7.** 다음 빈칸에 들어갈 말이 순서대로 짝지어진 것은?

① is - get
② are - gets
③ are - get
④ are - got
⑤ was - gets

The Academy Awards _____ one of the most well known and oldest awards shows. The first show took place on May 16, 1929. It is a ceremony that gives awards to the best films and performers of that year. Each winner _____ a gold statuette called an Oscar. The nickname Oscar came from a secretary who saw the statuette and said it looked like her Uncle Oscar.

*statuette 작은 조각품

EASY ENGLISH GRAMMAR COURSE FOR BEGINNERS

# BASIC
# English
# Grammar
## for Speaking & Writing

## 2

머리에 쏙쏙 들어오는
# 정답 및 해설

MENTORS

# BASIC
## English
## Grammar
*for Speaking & Writing*

# 2권

## 정답 및 해설

## Chapter 01 명사와 관사

### Unit 01_ 명사의 쓰임

| P.14

### Dialogue

A: 그는 누구입니까?
B: 그는 나의 남동생입니다.
A: 그의 이름이 무엇입니까?
B: 그의 이름은 Jack Daniel입니다.
A: 그는 어디 삽니까?
B: 밴쿠버에 살아요.
A: 그는 무엇을 좋아합니까?
B: 서핑을 좋아해요.

### Unit Test

**1.**

| | |
|---|---|
| 1. Ann, health | 2. Money, life |
| 3. Sally, music | 4. sky, sun |
| 5. Tokyo, capital, Japan | 6. Money, happiness |
| 7. friends | 8. father, lawyer |
| 9. Ann, restaurant | 10. secret |

**2.**

1. O  2. S  3. O  4. C  5. S
6. S  7. O  8. C  9. S  10. C

### Writing Pattern Practice

**1.**

The weather is nice.
My sisters are twins.
Roses are beautiful.
Eric is my boyfriend.
Jenny stayed at the Hilton Hotel.

**2.**

I like sports.
Jane loves her parents.
Daniel wrote a book.
An elephant has a long nose.
People watch TV a lot.

**3.**

I'm a student.
Today is Monday.
My favorite sport is soccer.
Yesterday was my birthday.

**4.**

Call me David.
People call me a fool.

**5.**

I'm interested in music.
Look at that girl.
We're waiting for the bus.
I'm looking for my cell phone.

### Unit 02_ 명사의 소유격

| P.17

### Dialogue

A: 네 핸드폰 좀 써도 되니?
B: 미안해, 오늘 안가지고 왔어.
   Mike 것을 쓰지 그래?
A: 이것이 Mike 핸드폰이야?
B: 맞아.

### Unit Test

**1.**

| | | |
|---|---|---|
| girls' | Judy's | women's |
| men's | mother's | children's |
| baby's | Scott's | |

**2.**

1. women's   2. men's   3. Mike's
4. girls'    5. teacher's

**3.**

1. Jacks → Jack's
2. Janets → Janet's
3. Mr. Kim → Mr. Kim's
4. Cindy → Cindy's
5. Sally → Sally's

**4.**

1. ( X ) → Peter's favorite food
2. ( O )                3. ( O )
4. ( X ) → my parents' house
5. ( O )                6. ( O )
7. ( X ) → your sister's phone number
8. ( X ) → Kate's nickname

### Writing Pattern Practice

**1.**

Tom's car

Is that Tom's car?

women's clothes

These are women's clothes.

driver's license

David has a driver's license.

Tim's cell phone

This is Tim's cell phone.

Jane's house

Jane's house is next to the post office.

## 2.

the title of this song

What's the title of this song?

the beginning of the movie

Hurry up, or we'll miss the beginning of the movie.

the author of this book

Tell me the author of this book.

## 3.

Mike's

This computer is Mike's (computer).

Mary's

You can use Mary's.

Shakespeare's

Is this play Shakespeare's?

## Unit 03_ 셀 수 있는 명사와 셀 수 없는 명사

| P.20

### Dialogue

A: 뭐 샀어?

B: 야채를 좀 샀어.

A: 쌀이 떨어져 가는데. 샀어?

B: 응.

### Unit Test

**1.**

star(C), ink(U), apple(C), car(C), money(U), bread(U), furniture(U), advice(U), music(U), book(C), salt(U), information(U), water(U), eye(C), foot(C), tooth(C), chair(C), man(C), boy(C), perfume(U), love(U), happiness(U), friend(C), key(C)

**2.**

1. It's milk.       2. It's an egg.
3. It's money.     4. It's a key.

5. It's a star.

**3.**

1. money          2. information
3. long           4. a hat
5. a car          6. a flower
7. a job          8. coffee
9. Money          10. meat

### Writing Pattern Practice

**1.**

I need an apple.

I need a girlfriend.

I need a cell phone.

I need a month.

**2.**

I need two chairs.

I need two pens.

I need two books.

I need two weeks.

**3.**

I need money.

I need food.

I need paper.

I need fresh air.

**4.**

I need a cup of coffee.

I need a piece of paper.

I need a glass of water.

I need a spoonful of sugar.

**5.**

I need two loaves of bread.

I need two boxes of cereal.

I need two bottles of Coke.

I need two bunches of grapes.

## Unit 04_ 명사의 복수형

| P.23

### Dialogue

A: 안경이 필요한데 찾을 수가 없어요.

B: 책상 위에 있어.

A: 셔츠와 청바지는 어디 있어요?

B: 그것들은 침대 위에 올려놨어.

## Unit Test

### 1.

| | |
|---|---|
| day - days | week - weeks |
| month - months | year - years |
| dish -dishes | flower - flowers |
| umbrella - umbrellas | baby - babies |
| woman - women | man - men |
| knife -knives | dictionary - dictionaries |
| party - parties | potato - potatoes |
| tomato - tomatoes | box -boxes |
| sheep - sheep | fish - fish |
| tooth - teeth | mouse - mice |

### 2.

1. Sheeps → Sheep      2. is → are
3. is → are            4. jean → jeans
5. sunglass → sunglasses
6. woman → women
7. Man → Men
8. tomatos → tomatoes
9. childs → children
10. benchs → benches

### 3.

| | | | |
|---|---|---|---|
| 1. are | 2. taste | 3. are | 4. are |
| 5. hurt | 6. are | 7. look | 8. are |
| 9. are | 10. are | | |

## Writing Pattern Practice

### 1.

There is a chair here.
There are chairs here.
There is a hat here.
There are hats here.

### 2.

There is a box here.
There are boxes here.
There is a tomato here.
There are tomatoes here.

### 3.

There is a baby here.
There are babies here.
There is a dictionary here.
There are dictionaries here.

### 4.

There is a knife here.

There are knives here.
There is a shelf here.
There are shelves here.

### 5.

There is a woman here.
There are women here.
There is a man here.
There are men here.
There is a child here.
There are children here.
There is a fish here.
There are fish here.

## Unit 05_ 부정관사

P.26

### Dialogue

A: 들고 있는 그림을 묘사해 봐요.
B: 날씨가 좋아요.
여자가 택시를 기다리고 있구요. 그녀는 손에 핸드폰을 들고 있어요. 소년이 그녀 옆에 서 있어요. 그는 모자를 쓰고 있네요.

## Unit Test

### 1.

| | | |
|---|---|---|
| 1.a | 2. an | 3. an |
| 4. an | 5. an | 6. a |
| 7. an | 8. a | |

### 2.

| | |
|---|---|
| 2. an animal | 3. a fruit |
| 4. a mountain | 5. a planet |
| 6. a country | 7. a vegetable |
| 8. a sport | |

### 3.

| | |
|---|---|
| 1. a firefighter | 2. a taxi driver |
| 3. a teacher | 4. a sales clerk |

## Writing Pattern Practice

### 1.

It's a pear.
It's a horse.

### 2.

It's an apple.
It takes an hour.

4

**3.**

I live in an apartment.

There is a telephone in the room.

**4.**

There is a student in the classroom.

I have a Japanese friend here.

**5.**

I work five days a week.

Call me once a day.

**6.**

A rose is beautiful.

An apple tastes good.

**7.**

Tennis is a sport.

A rose is a flower.

**8.**

I'm a teacher.

Tom is a firefighter.

## Unit 06_ 정관사

P.29

### Dialogue

A: 너 뭐 샀니?
B: 나는 시계를 샀어.
A: 그 시계 스위스제니?
B: 응, 맞아.

### Unit Test

**1.**

sun, earth, sky, world, same, moon

**2.**

1. the piano　　　　　2. the same
3. The sun

**3.**

1. Where is the nearest bank?
2. The sky is blue.
3. The sun is shining.
4. Let's play soccer.
5. Let's have dinner.
6. I played the piano.
7. The moon came out.
8. I'm working next Saturday.

9. We swam in the sea.
10. Look at the stars.

### Writing Pattern Practice

**1.**

The movie was boring.

The skirt was very cheap.

**2.**

I'll get the phone.

Close the door.

**3.**

The book on the desk is mine.

The man in black is my teacher.

**4.**

I live on the fifth floor.

We have the same tastes.

**5.**

The sun rises in the east.

The moon came out.

The sky is blue.

**6.**

My father gets paid by the week.

We can buy sugar by the pound.

**7.**

Let's play soccer.

Let's eat breakfast.

Let's go to France.

**8.**

I went to Europe last Christmas.

See you next Friday.

**9.**

The rich are not always happy.

I want to help the poor.

## Unit 07_ There be동사+명사

P.32

### Dialogue

A: 나 목말라.
B: 테이블에 주스가 좀 있어.
A: 물은 없니?
B: 냉장고에 좀 있을 거야.

## Unit Test

**1.**

1. is    2. was    3. are    4. were    5. Is

**2.**

1. There is one hospital.
2. There is one bakery.
3. There are two bus stops.
4. There is one movie theater.
5. There is no swimming pool.
6. There are two churches.
7. There is no book store.

**3.**

1. Are there    2. Is there    3. Are there
4. Is there    5. are there

## Writing Pattern Practice

**1.**

There is some Coke in the fridge.
There is an apple in the basket.
There is a beautiful lake there.
There is a train at 10 (o'clock).
There are a lot of people in the park.
There are twelve months in a year.

**2.**

There isn't much water.
There isn't any reason to get upset.
There aren't any people here.

**3.**

Is there a bank?
Is there any ice cream?
Are there many people?

**4.**

There was some bread here.
There was a great movie on TV last night.
There were thousands of people at the concert.
There were a lot of people at the party.

**5.**

There has been a lot of snow here.
There have been a lot of car accidents here.

**6.**

There will be a lot of snow this winter.
There is going to be a meeting on Monday morning.

**1.**

① women's clothes
② the title of the song
③ the beginning of the movie
④ a piece of paper
⑤ two loaves of bread

**2.**

① Jane은 아파트에 산다.
② 나는 한 마디도 못했다.
③ 테니스는 운동경기이다.
④ 내가 전화 받을 것이다.
⑤ 냉장고에 콜라가 좀 있다.

**3.**

① teacher → a teacher
② John → John's
③ Tom → Tom's
④ parents's → parents'
⑤ flower → flowers
⑥ My brother → My brother's
⑦ childs → children
⑧ Sky → The sky
⑨ a → an
⑩ foods → food

**해설**

① 직업명 앞에는 a(n)를 붙인다.
② John의 소유격은 John's이다.
③ 'Tom의 컴퓨터' 는 'Tom's computer'이다.
④ s로 끝나는 명사의 소유격은 ( )만 붙인다.
⑤ 「There are+복수명사」이다.
⑥ '남동생의 차' 는 'my brother's car' 이다.
⑦ child의 복수형은 children이다.
⑧ 세상에서 유일한 것 앞에 the를 붙인다.
⑨ 모음으로 시작하는 명사 앞에는 부정관사 an을 쓴다.
⑩ food은 셀 수 없는 물질명사이므로 복수형을 쓰지 않는다.

**4.**

① an    ② The    ③ X    ④ a    ⑤ a
⑥ an    ⑦ X    ⑧ X    ⑨ are    ⑩ the

1. ⑤    2. ②    3. ③    4. ④    5. ②
6. ④    7. ①    8. ④

1. these   2. this     3. this     4. These  5. This

**3.**
1. that    2. those   3. That    4. that     5. Those

**4.**
1. it      2. it       3. they    4. they

## 해설

1. 명사는 문장 안에서 주어, 목적어, 보어, 전치사의 목적어 역할을 한다.
2. ①, ③, ④, ⑤는 목적어 역할을 ②는 보어역할을 한다.
3. ① three bottle → three bottles
   ② best athlete → the best athlete
   ④ waters → water
   ⑤ the basketball → basketball
4. ④ 소유대명사로 쓰였고 나머지는 소유격으로 쓰였다.
5. ② photoes → photos
6. be동사가 복수형임을 유의한다.
7. '빨간색 옷을 입은 저 여자는 우리 선생님이시다'로 명사가 수식어의 꾸밈을 받을 때 the를 붙여야 하는 것과 be동사가 단수형임에 유의한다.
8. 서수 앞에 정관사 the를 붙여야하고 식사명 앞의 관사는 생략한다.

## 해석

인디언들은 오래전에 추수감사절을 기념했었다. 그들은 훌륭한 수확을 기념하기 위해 칠면조, 사슴고기, 옥수수, 그리고 빵을 준비했다. 오늘날 우리도 역시 추수감사절을 기념한다. 많은 가족들이 모여 저녁을 먹는다. 추수감사절은 항상 11월에 온다. 함께 모여 이야기를 나누는 시간이다.

---

Chapter
# 02 | 대명사

## Unit 08_ 인칭대명사와 지시대명사
P.38

## Dialogue

A: 나 Florida 간다.
B: 와, 멋지다! Florida는 해변이 유명하잖아.
A: 응, 아름다운 곳이지.
B: 부럽다.

## Unit Test

**1.**
1. it          2. them
3. She         4. He
5. him         6. it
7. her         8. his
9. my, them    10. they

## Writing Pattern Practice

**1.**
I'm a student.
We're doctors.
You're pretty.
You're lost.
He's here.
She studies English hard.
It's true.
They love each other.

**2.**
My name is Sonia.
I don't know his phone number.
What's your name?
Is your brother a student?
I like her smile.
Its tail is long.

**3.**
My parents love me.
Give us some money.
I miss you.
Cindy invited him.
I saw her.
I got it from my girlfriend.
I bought them yesterday.

**4.**
It's mine.
This car isn't ours.
Are these shoes yours?
My house is bigger than his.
That idea was hers.
Is this car theirs?

**5.**
What's this?
Look at this.
What are these?
Is that your umbrella?

Is that Mary?

Those are my books.

Are those your parents?

**6.**

This coat is very expensive.

I want this book.

I want these books.

Do you like these glasses?

These flowers are for you.

That girl is my daughter.

Who is that man?

Look at those skirts.

Those questions are pretty difficult.

## Unit 09_ 부정대명사

P.42

### Dialogue

A: 일식집에 가자. 스시가 먹고 싶어.

B: 좋아. 가자.

A: 돈 먼저 찾을께. 가까운 곳에 현금지급기 있나?

B: 응, 코너에 있어.

### Unit Test

**1.**

1. one          2. some          3. anything

4. some          5. are

**2.**

1. anything          2. something

3. anything          4. Somebody, something

5. something          6. anybody

7. anything          8. somebody

9. something          10. somebody

**3.**

1. Say something to me.

2. I didn't say anything.

3. Somebody called you.

4. There isn't anybody here.

5. Both are expensive.

6. You can have either of them.

7. Neither of us is hungry.

### Writing Pattern Practice

**1.**

"Yes, I have one."

Would you like one?

**2.**

I didn't eat any cookies, but Liz ate some.

"Do you need any money?"

"No, I don't need any."

**3.**

Somebody wants to see you.

Is there anybody here?

Where is everyone?

I need something warm.

I did something bad.

I want to meet somebody new.

Something happened.

**4.**

All of them are happy.

I invited all of my friends to my birthday party.

There are none here.

**5.**

Both are in the United States.

You can take either.

Neither of my parents speaks English.

## Unit 10_ 재귀대명사

P.46

### Dialogue

A: 너를 거울에 비추어봐. 끔찍해 보여.

B: 오다가 넘어져서 좀 다쳤어.

A: 네 무릎에서 피나고 있어. 병원에 가는 게 좋겠어.

B: 아니. 소독약이나 좀 바를 거야. 괜찮아 질 거야.

### Unit Test

**1.**

myself, yourself, yourselves, himself, herself, itself, ourselves, themselves

**2.**

1. yourself          2. themselves

3. yourselves          4. herself

5. himself          6. herself

7. herself          8. yourself

9. yourselves          10. himself

**3.**

1. by myself          2. by(for) yourself

3. yourself          4. yourself

5. herself

## Writing Pattern Practice

### 1.

Look at yourself.
I cut myself.
I hurt myself.
I'll introduce myself.
She looked at herself in the mirror.
We enjoyed ourselves.

### 2.

I want to do it myself.
I want to see it myself.
You'd better do the homework yourself.
He made the cake himself.

### 3.

I live by myself.
I finished it by myself.
Mary sometimes talks to herself.
We enjoyed ourselves at the party.
Help yourself.
Make yourself at home(=comfortable).

## Unit 11_ it의 특별한 쓰임

P.49

### Dialogue

A: 너무 춥다.
B: 응, 그래. 몇시야?
A: 3시 50분이야. 우리가 David을 한 시간 동안 기다렸어.
B: 가는 편이 낫겠다. 그는 우리 약속을 잊은 것 같아.
A: 알았어. 여기 버스 오네. 그냥 가자.

### Unit Test

### 1.

1. It's windy.
2. It's cloudy.
3. It's raining.

### 2.

1. What day is it today?
2. What date is it today?
3. What time is it?
4. How far is it?
5. How is the weather?

### 3.

1. It's nice to meet you.
2. It's impossible to finish it by then.
3. It's dangerous to travel by yourself.
4. It's easy to understand.

## Writing Pattern Practice

### 1.

What time is it?
It's six o'clock.

### 2.

It's hot.
It's warm.
It's cool.
It's chilly.
It's cold.
It's freezing.
It's dry.
It's hot and humid.
It's sunny.
It's foggy.
It's windy.
It's cloudy.

### 3.

It's Wednesday.
It's Saturday.
It's Sunday.

### 4.

It's February.
It's January 1st.
It's July 24th.

### 5.

It's five miles to the bank.
It's about ten kilometers from here.

### 6.

How is it going?
It's going well.

REVIEW I

### 1.

① a computer class    ② Mary
③ these shoes    ④ my party
⑤ that beautiful girl

**2.**
① 누군가 너를 보기를 원한다.
② 그들 모두가 행복하다.
③ 마실 것을 원하니?
④ 우리 둘 다 15살이다.
⑤ 부모님 중 아무도 영어를 말하실 수 없다.

**3.**
① me　　② his　　③ are
④ Jason and I　⑤ These are　⑥ those stars
⑦ they are　　⑧ any　　⑨ yourself
⑩ myself

### 해설
① love의 목적어가 필요하다.
② '그의 방' 은 'his room' 이다.
③ all은 구성원 모두를 가리킬 경우 복수취급 한다.
　 all이 '모든 것' 이라는 뜻으로 하나의 일을 나타낼
　 때는 단수취급 할 수 있다.
④ 주어자리이므로 I를 써야한다.
⑤ my sisters가 복수이므로 these are를 써야한다.
⑥ stars 때문에 that의 복수형인 those를 써야한다.
⑦ your pens를 가리키므로 they are를 써야한다.
⑧ 부정문에서는 some대신 any를 쓴다.
⑨ 주어를 반복해서 목적어자리에 쓰는 경우 재귀대
　 명사를 사용한다.
⑩ 주어를 반복해서 목적어자리에 쓰는 경우 재귀대
　 명사를 사용한다.

**4.**
① one　　② Its　　③ It
④ live　　⑤ myself

## REVIEW 2

1. ③　2. ②　3. ③　4. ⑤　5. ①
6. ③　7. ④　8. ⑤　9. ①

### 해설
1. 제 3자와 나는 우리(we)로 대신할 수 있다.
2. 제 3자와 너는 너희(you)로 대신할 수 있다.
3. 주어자리이고 여자이므로 she를 쓴다.
4. these나 those는 they로 받는다.
5. 특정한 펜이 아니라 일반적인 펜을 말하므로 부정
　 대명사 one을 쓴다.
6. some은 긍정문에서 some, 부정문이나 의문문에
　 서 any로 바꿔 쓴다.
7. ①, ②, ③, ⑤번은 주어를 다시 목적어자리에 쓰는
　 경우고 ④번은 강조재귀대명사로 생략할 수 있다.

8. ①, ②, ③, ④번은 해석하지 않는 비인칭 주어이고
　 ⑤번은 가주어이다.
9. 바로 앞문장의 Christmas trees를 가리킨다.

### 해석
크리스마스는 한국과 세계에 걸쳐 기념된다. 12월 25
일이다. 크리스마스시즌에 사람들은 집을 전등과 장신
구로 장식한다. 크리스마스트리도 역시 장식된다. 선
물들은 그 아래에 놓여진다. 크리스마스이브는 크리스
마스 전날이다. 그때 몇몇 아이들은 양말을 벽난로에
걸어놓고 산타로부터 선물을 기대한다. 우리 모두는
크리스마스를 무척 많이 좋아한다.

## Chapter 03 형용사와 부사

### Unit 12_ 형용사의 쓰임

P.56

### Dialogue

A: 정말 멋진 드레스야.
B: 오늘은 뭔가 특별한 것을 입고 싶었거든.
A: 잘 어울린다.
B: 고마워.

### Unit Test

**1.**
1. boring　　　　2. cold
3. raining　　　　4. surprised
5. Japanese

**2.**
1. interesting　　2. shocking
3. tired　　　　4. boring
5. exciting

**3.**
1. Laura has brown eyes.
2. They live in a new apartment.
3. Do I look tired?
4. I don't feel bored.
5. This book isn't interesting.

### Writing Pattern Practice

**1.**
You are a nice person.
She has a beautiful smile.

David has a great car.
It's an interesting book.
Jason is a boring person.

**2.**

I need something new.
She did something good.
We didn't do anything bad.
I met somebody new.

**3.**

I'm tired.
I'm afraid.
You're attractive.
You're skinny.
My brother is smart.
Life is short.
These flowers are so beautiful.
These bags are small.

**4.**

You look tired.
They look bored.
It feels soft.
I feel sick.
This fish smells bad.
Something smells good.
Does it taste good?
This soup tastes terrific.
It sounds good.
The music sounds fantastic.

## Unit 13_ 수량형용사

P.59

### Dialogue

A: 어디에서 우리 회의하죠?
B: 2층에서요.
A: 거기에 사람들이 많이 있어요?
B: 좀 있는데 많이는 없어요. 서두르시는게 좋겠어요.

### Unit Test

**1.**

first, two, three, fifth, eighth, ninth, twelfth, twentieth, forty

**2.**

| 1. much | 2. many | 3. much |
|---------|---------|---------|
| 4. much | 5. many | |

**3.**

| 1. a few | 2. little | 3. few |
|----------|-----------|--------|
| 4. a few | 5. little | 6. a few |
| 7. a few | 8. a few | 9. a few |
| 10. a little | | |

**4.**

1. I drank a little water.
2. Jack has little money.
3. There are few people here.
4. I know a few words of Japanese.
5. Sally makes few mistakes.

### Writing Pattern Practice

**1.**

Are there many people?
There aren't many people.
Is there much snow in Tokyo?
There isn't much snow in Tokyo.
Do you have much money?
I don't have much money.

**2.**

I know a few words of Japanese.
I'll be there in a few minutes.
I drank a little water.
I bought a little fruit.

**3.**

Sally makes few mistakes
There are few people here.
Jack has little money
There is very little money left.

**4.**

I have a lot of(=lots of) friends.
Bob makes a lot of(=lots of) money.

**5.**

Let's buy some milk.
There aren't any classes on Saturday.
Would you like some coffee?

**6.**

There is one apple.
There are two pears.

**7.**

I'm on the first floor.
This is my second try.

## Unit 14_ 부사의 쓰임

P.62

### Dialogue

A: 밖에 날씨 어때?
B: 비가 많이 와.
A: 정말? 아침에는 맑았었는데.
B: 갑자기 오기 시작 하더라구. 곧 그칠 것 같아.

### Unit Test

**1.**
1. early        2. well        3. heavily

**2.**
1. very        2. carefully        3. here
4. back        5. really

**3.**
1. quickly        2. careful        3. happily
4. fast        5. hard        6. nice
7. late        8. nervous

**4.**
1. there        2. much        3. he won the first prize
4. at night        5. well

### Writing Pattern Practice

**1.**
My family lives here.
People eat fast in Korea.
My father came home late.
Karen gets up early.
Go straight for two blocks.
Nina cooks well.
The train arrived five minutes late.
I've read an interesting book lately.

**2.**
You are so beautiful.
John works very hard.
Her silk scarf was very expensive.
It's really freezing tonight.
That movie was really shocking.

**3.**
I walked very carefully.
She speaks English very well.
Turtles walk very slowly.
I'll be right there.

You speak English quite well.

**4.**
Happily, he got all As.
Fortunately, she passed the exam.
Certainly, she'll get the job.

## Unit 15_ 부사의 종류

P.65

### Dialogue

A: 너는 테니스치니?
B: 응, 매우 자주. 나는 보통 퇴근하고 테니스를 쳐.
A: 잘치니?
B: 아니, 별로.

### Unit Test

**1.**
1. He always comes home late.
2. My mother is usually busy.
3. I can hardly believe it.
4. John sometimes calls me at night.
5. Kim is often late.
6. I never eat too much.
7. My grandfather rarely brushes his teeth.

**2.**
1. Where        2. When        3. How
4. Why

**3.**
1. too        2. enough        3. enough
4. too        5. too

**4.**
1. I like Italian food very much.
2. He left two days ago.
3. I will drive you there.
4. I will always remember you.
5. Do you usually walk to school?
6. This house isn't big enough.

### Writing Pattern Practice

**1.**
My brother came home 10 minutes ago.
I've never been to Hawaii before.
We're taking a break now.
Things will be different then.

12

**2.**

I've lived here since 1999.
I'll walk you there.
Do you live near here?

**3.**

I must always get up early.
I usually eat breakfast.
I often play basketball with my friends.
I sometimes eat Chinese food.
My father rarely gets angry.
I'm hardly ever late for school.
I never cheat.

**4.**

Where do you live?
When do you study English?
How does your father get to work?
Why do you go to bed late every night?

**5.**

You're so beautiful.
I'm getting along very well.
I was much bored at the concert.
Your English is good enough.

## REVIEW 1

**1.**

① exciting     ② excited     ③ tiring
④ tired     ⑤ boring     ⑥ bored

**2.**

① 나는 새로운 사람을 만났어.
② 그녀는 뭔가 나쁜 짓을 했다.
③ 뭔가 냄새가 나쁘다.
④ 그것은 촉감이 부드럽다.
⑤ 그것은 맛이 좋니?

**3.**

① much → many     ② some → any
③ little → few     ④ much → many
⑤ few → little     ⑥ book → books
⑦ any → some     ⑧ a little → a few
⑨ many → much     ⑩ much → many

**해설**

① people은 셀 수 있는 명사이므로 many를 써야한다.
② 부정문에서 some은 any로 바꿔 쓴다.
③ friends는 셀 수 있는 명사의 복수형태이므로 few

를 써야한다.
④ CDs는 셀 수 있는 명사의 복수 형태이므로 many
　를 써야한다.
⑤ time은 셀 수 없는 명사이므로 little을 써야한다.
⑥ book은 셀 수 있는 명사이므로 a few와 함께 복수
　형태를 써야한다.
⑦ 평서문에서는 any 대신 some를 쓴다.
⑧ hours는 셀 수 있는 명사의 복수 형태이므로 a
　few를 써야한다.
⑨ food은 셀 수 없는 명사이므로 much를 써야한다.
⑩ students는 셀 수 있는 명사의 복수 형태이므로
　many를 써야한다.

**4.**

① carefully     ② late     ③ probably
④ Happily     ⑤ curly     ⑥ lovely
⑦ terribly     ⑧ well     ⑨ very bored
⑩ good enough

## REVIEW 2

1. ②, ③, ④, ⑤    2. ①    3. ④    4. ④    5. ③
6. ⑤    7. ④    8. ⑤    9. ①

**해설**

1. 부사는 형용사, 동사, 다른 부사, 문장전체를 수식
　한다.
2. hardly(거의~하지 않는다), lately (최근에)
　highly(매우), fastly(X) → fast(O: 빠르게)
3. 빈도부사 hardly는 be동사 다음에 위치한다.
4. friendly는 형용사로 뜻은 '정다운, 친한'이다.
5. ① forth → fourth, ② fiveth → fifth,
　④ nineth → ninth, ⑤ twelveth → twelfth
6. 빈칸에는 interesting을 수식하는 부사가 들어가야
　한다.
7. homework은 셀 수 없는 명사로 many를 쓸 수 없다.
8. apples는 셀 수 있는 명사의 복수형으로 a little를
　쓸 수 없다.
9. during은 전치사, 나머지는 부사이다.

**해석**

낮에 하늘을 보십시오. 당신은 아마 해를 볼 수 있을
것입니다. 해는 사실 별들 중에 하나입니다. 그것은 우
리에게 빛과 열을 줍니다. 하지만 당신은 달과 다른 별
들을 낮에 볼 수 없습니다. 왜냐하면 해가 너무 밝게
빛나기 때문이죠.
밤에 해는 지구의 다른 편에서 빛납니다. 그래서 우리
는 그때 달을 볼 수 있습니다. 별들은 그들 자신의 이름
이 있습니다. 지금 하늘을 보세요. 무엇이 보이십니까?

## Chapter 04 비교

## Unit 16_ 형용사와 부사의 비교급

P.72

### Dialogue

A: 이 카메라 너무 비싸요. 나는 덜 비싼게 필요한데요.
B: 알겠습니다. 제가 다른 것을 보여드리죠.
   이건 어때요?
A: 이것은 얼마인데요?
B: 저것보다 20달러 싸요.

### Unit Test

**1.**

1. bigger
2. farther
3. fatter
4. more comfortable

**2.**

older, stronger, happier, more important, better, better, worse, larger, more serious, prettier, more beautiful, more crowded, more tired, more embarrassing, thinner, earlier

**3.**

1. bigger
2. taller
3. more interesting
4. better
5. better

### Writing Pattern Practice

**1.**

I feel better.
I feel worse.
Be more careful.
You're getting prettier.
My father wants a bigger car.
Carol runs faster.
I want a less expensive one.
This cake tastes better.
Your idea is better.

**2.**

I'm taller than my brother.
Athens is older than Rome.
Karen speaks English better than me.
She gets up earlier than me.
It takes less than an hour.
I can swim better than him.
I came here earlier than Sue.

Sarah is healthier than before.

**3.**

This book is more interesting than that one.
Can you speak more slowly?
This chair is more comfortable than that one.
This song is more famous than that one.

**4.**

You're more beautiful than Susan.
This watch is more expensive than that one.
This movie is more touching than that one.
You look more tired than before.

## Unit 17_ 비교급을 이용한 표현

P.75

### Dialogue

A: 오늘 기분 어떠세요?
B: 어제보다 훨씬 기분 좋아요.
A: 잘됐네요. 가능한 많이 쉬셔야 해요.
B: 네. 그럴께요.

### Unit Test

**1.**

3. Her sister is taller than her.
4. She dances better than her sister.
5. Her sister is more diligent than her.
6. Her sister gets up earlier than her.
7. Her sister is prettier than her.

**2.**

1. as good as yours.
2. as big as mine.
3. as fast as me.
4. as early as Jane.
5. as expensive as this one.

**3.**

1. It's getting colder and colder.
2. I don't sleep as much as you.
3. You watch TV more than me.
4. Australia is much bigger than New Zealand.
5. I'll be there as soon as possible.

### Writing Pattern Practice

**1.**

You look even more tired.

The United Kingdom is much older than the United States.
The Hyatt Hotel is a lot more expensive than the Holiday Inn.

**2.**

It's getting hotter and hotter.
It's getting darker and darker.
It's getting more and more interesting.
You're getting more and more beautiful.

**3.**

I am as tall as my mother.
I can swim as well as you.
Jessy weighs twice as much as me.

**4.**

Jeju Island isn't as big as Hawaii.
Basketball isn't as popular as soccer in Korea.
I don't eat as much as you.

**5.**

Call me as soon as you can.
I'll e-mail you as soon as I can.
I always study as hard as I can.
Speak English as slowly as you can.

**6.**

Nothing is more important than health.
Health is more important than any other thing in the world.

## Unit 18_ 형용사와 부사의 최상급

P.78

### Dialogue

A: 네가 본 영화 중에 무엇이 최고의 영화니?
B: 내 생각에 Harry Potter가 최고의 영화인 것 같아.

### Unit Test

**1.**

oldest, strongest, happiest, best, best, worst, most serious, prettiest, most beautiful, most tired, most embarrassing, thinnest

**2.**

1. A is the youngest. C is the oldest.
2. A is the cheapest. C is the most expensive.
3. C is the shortest. A is the tallest.

**3.**

1. the most important     2. the longest
3. the most boring        4. the shortest
5. the biggest

### Writing Pattern Practice

**1.**

Carol is the youngest person.
Jason is the smartest person.
Monopoly is the most exciting game.
Grammar is the most important thing to study.
Paris is the most beautiful city.
Peter is the best-looking guy.
Where is the nearest bank?
I speak English the best.
Sally runs the fastest.
This is the most delicious food.
Richard works the hardest.
King Sejong was the greatest leader.
What is the worst movie you've ever seen?

**2.**

Heather is my best friend.
Most women like shopping.

**3.**

Carol runs (the) fastest of us all.
Winter is the coldest of the four seasons.
My father is the shortest of them.
David is the tallest of them all.

**4.**

Seoul is the biggest city in Korea.
The Nile River is the longest river in the world.
Bill Gates is the richest man in the world.
It's the oldest building in this city.

### REVIEW I

**1.**

① older                  ② more difficult
③ worse                  ④ cheapest
⑤ most important

**2.**

① 너는 Dave보다 수영을 잘하는 사람이다.
② 너 지난번보다 덜 먹는구나.
③ 나는 너만큼 자주 영화를 보지 않는다.
④ Kevin은 우리 모두 중에서 가장 작다.

⑤ 건강은 인생에서 가장 중요한 것이다.

## 3.

① more early → earlier
② more cheaper → cheaper
③ more better → better
④ interestinger → more interesting
⑤ taller → tall
⑥ pretty → prettier
⑦ the most shortest → the shortest
⑧ the most large → the largest
⑨ the my best → my best
⑩ the most tall → the tallest

## 4.

| | |
|---|---|
| ① Tom's | ② much |
| ③ longer | ④ much |
| ⑤ soon | ⑥ large |
| ⑦ largest | ⑧ most expensive |
| ⑨ quickly | ⑩ hers |

## REVIEW 2

1. ⑤   2. ④   3. ③   4. ③   5. ④
6. ⑤   7. ②   8. ⑤   9. ④

**해설**

1. ① wise - wiser     ② crazy - crazier
   ③ tall - taller     ④ pretty - prettier
2. ① big - biggest     ② easy - easiest
   ③ thin - thinnest     ⑤ bad - worst
3. ① better → the best  ② taller → tall
   ④ the most → more 또는 better
   ⑤ biggest → the biggest
4. 「as 형용사/부사 as ~」 '~ 만큼 …한' 의 뜻이다.
5. 「as 형용사/부사 as possible」은 「as 형용사/부사 as 주어 can/could」로 바꿔 쓸 수 있다.
6. little - less - least
7. '뉴욕과 시카고 중에 어디가 더 큰가요?' 라는 비교 문장이다.
8. '모든 소녀들 중에 누가 가장 노래를 잘 하나요?' 라는 최상급 문장이다.
9. '태평양이 세계 5대양 중 가장 넓다' 라는 최상급 문장과 '태평양의 총 표면이 대서양의 두 배 만큼이다' 라는 원급 비교문장이다.

**해석**

태평양은 세계의 5대양(이어 대서양, 인도양, 남극해, 북극해순) 중에 가장 넓다. 태평양의 총 표면은 1억 7

천만 평방 km이다. 그것은 대서양의 두 배 만큼 넓이이고 지구 표면의 1/3이다.

## Chapter 05 | 접속사

### Unit 19_ 접속사 and/ but/ or/ so

| P.84

### Dialogue

A: 너 아파 보인다.
B: 감기 걸렸는데 괜찮아요.
A: 수업 끝나고 전화해. 데리러 갈게.
B: 고마워요, 엄마.

### Unit Test

## 1.

| | | |
|---|---|---|
| 1. but | 2. and | 3. but |
| 4. but | 5. but | |

## 2.

| | | |
|---|---|---|
| 1. or | 2. so | 3. so |
| 4. so | 5. or | |

## 3.

1. Seoul, New York
2. a pair of jeans, a skirt
3. Wednesday, Thursday
4. Sue, I
5. young, rich
6. It rained heavily, they didn't go out
7. I helped her, she didn't thank me
8. tennis, badminton
9. It was very hot, I took off my jacket.
10. coffee, tea

## 4.

| | | |
|---|---|---|
| 1. or | 2. are | 3. is |
| 4. have | 5. and | |

### Writing Pattern Practice

## 1.

It's hot and humid.
Sue and I are friends.
My father loves fishing and hiking.
I like Coke, and my sister does too.

**2.**

I like watching movies, but Paul doesn't.
Maria is rich, but she isn't happy.
I helped her, but she didn't thank me.

**3.**

She may become a model or an actress.
Do you want to stay or go?
Which city is bigger, Seoul or New York?
Is it Wednesday or Thursday today?

**4.**

I stayed up all night, so I am very tired.
It rained heavily, so they didn't go out.
It was very hot, so I took off my jacket.

**5.**

Both she and I are from Canada.
Both Jane and Susan are living in Seoul.

**6.**

Either Jane or I am going to attend the meeting.
Either he or you have to finish it.

**7.**

They can speak neither English nor Korean.

---

## Unit 20_ 명사절을 이끄는 접속사

P.87

**Dialogue**

A: 나는 아빠와 함께 여행가.
B: 어디 가는데?
A: 확실히 모르겠어. 아빠가 그러시는데 차로 여기저기 가고 싶으시대.

**Unit Test**

**1.**

1. is ✓you
2. hope ✓you
3. glad ✓I
4. sure ✓he's
5. me ✓she
6. know ✓Beth
7. is ✓he

**2.**

1. 목
2. 주
3. 보
4. 목
5. 주

**3.**

1. I wonder how far it is.
2. I'd like to know what his name is.
3. Please tell me how you lost weight.

4. Does he think that she is beautiful?
5. I think that the prices are going up.
6. Do you know who lives there?
7. I wonder how she made it.
8. I'm sure that she'll be here on time.
9. Could you tell me where you exercise?
10. Nobody told me why we lost the game.

**Writing Pattern Practice**

**1.**

It is true that he passed the test.
I think that he is a liar.
The problem is that I have no money.

**2.**

Whether you like me or not isn't important.
Do you know whether(or if) Mary won the game or not?
The question is whether(or if) Tom got fired or not.

**3.**

How you study English is important.
Where he lives shows that he is very rich.
Do you know what it means?
I don't know when he came back last night.
The question is why he stole it.
The important thing is who she loves.

---

## Unit 21_ 부사절을 이끄는 접속사

P.90

**Dialogue**

A: 나 빈털터리야.
B: 네가 돈이 좀 필요하면 내가 좀 빌려줄게.
A: 정말? 어떻게 고맙다고 해야 할 지.
B: 뭘. 친구 좋다는 게 뭐니?

**Unit Test**

**1.**

1. Because I didn't sleep well, I feel sleepy
2. Because I was sick, I went to see a doctor.
3. Because it was very hot, I opened the window.
4. Because I didn't eat anything today, I'm hungry.
5. Because I got all As, my mother is very happy.

**2.**

1. if you don't hurry
2. after you go out
3. while I was walking down the street
4. when you're sleepy
5. after we had a fight
6. although he's very old

**3.**

| | | |
|---|---|---|
| 1. I finish | 2. rains | 3. stops |
| 4. am | 5. will be | 6. blow |
| 7. will give | | |

## Writing Pattern Practice

**1.**

When I went out, it was cold.
When you come back, I'll be at home.
While you were sleeping, Kate called.
While I was taking a shower, my brother came home.
Before you go to bed, brush your teeth
Before you go out, turn off the lights.
After I got home, I ate dinner.
After I ate dinner, I watched TV.
I'll be here until you come back.

**2.**

Because it was very hot, we opened a window.
Because Susie was sick, she couldn't sing well.
As Ted is underage, he can't drink at a bar.
Since I had a big lunch, I don't feel hungry.

**3.**

If we take the bus, it will be cheaper.
If it rains, we won't go on a picnic.
If it rains, what will we do?
If you come here, I will be happy.
Although my brother is young, he is wise.
Although he is only 15 years old, he can speak 5 languages.

## REVIEW 1

**1.**

① I like apples and pears.
② I like movies but Paul doesn't.
③ Mary is rich but she isn't happy.
④ Do you want to stay or go?

⑤ It was very cold so I closed the door.

**2.**

① 그녀와 나는 모두 한국 출신이다.
② Jim 또는 내가 거기에 갈 것이다.
③ 그들은 영어도 한국말도 못한다.
④ Mary가 게임이 이겼는지 아니?
⑤ 네가 가는지 가지 않는지는 중요하지 않다.

**3.**

① me → I
② or → and
③ or → nor
④ If → Whether
⑤ How do you study → How you study
⑥ what does it mean → what it means
⑦ why did he steal → why he stole
⑧ you will come → you come
⑨ the train will arrive → the train arrives
⑩ we'll take the bus → we take the bus

**해설**

① 주어자리이므로 인칭대명사 주격 I를 써야한다.
② 「both A and B」는 'A와 B 둘 다' 라는 뜻이다.
③ 「Neither A nor B」는 'A도 B도 아닌' 이라는 뜻이다.
④ If가 '~인지 아닌지' 의 뜻으로 쓰였을 경우 주어자리에 올 수 없기 때문에 대신 whether을 써야 한다.
⑤ ⑥ ⑦ 의문사(what, where, when, how, why, who)가 간접의문문의 형식으로 문장 안에서 명사절을 이끌 때 어순은 평서문 어순을 쓴다.
⑧ ⑨ ⑩ 시간이나 조건을 나타내는 부사절은 현재가 미래를 대신한다.

**4.**

| | | |
|---|---|---|
| ① so | ② and | ③ or |
| ④ so | ⑤ or | ⑥ and |
| ⑦ Because | ⑧ Although | ⑨ is |
| ⑩ X | | |

## REVIEW 2

1. ② 2. ③ 3. ④ 4. ① 5. ④
6. ⑤ 7. ④ 8. ③ 9. ④ 10. ④

**해설**

1. '나는 항상 저녁을 먹지만 오늘 먹지 않았다.' 라는 문장으로 but이 가장 자연스럽다.
2. '너무 추워서 나는 재킷을 입었다.' 라는 문장으로

so가 가장 자연스럽다.

3. '너는 영화 보는 것을 좋아하니, 또는 TV보는 것을 좋아하니?' 라는 문장으로 or가 가장 자연스럽다.

4. think의 목적어로 Susan is a genius를 명사절로 묶어줄 수 있는 that이 정답이다.

5. '나는 Tom이 누구를 사랑하는지 알고 싶다.' 라는 문장으로 who가 가장 자연스럽다.

6. '안이 너무 더워서 우리는 창문을 열었다.' 라는 문장으로 Because가 가장 자연스럽다.

7. '네가 집에 도착한 후에 손을 씻어라.' 라는 문장으로 after가 가장 자연스럽다.

8. 「either A or B」는 'A 또는 B 둘 중 하나' 라는 뜻이다.

9. 절이 목적어나 보어자리에 올 수 있도록 명사절로 묶어줄 수 있는 that이 정답이다.

10. '화재가 발생할 때 소방관은 황급히 그곳으로 가 불을 끈다.' 의 '소방관은 근무 중일 때 항상 불과 싸울 준비가 되어 있어야한다.' 라는 문장이다.

해석

미래에 무엇이 되고 싶습니까? 여러분 중 몇몇은 미래에 소방관이 되고 싶을 것이다. 소방관이 하는 일은 위험하다. 화재가 발생할 때 소방관이 황급히 달려가 진화한다. 소방관은 특수복장을 착용한다. 그리고 그 옷은 소방관을 열과 물로부터 보호한다. 소방관이 근무 중일 때 그는 항상 불과 싸울 준비가 되어있다. 그는 많은 생명들을 구한다.

## Chapter 06 전치사(구)

### Unit 22_ 시간전치사 1

| P.96

#### Dialogue

A: 언제가 콘서트인가요?
B: 12월 31일에 해요.
A: 몇시요?
B: 7시 30분에 시작해요.

#### Unit Test

**1.**
in, in, at, at, on, on, on, in, at, in, on, on, in, at, on

**2.**
1. F   2. T   3. T   4. F   5. F
6. T   7. F   8. T   9. T   10. F

**3.**
1. I met Jack last Christmas.
2. Do you work on Saturdays?
3. Lisa saw you on Friday night.
4. I can't meet him on Saturday evening.
5. Paul is leaving on September 22nd.
6. The movie starts at 3:30.
7. I've waited for your call all day.

#### Writing Pattern Practice

**1.**
at 8 (o'clock)
at dawn
at noon
at night
at midnight

**2.**
in the morning
In the afternoon
in the evening
in the middle of the night
in April
in the spring
in 2006

**3.**
on Wednesday
on Sundays
on Friday night
on January 5th
on Christmas day
on my birthday

**4.**
next week
last Christmas
this Friday
every Sunday
all day
all morning
all afternoon
all night

### Unit 23_ 시간전치사 2

| P.99

#### Dialogue

A: 여름방학 동안에 뭐 할 거야?

B: 나는 파리 갈 거야.
A: 얼마나 오래 거기에 있을 거니?
B: 이 삼주 정도.

## Unit Test

**1.**
1. for      2. during      3. during
4. for      5. for

**2.**
1. by      2. until      3. by
4. by      5. until

**3.**
1. from      2. since      3. since
4. from      5. since

**4.**
1. It's rained for a week.
2. Beth felt sleepy during the class.
3. The results will come out by tomorrow.
4. I will be there in an hour.
5. He will be back within two hours.
6. Do you work from Monday to Friday?
7. I'll be here until then.

## Writing Pattern Practice

**1.**
I'll stay in Japan for a month.
It has rained for a week.
We played badminton for three hours.

**2.**
I went to Malaysia during the vacation.
Jack didn't say anything during the meal.
Beth felt sleepy during the class

**3.**
I have to go back home by 10.
Jane has to get home by 11.
I have to finish the report by tomorrow.
You have to hand in your homework by Friday.

**4.**
I'll stay here until Friday.
I stayed in bed until noon.

**5.**
I'll be there in an hour.
Jason will get here in 30 minutes.

**6.**
I'll be there within an hour.
You have to finish this exam within 30 minutes.

**7.**
Jack works from nine to five.
Do you work from Monday to Friday?

**8.**
I've lived in Seoul since 1990.

## Unit 24_ 장소전치사

### Dialogue

A: 내 코트는 어디 있어요?
B: 옷장에 있어.
A: 내 안경은 어디 있나요?
B: 아마 책상위에 있을거야.

## Unit Test

**1.**
1. at the party    2. at Susie's    3. in Chicago

**2.**
1. At      2. in      3. at      4. at
5. in      6. in      7. in

**3.**
1. on      2. next to(=by, beside)
3. on      4. under      5. behind

## Writing Pattern Practice

**1.**
There are some books in the box.
He's in his room.
I've lived in Seoul since I was born.
People are swimming in the pool.
I walked my dog in the park.
This building is the tallest in this city.

**2.**
I'm at home.
Somebody is at the door.
Sally's talking on the phone at her desk.
I had a great time at the party.
My friends and I did our homework at Jane's.
I'm waiting for the bus at the bus stop.

**3.**

The plane flew above the clouds.

**4.**

There is a bee over your head.

**5.**

Your cell phone is on the table.

**6.**

I lay down under the tree.

**7.**

The sun dipped below the horizon.

**8.**

Who parked in front of the entrance?

**9.**

He's standing behind the chair.

**10.**

Can I sit next to you?

## Unit 25_ 그 밖의 주요 전치사

| P.105

### Dialogue

A: KTX 타고 여행해본 적 있어?
B: 아니, 아직요.
A: 그 기차 정말 빨라. 시속 300km로 달릴 수 있지.
B: 와, 멋지다!

### Unit Test

**1.**

| 1. into | 2. between | 3. by |
|---|---|---|
| 4. with | | |

**2.**

| 1. for | 2. by | 3. with |
|---|---|---|
| 4. by | 5. at | 6. out of |
| 7. into | | |

**3.**

| 1. to → for | 2. for → with | 3. for → with |
|---|---|---|
| 4. among → between | | |

### Writing Pattern Practice

**1.**

Let's jump into the water.

Something got into my eye.

**2.**

Get out of the car.
He went out of the room.

**3.**

We went up the hill.

**4.**

We came down the hill.

**5.**

I bought the CDs for $20.

**6.**

I'll pay by check.
Karen goes to school by bus.

**7.**

I live with my parents.
I need someone to talk with.

**8.**

Eat the fish with the chopsticks.
I need something to write with.

**9.**

I sat between Julin and Mary.

**10.**

There is a cottage among the trees.

### REVIEW I

**1.**

| ① in the morning | ② in April |
|---|---|
| ③ in the summer | ④ in 2000 |
| ⑤ on Sunday morning | ⑥ on January 31st |
| ⑦ on Sunday | ⑧ on Christmas day |
| ⑨ next week | ⑩ last Friday |

**2.**

① Jane은 일주일 동안 멀리 있을 것이다.
② 나는 방학동안 일본에 갔었다.
③ 나는 내일까지 뉴욕에 머무를 것이다.
④ 너는 30분 내에 그것을 끝마쳐야 한다.
⑤ 그는 한 시간 후에 여기에 올 것이다.

**3.**

| ① during → for | ② for → during |
|---|---|
| ③ until → by | ④ by → until |

⑤ since → from       ⑥ from → since
⑦ in → at            ⑧ on → at
⑨ of → at            ⑩ in → at

**해설**

① ② '~동안'의 뜻인 for은 주로 뒤에 「숫자+명사」가 오고 during은 「the+특정기간을 나타내는 명사」가 온다.

③ ④ '~까지'의 뜻인 by는 동작의 완료를 의미하고 until은 동작이 ~까지 계속 진행됨을 의미한다.

⑤ ⑥ from은 '~부터'라는 뜻으로 완료형을 제외한 모든 시제에 쓸 수 있다. since는 '~이래로'라는 뜻으로 주로 완료시제와 함께 쓴다.

⑦ ⑧ ⑨ ⑩ in은 '~안에'라는 뜻이고 at은 '~에'라는 뜻으로 장소를 한 지점으로 말할 때 또는 (비교적 좁은) 장소나 같은 목적을 가지고 모인 장소에도 쓴다.

**4.**
① at       ② in       ③ at       ④ in
⑤ at       ⑥ at       ⑦ at

**REVIEW 2**

1. ⑤  2. ④  3. ①  4. ②  5. ⑤
6. ⑤  7. ①  8. ④  9. ①  10. ①

**해설**

1. among은 '셋 이상의 사이'라는 뜻이다.
2. ④번의 in은 장소를 나타내고 나머지는 시간을 나타내는 전치사다.
3. in front of~는 '~앞에'라는 뜻이다.
4. next to~는 '~옆에'라는 뜻이다.
5. with~는 '~을 가지고'라는 뜻이 있다.
6. among은 '셋 이상의 사이'라는 뜻이다.
7. at ~은 '~의 속도로'라는 뜻이 있다.
8. 날짜나 '~층에'라는 표현 앞에는 전치사 on을 쓴다.
9. 시각이나 같은 목적을 가지고 모인 장소 앞에는 전치사 at을 쓴다.
10. 나라나 대륙이름 앞 또는 달 앞에는 전치사 in을 쓴다.

**해석**

북미와 유럽에서 사람들은 특정한 날에 시간을 바꾼다. 3월이나 4월에 그들은 시계를 한 시간 앞으로 맞춘다. 10월에 그들은 시계를 한 시간 뒤로 맞춘다. 시간을 바꾸는 것은 사람들을 많이 돕는다. 우선 사람들은 낮 시간에 더욱 일할 수 있고 두 번째로 사람들은 전력을 덜 사용할 수 있다.

**Unit 26_ 관계대명사 who**

P.112

**Dialogue**

A: 어떤 여자애를 좋아해?
B: 많이 웃는 여자애를 좋아해. 머리가 긴 여자를 좋아하고 또한 내가 믿을 수 있는 여자애를 좋아해.

**Unit Test**

**1.**
1. who(m)
2. whose
3. who

**2.**
1. who
2. who(m)
3. who(m)
4. whose
5. who

**3.**
1. That is the man who(m) I wanted to see.
2. I know a man who cooks very well.
3. That is a girl whose father is a pilot.

**Writing Pattern Practice**

**1.**
I know a boy who can sing well.
I like people who can dance well.
I know some people who could help you.
I like neighbors who are kind.
The people who live in China speak Chinese.

**2.**
The girl whose hair is brown is my friend.
Janet is my friend whose father teaches art.

**3.**
Janet is a girl who(m) I like.
I need a friend who(m) I can trust.
The girl who(m) I like is Mary.
Hyo Ree Lee is a singer who(m) we know very well.

# Unit 27_ 관계대명사 which, that

## Dialogue

A: 어디 살아?
B: 예쁜 정원이 있는 집에서 살아. 넌 어디서 살아?
A: 전망이 아주 좋은 아파트에서 살고 있어.

## Unit Test

### 1.

| | | |
|---|---|---|
| 1. which | 2. that | 3. that |
| 4. that | 5. whose | 6. which |
| 7. that | 8. that | 9. whose |
| 10. the key | 11. which | 12. that |
| 13. who | | |

### 2.

1. This is the book that I read 5 times.
2. This is a book whose cover is red.
3. You can eat anything that is on the table.
4. This is the only pencil that I have.

## Writing Pattern Practice

### 1.

This is the watch which I bought yesterday.
This is the house which has a great view.
Do you know a shop which sells good coffee?
This is the dog whose ears are big.

### 2.

This is the person that I told you.
This is all that I have.
This is the movie that I saw.
I lost the book that I borrowed yesterday.
He's the only person that I respect.

# Unit 28_ 관계대명사의 생략

P.118

## Dialogue

A: 왜 그렇게 화났어?
B: 저기서 놀고 있는 내 형한테 화가 났어. 형이 아버지가 어제 내게 사주신 공을 잃어버렸어.

## Unit Test

### 1.

| | | |
|---|---|---|
| 1. ③ | 2. × | 3. ③ |
| 4. ② | 5. ② | 6. × |
| 7. ③ | 8. ② | 9. × |
| 10. ② | 11. × | 12. ② |

### 2.

1. The girl sleeping there is my sister.
2. This is the book I borrowed yesterday.
3. Tell me everything you heard.

## Writing Pattern Practice

### 1.

This is the bag I bought yesterday.
This is a person I like a lot.
Do you remember the man we met in New York?
The fan I bought broke.
I lost the watch you gave me.
This is everything I have.
I have a lot of friends I play with.
This is the book I wrote.

### 2.

The boy playing soccer is my brother.
This is a car made in Japan.
The woman wearing sunglasses is my mother.
The dog wagging its tail is my dog.

## REVIEW I

### 1.

① → the woman who lives next door
② → the computer which I wanted to buy
③ → the train which leaves at 3:00
④ → the dress which she wore
⑤ → the boy whose father is a fire fighter

### 2.

① whose → who(m)
② whose → which 또는 that
③ who → which 또는 that
④ whom → who
⑤ who → which 또는 that
⑥ who → which 또는 that
⑦ whom → whose

**해설**

① 선행사 the girl이 사람이고 관계대명사절에서 목적격 역할을 하므로 who(m)이나 that을 쓴다.

② 선행사 an amusement park가 사물이고 전치사 to의 목적어 역할을 하므로 which나 that을 쓴다.

③ 선행사 a country가 사물이고 관계대명사절에서 주격 역할을 하므로 which나 that을 쓴다.

④ 선행사 a person이 사람이고 관계대명사절에서 주격 역할을 하므로 who나 that을 쓴다.

⑤ 선행사 a flower가 사물이고 관계대명사절에서 주격 역할을 하므로 which나 that을 쓴다.

⑥ 선행사 a country가 사물이고 관계대명사절에서 주격 역할을 하므로 which나 that을 쓴다.

⑦ 선행사 someone이 사람이고 관계대명사절에서 소유격 역할을 하므로 whose를 쓴다.

## REVIEW 2

1. ⑤ 2. ① 3. ② 4. ① 5. ③ 6. ① 7. ⑤ 8. ①

**해설**

1. 선행사 a girl이 사람이고 관계대명사절에서 소유격 역할을 하므로 whose를 쓴다.
2. 선행사 the boy가 사람이고 관계대명사절에서 목적격 역할을 하므로 who(m)이나 that을 쓴다
3. Look at the man dances on the stage. 라는 문장에서 선행사 the man을 꾸며주는 관계대명사절의 관계대명사가 빠져있다. dances 앞에 who나 that이 필요하다.
4. 선행사 people이 사람이고 관계대명사절에서 주격 역할을 하므로 who나 that을 쓴다.
5. 선행사 the mountain이 사물이고 관계대명사절에서 소유격 역할을 하므로 whose를 쓴다.
6. 목적격관계대명사는 생략 가능 하므로 선행사 the book이 관계대명사절에서 목적격 역할을 하는 ① 번이 답이다.
7. 주격관계대명사와 be동사가 생략 가능 하므로 ⑤ 번이 답이다.
8. 둘 다 선행사가 관계대명사절에서 주격역할을 하므로 ①번이 답이다.

**해석**

해적은 배가 운반하는 물건들을 훔치는 범죄자다. 수년전, 해적들은 정부를 위해 일했고 적들의 배를 공격했다. 이후에 그들은 모든 배들을 공격했고 모두 사형 당하거나 감옥으로 보내졌다. 몇몇의 해적들은 자유롭게 남아 부자가 되었다. 요즈음 해적들은 현대적인 보트와 총과 컴퓨터를 사용한다. 어떤 회사는 도난당한 배를 되찾기 위해 수백만 달러를 지불한다.

## Unit 29_ 가정법 과거, 과거완료

P.124

### Dialogue

A: 데이빗이 여기 산다면 내가 더 기쁠텐데.
B: 네가 걜 화나게 하지 않았더라면 여기 왔을 텐데.

### Unit Test

**1.**

| | |
|---|---|
| 1. were | 2. could |
| 3. had played | 4. miss |
| 5. had | 6. had studied |
| 7. had | 8. could |
| 9. had | 10. would |
| 11. wouldn't have had | 12. hadn't missed |

**2.**

| | |
|---|---|
| 1. were, wouldn't | 2. were, could |
| 3. ate, could | 4. had sent, would have |
| 5. had not been, could have | |

### Writing Pattern Practice

**1.**

If I were you, I wouldn't go there.
If I were a doctor, I could help you.
If he were here, I would be happy.
If it were not rainy, we could go out.
If I had money, I could buy it.
If he quit smoking, he would be healthy.
If it were Sunday, we would go on a picnic.

**2.**

If I had finished my homework, I could have gone there.
If he had hurried, he could have arrived here on time.
If Neil had played well, the team would have won.

## Unit 30_ I wish 가정법, as if 가정법

P.127

### Dialogue

A: 쟤가 여기 오지 않았으면 좋았을 텐데. 누가 걜 초대한거야?

B: 몰라. 나도 쟤 싫어해. 마치 모든 걸 알고 있는 것처럼 말한단 말이야.

## Unit Test

### 1.

1. I wish I spoke Chinese.
2. I wish I were handsome.
3. He wishes he were tall.
4. I wish I were skinny like a model.
5. I had studied hard.
6. I wish I had been there.
7. I wish I had known the answer.

### 2.

1. were
2. as if I were a baby
3. had seen
4. as if he had finished his homework.

## Writing Pattern Practice

### 1.

I wish I were you.
I wish I were tall.
I wish I had a cell phone.
I wish I had a pet.
I wish I spoke English well.

### 2.

I wish I had finished my homework.
I wish I had known the answer.
I wish I had taken a subway.

### 3.

She acts as if she were a princess.
He acts as if he knew everything.

### 4.

He talks as if he had finished his homework.
He talks as if he had seen a ghost.

## REVIEW 1

### 1.

① is → were
② O
③ knows → knew
④ have → had
⑤ O

⑥ know → knew
⑦ am → were
⑧ have → had
⑨ O
⑩ finished → had finished

### 해설

① ⑥ ⑦ ⑧ 「If+주어+동사과거형(be동사:were), 주어+조동사과거형+동사원형」은 현재의 사실과 반대되는 일을 가정할 때 사용하며, 뜻은 '~라면, … 할텐데.' 이다.

③ 「as if+가정법과거(주어+동사과거형)」은 현재 사실과 다른 상황을 가정할 때 사용하며, 뜻은 '마치 ~ 인 것처럼' 이다.

④ 「I wish+가정법 과거(주어+동사과거형)」은 현재 사실과 다른 상황을 소원할 때 사용하며, 뜻은 '~ 하면 좋을 텐데' 이다.

⑩ 「I wish+가정법 과거완료(주어+had+과거분사)」는 과거 사실과 다른 상황을 소원할 때 사용하며, 뜻은 '~했다면 좋을 텐데' 이다.

### 2.

① 내가 너라면, 거짓말을 하지 않을 텐데.
② 네가 내게 물어봤다면 내가 말했을 텐데.
③ 남동생 아기가 있다면 좋을 텐데.
④ 일을 다 했더라면 좋을 텐데.
⑤ 그녀는 마치 자신이 모델인 것처럼 행동한다.
⑥ 그는 마치 자신이 정직했던 것처럼 말한다.

## REVIEW 2

1. ③  2. ④  3. ④  4. ⑤  5. ② 6. ⑤ 7. ③

### 해설

1. 가정법 과거에서 주절의 형태는 「주어+조동사과거형+동사원형」이다.

2. 「as if+가정법과거(주어+동사과거형(be동사:were))」은 현재 사실과 다른 상황을 가정할 때 사용하며, 뜻은 '마치 ~ 인 것처럼' 이다.

3. 「as if+가정법과거완료(주어+had+과거분사)」는 과거 사실과 다른 상황을 가정할 때 사용하며, 뜻은 '마치 ~ 이었던 것처럼' 이다.

4. I didn't walk here.의 내용을 후회하는 문장은 I wish I would have walked here.이다.

5. 「as if+가정법과거(주어+동사과거형)」은 현재 사실과 다른 상황을 가정할 때 사용하며, 뜻은 '마치 ~ 인 것처럼' 이다.

6. 현재 사실과 다른 상황을 가정하여 '마치 ~인것처

럼'이라고 말할 때는 「as if+가정법과거(주어+동사 과거형(be동사:were))」을 쓴다.

7. 현재 사실과 반대되거나 일어날 것 같지 않은 일을 소망할 때는 「I wish+가정법 과거」를 쓴다.

### 해석
내 집 옆에는 큰 호수가 있다. 봄, 가을마다 많은 오리가 호수에 모인다. 그들은 며칠만 머무른다. 보통 큰 소음을 낸다. 그들은 계절에 따라 남쪽으로 가거나 북쪽으로 온다. 눈 오는 겨울에는 오리들이 부럽다. 나도 따뜻한 남쪽으로 갈 수 있으면 좋겠다.

# Chapter 09 일치와 특수구문

## Unit 31_ 수의 일치

P.134

### Dialogue
A: 잭이 네 친구니?
B: 응. 나하고 매우 가까운 친구야. 잭 뿐만 아니라 에릭도 내 절친 중의 하나야.

### Unit Test

**1.**
| | | |
|---|---|---|
| 1. is | 2. is | 3. is |
| 4. are | 5. is | 6. are |
| 7. is | 8. am | 9. were |
| 10. come | | |

**2.**
| | | |
|---|---|---|
| 1. understands | 2. went | 3. am |
| 4. is | 5. is | 6. has |
| 7. is | | |

### Writing Pattern Practice

**1.**
Five dollars is all I have.
Two hours is a long time to wait.
Measles gives us a high fever.
Physics is my favorite subject.
Every student is in the classroom.

**2.**
Yuki and David are close friends.
A number of people are running.

**3.**
Either you or your sister has to go there.
Neither my parents nor my sister are here.
Not only Jane but also I am satisfied.

## Unit 32_ 시제의 일치

P.137

### Dialogue
A: 닐, 정시에 맞춰 왔네. 네가 늦을 줄 알았는데.
B: 제니가 여기까지 태워다 줘서 일찍 올 수 있었어.

### Unit Test

**1.**
| | |
|---|---|
| 1. looked | 2. boils |
| 3. broke out | 4. was |
| 5. would | |

**2.**
1. You told me that you would be absent.
2. She told me that she had a cold.
3. They thought that they were happy together.

**3.**
1. ② will → would
2. ④ was → is
3. ③ discovers → discovered

### Writing Pattern Practice

**1.**
I know that she has a cold. ·
I think that he finished his homework.
She says that she would lose her weight.

**2.**
I thought he would help me.
I knew she had been to Japan.
She said that she would be absent.

**3.**
We know that the Earth is round.
She said that she jogs everyday.

**4.**
My teacher said that the Korean war broke out in 1950.
We know that Columbus discovered the Americas.

## Unit 33_ 강조구문과 부정구문

| P.140

### Dialogue

A: 밥을 사랑해?
B: 어, 그래. 정말 걜 사랑해.
A: 언제 첨 걜 만난거야?
B: 내가 걜 처음 만난 건 바로 지난 성탄절 때야.

### Unit Test

**1.**
1. I do love my parents.
2. She does like movies.
3. I did finish my homework.

**2.**
1. It was Jane          2. It was Tom
3. It was at a cafe      4. It was yesterday

**3.**
1. not always          2. cannot be always
3. No one likes him.

### Writing Pattern Practice

**1.**
I do love you.
She does hate sports.
I did finish my homework.

**2.**
It's you that I like.
It was Jane that I met in Chicago last year.
It was in Chicago that I met Jane last year.
It wasn't Tom that I saw in the park.
It wasn't in the park that I saw Tom.

**3.**
No one was hurt.
The poor are not always unhappy.

## Unit 34_ 생략과 도치

| P.143

### Dialogue

A: 어, 이런! 저기 케이티가 온다.
B: 어, 나 가야 되겠어. 난 정말이지 쟤 싫어하거든.
A: 나도 그래.

### Unit Test

**1.**
1. (I) had          2. (is allowed here)
3. (This is)

**2.**
1. did I          2. is your bag
3. so do I        4. neither did I

**3.**
1. So am I          2. So did I
3. Neither do I     4. Neither did I

### Writing Pattern Practice

**1.**
I washed my face and brushed my teeth.
She speaks English and Japanese.

**2.**
When young, she was slim.
I want to see you if possible.

**3.**
No swimming.
No parking.
Not for sale.

**4.**
On the desk is your book.
Under the tree stood a handsome man.
Never can I believe the news.

**5.**
So am I.
So was I.
Neither does she.
Neither did she.

### REVIEW I

**1.**
1. is          2. are
3. is          4. is
5. were        6. rises
7. rains       8. broke out

**2.**
1. he was in trouble .
2. he was going to be absent.

**3.**

Not

**4.**

Neither

**5.**

a strange-looking man stood → stood a
strange-looking man

1. ① 2. ② 3. ② 4. ④ 5. ② 6.

**해설**

1. 선행사가 사람일 때 주격관계대명사는 that이나
   who를 쓴다.
2. '~도 역시 그렇다'는 의미로 긍정문 (현재시제/일
   반동사) 뒤에는 「So+do/does+주어」를 쓴다.
3. Anny doesn't always play computer games.
   이라는 문장에서 앞의 문장과 반복되는 부분은 생
   략하고 Anny doesn't.라고 쓴다.
4. do가 강조의 의미로 쓰인 문장은 We do exercise
   everyday.이다.
5. do가 강조의 의미로 쓰이는 경우는 「do/does/did
   +동사원형」이다.
6. 「not only A but also B」와 「either A or B」의 경
   우, B에 동사의 수를 일치시킨다.
7. Academy Awards를 하나의 개념으로 보아 단수
   취급하고 Each는 항상 단수취급 한다.

**해석**

아카데미 시상식은 가장 잘 알려지고 오래된 대회다.
첫 번째 대회는 1929년 5월 16일에 개최되었다. 아카
데미 시상식은 그해의 최고의 영화와 연기에 상을 주
는 대회다. 각 수상자는 오스카라 불리는 금상을 받는
다. 오스카라는 이름은 그 상을 본 비서가 그녀의 삼촌
오스카를 닮았다고 한데서 비롯되었다.

# BASIC
## English Grammar
*for Speaking & Writing*

# 1권

## 정답 및 해설

# Chapter 01 | 문장의 기본개념

## Unit 1_ 문장의 구성

P.14

### Dialogue

A: 생일축하해. 줄 것이 있어.
B: 고마워. 와, 예쁜 모자네!
A: 마음에 들어?
B: 응, 정말 마음에 들어. 네 선물은 항상 나를 행복하게 해.

### Unit Test

**1.**
1. X   2. O   3. X   4. O   5. X

**2.**
1. I                        2. Mary
3. My parents              4. The weather
5. This bicycle

**3.**
9개 (have, lives, takes, lives, studies, lives, likes, wants, miss)

**4.**
1. mathematics            2. Coke
3. cereal                  4. soccer
5. the room

**5.**
1. 주격보어                2. 목적격보어
3. 주격보어                4. 주격보어
5. 목적격보어

### Writing Pattern Practice

**1.**
I work.
My brother studies hard.
My father smokes.
We eat a lot.
They exercise every day.

**2.**
I eat breakfast every day.
Susan studies English hard.
We like movies.

**3.**
I am happy.
You look pretty.
Mary is tired.
The car is expensive.
He always makes me happy.
Call me Liz.

**4.**
Fortunately, the weather is very nice.
I get up at 6.
Try everything possible.
Look at the girl with blonde hair.
We play tennis on the tennis courts.

## Unit 2_ 단어의 종류

P.17

### Dialogue

A: Daniel에 대해서 뭐가 좋아?
B: 음...유머감각이 좋고 나를 많이 웃겨.
A: 어떻게 생겼는데?
B: 꽤 잘생겼어.

### Unit Test

**1.**
1. 전치사   2. 감탄사   3. 동사   4. 접속사
5. 형용사   6. 명사    7. 명사   8. 부사
9. 동사    10. 전치사  11. 형용사  12. 전치사
13. 형용사  14. 접속사  15. 대명사

**2.**
1. I(주어) eat(동사)
2. Jane(주어) exercises(동사)
3. This bag(주어) is(동사)
4. You(주어) look(동사)
5. Tom and I(주어) go(동사)
6. David's family(주어) has(동사)
7. You(주어) have(동사)

### Writing Pattern Practice

**1.**
Anne lives in Canada.
I have a cell phone.
This is my computer.

**2.**
He's my teacher.

2

This is my bag.
They're my friends.

**3.**
I have a girlfriend.
She drives to work.

**4.**
I'm tired.
The weather is nice.
Have a good time.

**5.**
Please listen carefully.
Sally eats a lot.

**6.**
The keys are on the table.
Let's talk about it.

**7.**
Jack is young, but he's smart.
Say yes or no.

**8.**
Wow, your car is great!
Oh, you have a cold!

## REVIEW 1

**1.**
① I / am a little tired.
② Kate and her family / live in Seattle.
③ Cindy and I / are good friends.
④ Steve / goes to bed late every night.
⑤ Your bag / is under the table.
⑥ It / is sunny today.
⑦ Sandra / speaks Spanish and English.
⑧ I / drink tea.
⑨ These shoes / are mine.
⑩ You and your sister / look just like your mother.
⑪ The weather / is really nice.
⑫ John and Mary / stay in China.
⑬ I / have something for you.
⑭ My brothers and I / play tennis on Saturdays.
⑮ Your handwriting / is terrible.

**2.**
① 주어   ② 보어   ③ 동사   ④ 목적어
⑤ 보어   ⑥ 수식어   ⑦ 주어   ⑧ 보어

⑨ 목적어   ⑩ 수식어

## REVIEW 2

1. ⑤      2. ③      3. ⑤      4. ④      5. ⑤
6. ①, ③   7. ①      8. ②      9. ⑤      10. ⑤

**해설**
1. 문장의 기본요소는 주어, 동사, 목적어, 보어, (수식어)이다.
2. eat은 '먹다' 라는 뜻으로 동사로 쓴다.
3. there은 '저기' 라는 뜻으로 부사로 쓴다.
4. carefully는 '조심스럽게' 라는 뜻으로 부사로 쓴다.
5. ouch는 '아야' 라는 뜻으로 감탄사로 쓴다.
6. 전치사 다음에는 명사와 대명사가 올 수 있다.
7. Anne은 고유명사로 명사에 속한다.
8. happy는 '행복한' 이라는 뜻으로 형용사로 쓴다.
9. wow는 놀라움을 나타내는 감탄사이다.
10.① Easter(부활절) ② Sunday(일요일) ③ holiday(휴일) ④ homes(가정들)은 명사고 ⑤ brings(가져오다)는 동사다.

**해석**
부활절은 매년 다른 일요일이다. 하지만 항상 3월 또는 4월에 있다. 부활절이 국경일은 아니다. 그것은 기독교인들이 종교적 휴일이다. 아이들은 상상의 토끼, 즉 부활절 토끼가 존재한다고 믿는다. 부활절 전날 밤, 부활절 토끼는 많은 집들을 방문한다. 그는 달걀과 사탕이 들어있는 부활절 바구니를 가져다준다.

Chapter **02** | **문장의 종류**

**Unit 3_ 평서문**

P.24

### Dialogue
A: 소개 좀 해주세요.
B: 저는 David Whitman이고, Madison 중학교에 다닙니다. 저는 스포츠에 관심이 있습니다. 제가 좋아하는 스포츠는 축구와 수영입니다. 미래에 축구선수가 되고 싶습니다.

### Unit Test

**1.**
3, 5, 6, 7

**2.**
1, 3, 4, 6

**3.**

1. I'm        2. She's      3. can

4. don't      5. live       6. have       7. like

## Writing Pattern Practice

**1.**

I'm from Korea.
You're pretty.
David is in the States.

**2.**

I can speak English.
It will snow.
You must fasten your seatbelt.

**3.**

I like to learn English.
You get up early.
My father smokes.

**4.**

I'm not free.
You aren't fat.
Your sister isn't here.

**5.**

I can't go to the movies.
It won't rain.
People shouldn't drink and drive.

**6.**

Sometimes, I don't like to study.
You don't exercise.
My mother doesn't work.

\* 특별히 강조할 때를 제외하면 do/does not을 축약하지 않는 경
우는 없다.

## Unit 4_ 명령문과 Let's

P.27

### Dialogue

A: 오늘밤 영화보자.
B: 좋아. 6시에 데리러와. 알았어?
A: 그래. 이번에는 공포영화보지말자.
B: 알았어. 늦지마.

### Unit Test

**1.**

1. Be happy.          2. Be quiet.

3. Have some more coffee.

4. Take care of my son.

5. Get up early.          6. Don't be late for school.

7. Don't get in the car.

8. Don't play soccer after school.

9. Don't stay up all night.

10. Don't play computer games too much.

**2.**

1. Let's        2 Let's not

3. Let's        4. Let's          5. Let's not

**3.**

1. Have a good trip.

2. Wait for me.

3. Don't be late.

4. Let's see a movie.

5. Turn off your cell phone.

6. Let's not go out.

7. Let's be careful.

8. Don't bother your brother.

9. Let's be quiet.

10. Let's not be absent.

## Writing Pattern Practice

**1.**

Be happy.
Be good.
Come in.
Listen to this music.
Have a good trip.
Wait for me.
Turn off your cell phone.
Help yourself, please.

**2.**

Don't be late.
Don't be sorry.
Don't do that again.
Don't say anything.
Don't bother your brother.
Never give up.

**3.**

Let's go to school.
Let's go out.
Let's study English.
Let's see a movie.
Let's eat dinner.
Let's be careful.

4

Let's be quiet.

**4.**
Let's not go out.
Let's not be absent.
Let's not see a movie.
Let's not cheat.
Let's not talk about it now.

## Unit 5_ 동사로 시작하는 의문문

### Dialogue

A: 당신은 매일 요리를 합니까?
B: 예, 그래요.
A: 요리를 잘하나요?
B: 예, 그래요.
A: 스파게티를 만들 수 있나요?
B: 물론 할 수 있죠.

### Unit Test

**1.**
1. Is it a nice coat?
2. Is the movie boring?
3. Does Jin go hiking every weekend?
4. Do Tom and John live near here?
5. Can they make it on time?

**2.**
1. You can speak English.
2. Mark is interested in music.
3. It is cold outside.
4. Mr. and Mrs. Smith live in Hawaii.
5. They are sorry for being late.

**3.**
1. Do   2. Does   3. Does   4. Do   5. Do

**4.**
1. Do you have a sister?
2. Is your sister pretty?
3. Do your sister and you go to the same middle school?
4. Do you live with your parents?
5. Do your parents go to church?
6. Is your father strict?
7. Does your mother work?

### Writing Pattern Practice

**1.**
Am I pretty?
Are you free?
Are we lost?
Is she a model?
Is it cold here?
Are they nurses?

Am I fat?
Are you a student?
Are we late?
Is he a lawyer?
Is this your bag?

**2.**
Can you speak English?
Can he swim?
Can Tom cook well?
Can they ski?
Can the children sing well?

**3.**
Do I know you?
Do you cook every day?
Do you have a lot of money?
Does he get up early?
Does she eat breakfast?
Does your brother like English?
Does Jin go hiking every weekend?
Do they go to church every Sunday?
Do Tom and John live near here?

## Unit 6_ 의문사로 시작하는 의문문 1
P.33

### Dialogue

A: 직업이 뭐에요?
B: 저는 교사입니다.
A: 어디에서 근무를 하시나요?
B: 민선고등학교에서 가르칩니다.
A: 몇 시에 출근을 하시나요?
B: 아침 7:30분에 일하러 갑니다.
A: 어떻게 학교까지 가시죠?
B: 차를 몰고 다닙니다.

### Unit Test

**1.**
1. Who  2. Where  3. Where  4. How  5. Why

**2.**
1. Where does David live?
2. Why are you late?
3. What is your favorite color?

정답 및 해설 **5**

4. Where do you exercise?

5. Who do you live with?

### 3.

1. What's your name?-Kathy Kim

2. Who wants to play the role of the princess?-I do.

3. Do I look pretty?-Yes, you do.

4. Does it taste like pizza?-No, it doesn't.

5. Do your parents go to church?-Yes, they do.

### 4.

1. Where do          2. When does

3. Who do           4 How does

5. What do

## Writing Pattern Practice

### 1.

What's your name?

What's your favorite color?

What can I do?

What do you eat for breakfast?

What does Julie look like?

What do Jack and Molly study?

What should I do?

What bothers you?

### 2.

Where are you?

Where am I?

Where is my coat?

Where do you live?

Where does David exercise?

Where do they have parties?

### 3.

Who's your friend?

Who do you like?

Who do you live with?

Who does Jack love?

Who do they miss?

Who likes chocolate?

Who knows his phone number?

Who has a lot of money?

### 4.

Why are you angry?

Why are they absent?

Why do you study English?

Why does John get up early?

Why does your uncle live in New York?

Why do they work so hard?

### 5.

How are you?

How can I get there?

How do I look?

How do you study English?

How does it taste?

How does Tom get to school?

### 6.

When is your birthday?

When do you study English?

When does Mary eat dinner?

When does the movie begin?

When do they have a meeting?

## Unit 7_ 의문사로 시작하는 의문문 2

P.37

### Dialogue

A: 좋아하는 명절이 뭐야?

B: 추수감사절.

A: 왜 추수감사절이 가장 좋은데?

B: 왜냐하면 맛있는 칠면조 저녁을 먹을 수 있기 때문이지.

### Unit Test

### 1.

1. 주어역할          2. 목적어역할

3. 주어역할          4. 목적어역할

5. 목적어역할

### 2.

1. Who has a lot of money?

2. Who is late for school?

3. Who isn't at work?

4. Who goes to bed early?

5. Who doesn't like shopping?

### 3.

1. What do you have?

2. What does Mary like?

3. What does Jane need?

4. What do I enjoy?

5. What do Jack and Liz eat for breakfast?

### 4.

1. Where is the phone booth?

2. What color do you like best?

3. Why are you late?
4. When does Mary go to bed?
5. How is your father?
6. Which doctor do you want to see?

## Writing Pattern Practice

**1.**
Who likes you?
Who wants to eat ice cream?
Who will come to the party?

**2.**
Who do you like?
Who does she want to invite?

**3.**
What bothers you?
What makes him tired?

**4.**
What do you eat for dinner?
What does that mean?
What does she want for Christmas?

**5.**
Which has a pocket?

**6.**
Which do you want to buy?
Which does he prefer?

**7.**
Why do you get up so early?
When do they get off work?

**8.**
What day do you have a meeting?
Which color do you prefer, pink or purple?

## Unit 8_ 부정의문문과 부가의문문

P.40

### Dialogue
A: 저 소녀를 봐, 정말 예쁘지 않니?
B: 맞아. 내 스타일이야.
A: 너랑 같은 중학교 나니지, 그렇지 않니?
B: 그런 것 같아.

### Unit Test

**1.**

1. Can't you swim?
2. Doesn't Harry like hiking?
3. Isn't this your hat?
4. Isn't he your roommate?
5. Aren't Paul and Jack close friends?

**2.**
1. Isn't he a good swimmer?
2. Don't women like shopping?
3. Can't you park here?
4. Don't they live in that apartment?
5. Don't his parents enjoy hiking?

**3.**
1. doesn't he          2. can you
3. aren't you          4. does it
5. aren't they

**4.**
1. Aren't you tired?
2. Doesn't your boyfriend live in Florida?
3. Isn't Nicole from New York?
4. Isn't Jack late for class?
5. Can't I sleep a little longer?

## Writing Pattern Practice

**1.**
Aren't you bored?
Isn't he your roommate?
Isn't the weather nice?
Aren't Nicole and you from New York?

**2.**
Can't I borrow your book?
Can't you stay a little longer?
Can't he give us a ride?
Can't we talk about it later?

**3.**
Don't you get up early?
Doesn't your father smoke?
Doesn't Sally work?
Don't they like music?

**4.**
You are sick, aren't you?
The weather is nice, isn't it?
Mary isn't at home, is she?
Gary and you are friends, aren't you?

**5.**

You can come to my birthday party, can't you?
Jane can't be here on time, can she?
Tom and you can stay with me, can't you?

**6.**
You like playing soccer, don't you?
Mary doesn't like math, does she?
They wear school uniforms, don't they?

## Unit 9_ 감탄문

P.43

**Dialogue**
A: 멋진 자전거다!
B: 삼촌이 내게 사주셨어.
A: 우리 내일 자전거 타러 가자.
B: 좋아.

**Unit Test**

**1.**

| | | | |
|---|---|---|---|
| 1. What | 2. How | 3. How | 4. What |
| 5. How | 6. What | 7. What | 8. How |
| 9. What | 10. How | | |

**2.**
1. a touching movie  2. a pretty girl
3. beautiful flowers  4. cute
5. interesting

**3.**
1. What a small world!
2. What a beautiful day!
3. How lovely the baby is!
4. What a pity!
5. How kind he is!
6. What a long day!
7. What nice shoes!

**Writing Pattern Practice**

**1.**
How beautiful you are!
How exciting the game is!
How boring the movie was!
How kind he is!
How tall the models are!

**2.**
How fast she ran!
How wonderfully they sang!

**3.**
What a great bike it is!
What pretty flowers they are!
What a great car you have!
What a nice bike it is!
What great students you are!
What expensive cars they are!
What a small world it is!
What a beautiful day it is!

**4.**
What a surprise!
What a shame!
What a play!
What a day!
What a pity!

## REVIEW I

**1.**
① gives → give        ② sees → see
③ being → be          ④ Do → Does
⑤ swims → swim        ⑥ Do → Does
⑦ eat → eats          ⑧ starts → start
⑨ my backpack is → is my backpack
⑩ goes → go

**해설**
① 「Never+동사원형」은 '절대 ~하지마라' 이다.
② 「Let's not+동사원형」은 '~하지말자' 이다.
③ 「Don't+동사원형」은 '~하지마라' 이다.
④ 「Does+she/he/it+동사원형」은 '~하니?' 이다.
⑤ 조동사가 들어간 문장의 의문문의 구조는 「조동사+ 주어+동사원형?」이다.
⑥ 일반동사가 들어간 문장의 주어가 3인칭 단수일 경 우 구조는 「Does+she/he/it+동사원형?」이다.
⑦ '누가 ~하니?' 는「Who+동사(e)s ~?」이다.
⑧ '~하지 않니?'는 주어가 3인칭 단수일 경우 구조는 「Doesn't+she/he/it+동사원형?」이다.
⑨ 「Where+be동사+주어?」는 '~가 어디있니?' 이다.
⑩ '어떻게 ~하니?' 는 주어가 3인칭 단수 일 경우 구 조는 「How does+she/he/it+동사원형?」이다.

**2.**
① Let's not be late.
② Where will they have a party?
③ How was the movie?
④ Don't you do your homework every day?
⑤ Jack can swim, can't he?

**3.**

① 냄새가 좋지 않니?

② 누가 Charlie와 머물고 싶니?

③ 너의 부모님은 부산에 사시지, 그렇지 않니?

④ 정말 예쁜 스커트구나!

⑤ 정말 그 영화는 지루했다!

**4.**

① Am I late for work?

② Is Janet raising two kittens?

③ Don't you stay up late?

④ He practices English every day.

⑤ What beautiful hair you have!

⑥ How exciting the concert was!

⑦ Brush your teeth.

⑧ Don't drink too much.

---

## REVIEW 2

1. ④　　2. ④　　3. ①, ②　　4. ② 　　5. ④

6. ③　　7. try, Do, know

**해설**

1. ① 감탄문 ② 의문문 ③ 명령문 ⑤ 의문문

2. ① Don't late.→Don't be late.

　② Let's not going there.→Let's not go there.

　③ How can I getting to the airport? → How can I get to the airport?

　⑤ Do she know the truth? → Does she know the truth?

3. what은 문장 안에서 주로 의문대명사나 의문형용사역할을 한다.

4. 보기의 who는 주어역할을 한다.

　① who-전치사의 목적어역할

　③ who-목적어역할

　④ who-목적어역할

　⑤ who-전치사의 목적어

5. ④주어가 they이므로 Isn't 를 Aren't로 고쳐야 한다.

6. 빈칸에 각각 들어갈 말은 ① isn't she? ② is she? ④ doesn't she? ⑤ do they? 이다.

7. '~하지마라' 는 「Don't+동사원형」이고 일반동사가 있는 문장의 의문문은 주어가 you 일 경우 「Do+you+동사원형?」을 쓴다.

**해석**

중국의 많은 사람들은 만리장성을 따라서 걷곤 합니다. 하지만 전체를 따라 걸으려는 시도는 하지 마십시오. 너무 깁니다. 당신은 그 길이를 아십니까? 로스엔젤레스에서 뉴욕까지 4000km를 걷는다고 상상해보십시오. 만리장성은 그것보다 훨씬 깁니다. 6000km 이상입니다.

---

## Chapter 03 | 문장의 5형식

### Unit 10_ 1형식 2형식

### Dialogue

A: 나 어때 보여?

B: 오늘 달라 보인다. 머리잘랐구나, 그렇지?

A: 응, 그래.

B: 전보다 훨씬 젊어 보여.

### Unit Test

**1.**

1. 1형식　2. 1형식　3. 1형식　4. 2형식　5. 2형식

6. 2형식　7. 1형식　8. 1형식　9. 1형식　10. 2형식

**2.**

become, be, sound, feel

**3.**

1. I exercise everyday.

2. You look tired.

3. I'll become a teacher.

4. The juice is in the fridge.

5. I was at the party last night.

6. My father smokes a lot.

7. Does it taste good?

8. James drives to work.

9. Does it sound good?

10. Is that singer famous?

### Writing Pattern Practice

**1.**

The sun rises in the east.

Jane works.

My mother cooks.

There are a lot of people here.

**2.**

I am tall.

Susan is very tired.

They are nurses.

**3.**

You look different today.

You look very tired.
Something smells bad.
The soup smells good.
Does it taste good?
It tastes terrific.
It sounds good.
The fur coat feels soft.
It doesn't feel good.
They seem kind.

**4.**

I'll become a doctor.
Susan became a singer.
I got hungry.
Laura got bored.
The leaves turned red.
It grew dark.

## Unit 11_ 3형식

P.53

### Dialogue

A: 이번 주말에 뭐 할 거니?
B: TV로 야구경기 볼 거야. 너는?
A: 영화 보러 갈 것 같아.
B: 좋겠다.

### Unit Test

**1.**
1. 3형식  2. 1형식  3. 1형식  4. 3형식  5. 2형식
6. 1형식  7. 3형식  8. 3형식  9. 1형식  10. 3형식

**2.**
1. a coat.                    2. three languages
3. how to say this       4. dinner
5. to travel                 6. that I'm stupid
7. that money is not everything

**3.**
1. He enjoys swimming.
2. Most people eat too much fast food.
3. Do you know how to make spaghetti?
4. I know what your name is.
5. Do you think that money is important?

### Writing Pattern Practice

**1.**

I have a car.
I like apples.

You're wearing a hat.
Janet speaks three languages.
Most people eat too much meat.

**2.**

Yes, I like them very much.
No, I didn't bring it.

**3.**

I finished working.
Neil enjoys swimming.
Would you mind opening the window?

**4.**

I want to go on a diet.
I decided to move to New York.
Henry would like to eat out.

**5.**

I learned how to use this machine.
Do you know where to go?

**6.**

I hope that you have a great time.
I want to know if he likes me.
I want to know what her phone number is.
I think that I will see a movie this weekend.

## Unit 12_ 4형식

P.56

### Dialogue

A: 마실 것 좀 가져다줘.
B: 알았어. 오렌지주스 가져다줄게.
A: 커피 마시고 싶은데. 좀 만들어 줄래?
B: 물론이지.

### Unit Test

**1.**
1. 4형식  2. 3형식  3. 3형식  4. 1형식  5. 2형식
6. 4형식  7. 4형식  8. 3형식  9. 4형식  10. 4형식

**2.**
1. Can you lend some money to me?
2. Pass the salt to me, please.
3. Tell a funny story to me.
4. I bought this watch for you.
5. Can you give the books to her?
6. My girlfriend wrote a letter to me.
7. John made some coffee for me.

**3.**

1. Can you lend me 20 dollars?
2. I'll buy you a present.
3. I showed the police officer my driver's license.

## Writing Pattern Practice

**1.**

I gave him a book.
My friend sent me a postcard.
The students asked me some questions.
Would you lend me a pen?
Grandma told me a story.
A man showed me the way to the bank.
She made her daughter a new dress.
Buy me dinner.
Mrs. White teaches us English.
Sue writes him a letter every week.
Please get me some water.
I asked her what to do next.

**2.**

She told a funny story to us.
Lend some money to me.
He taught English to me.
I gave a book to him.
Send it to me.

**3.**

My boyfriend bought a ring for me.
She got some water for me.
I made some coffee for my uncle.

## Unit 13_ 5형식

P.59

### Dialogue

A: 오늘 좋아 보이는데.
B: 파마 했어.
A: 더 예뻐 보인다.
B: 정말? 고마워.

### Unit Test

**1.**

1. 4형식  2. 5형식  3. 5형식  4. 5형식  5. 1형식
6. 2형식  7. 5형식  8. 3형식  9. 5형식  10. 4형식

**2.**

1. dance  2. smile  3. wash  4. go  5. fight

**3.**

1. Richard always makes me happy.
2. Did you see me dance?
3. My mother had me clean up the room.
4. I watched the baby sleeping.
5. People call him Mr. Perfect.
6. I found him to be a liar.
7. Let me introduce myself.

## Writing Pattern Practice

**1.**

I saw you doze/dozing.
Did you see Lisa cheat/cheating?
I like to watch you dance/dancing.
People watched me sing/singing.
I felt Sally cry/crying.
I felt something move/moving.
I heard them fight/fighting.
Did you hear him go out/going out?

**2.**

You always make me smile.
Did I make you feel tired?
I had my son do the laundry.
Please let me go.
Let me introduce myself.

**3.**

Call me Katie.
People call him a fool.
I named the dog Mary.
Who named you Christine?

**4.**

I found Mike nice.
Did you find Cindy a liar?

**5.**

Coffee keeps me awake.
I'm sorry to keep you waiting.

**6.**

Do you want me to vacuum the floor?
I want you to be a singer.

## REVIEW I

**1.**

① 1형식  ② 5형식  ③ 4형식  ④ 3형식

⑤ 2형식  ⑥ 3형식  ⑦ 5형식  ⑧ 2형식
⑨ 3형식  ⑩ 3형식  ⑪ 4형식  ⑫ 5형식
⑬ 1형식  ⑭ 2형식  ⑮ 5형식

**2.**
① tired          ② interesting
③ happy          ④ soft
⑤ eating         ⑥ playing
⑦ to             ⑧ to
⑨ for            ⑩ for

**3.**
① one of my friends  ② to know, if he will leave
for Florida.
③ me             ④ to leave
⑤ Susie

**REVIEW 2**

1. ④   2. ①   3. ③   4. ①
5. ④   6. ③   7. ②   8. ③

해설

1. 부사구란 두개이상의 단어가 모여서 문장 안에서
   부사역할을 하는 것이다.
   예 Once upon a time, there lived an old king.
      I came here to see you.
      My church stands on the hill.
      The movie starts at 4.
      부사나 부사절은 형식에 영향을 미치지 않는다.
2. smell은 '~냄새가 나다' 라는 감각동사로 쓰일 경
   우 2형식 문장을 만든다.
3. ③번 문장에서 he is a single은 that이 생략된 목
   적절이다.
4. ①번 문장은 'Sally는 나에게 편지를 썼다' 라는 뜻
   으로 간접목적어 me와 직접목적어 letter를 쓴 4형
   식 구조다.
5. ④번 문장은 사역동사를 쓴「let+목적어+목적어보
   어」구조이다.
6. 빈칸은 간접목적어 자리이므로 인칭대명사의 목적
   격이 들어가야 한다.
7. want는 5형식문장에서 '~가 …하기를 원한다' 라
   는 뜻으로 쓰면서 to 부정사를 목적격보어로 취한다.
8. ③번 문장은 '그것은 우리를 행복하고 신나게 만든
   다' 라는 뜻으로 목적어 us와 목적격보어 feel
   happy and excited를 쓴 5형식 구조이다.

해석

많은 사람들은 그들의 사랑을 초콜릿을 주는 것으로

보여줍니다. 그들은 초콜릿을 사랑의 어떤 상징으로
생각합니다.
그런데 말이죠. 초콜릿이 정말 사랑과 연관될 수도 있
습니다. 연구원들은 초콜릿을 먹는 것이 우리 뇌에 어
떤 작용을 일으킨다는 것을 알아냈습니다. 그것은 우
리를 행복하고 신나게 만들어 줍니다. 초콜릿은 우리
가 누군가를 사랑할 때와 같은 감정을 생성합니다.
그러므로, 지금 외로우신가요? 남자친구나 여자친구
가 없으세요? 그럼 초콜릿을 드세요.

**Chapter 04 | 동사**

**Unit 14_ Be동사**

P.66

## Dialogue

A: 이름이 뭐예요?
B: 제 이름은 Jack입니다.
A: 미국에서 오셨나요?
B: 아니오. 캐나다에서 왔어요.
A: 결혼 하셨어요?
B: 예, 했어요. 제 아내는 영어교사예요.

## Unit Test

**1.**
1. am   2. is   3. is   4. are   5. are

**2.**
1. is Jack              2. is not
3. is from Canada       4. is
5. is an English teacher

**3.**
1. is hungry            2. are married
3. is upstairs

**4.**
1. is nice              2. aren't fun
3. isn't diligent       4. are Australian
5. isn't poor           6. is ugly
7. is six               8. are heavy
9. is upstairs          10. is closed

## Writing Pattern Practice

**1.**
I'm tired today.
You're pretty.

You're very diligent.
Sally is afraid of dogs.
It's eight thirty. You're late again.

## 2.

I'm not hungry.
She isn't sad.
The weather isn't nice today.
We aren't healthy.

## 3.

I'm a student.
You're a fool.
They're lawyers.
Tom and I are close friends.

## 4.

I'm not fat.
You aren't a genius.
He isn't a police officer.
Those people aren't American.

## 5.

I'm upstairs.
You're home.
He's inside.
Tom and Jerry are outside.
Nobody's here.

## 6.

I'm not home.
John isn't downstairs.
Tom isn't here.
They aren't outside.

## Unit 15_ 일반동사

| P.69

### Dialogue

A: 커피 드실래요?
B: 아니 됐어요. 커피는 안 마셔요. 차 좀 마실께요.
Q: 그녀는 커피를 좋아해요?
A: 아니오, 그녀는 커피 안 마셔요.
Q: 그녀는 무엇을 마시기를 원해요?
A: 그녀는 차를 마시기를 원해요.

### Unit Test

#### 1.

1. listens  2. likes  3. love  4. rains  5. do

#### 2.

1. am believing → believe
2. is belonging → belongs
3. are you preferring → do you prefer
4. is wanting → wants
5. is understanding → understands
6. am hating → hate
7. Is Kate liking → Does Kate like
8. is knowing → knows
9. are seeming → seem
10. is fitting → fits

#### 3.

works, likes, cost, hope, achieve

#### 4.

1. I don't play the violin very well.
2. My sister doesn't play the piano very well.
3. John doesn't hate to cook.
4. You don't work very hard.
5. My parents don't enjoy playing golf.

### Writing Pattern Practice

#### 1.

I like soccer.
I know his phone number.
You have a girlfriend.
We go jogging every day.
They always eat breakfast.

#### 2.

Everybody likes music.
Nobody cares.
Cindy walks her dog every day.
My father drinks coffee a lot.
James likes movies.
It snows a lot in the winter.
It rains a lot on Jeju Island.

#### 3.

I don't exercise.
You don't eat vegetables.
We don't watch television very often.
They don't have much money.
My parents don't sleep in.

#### 4.

Sally doesn't eat meat.
My brother doesn't drink Coke.
It doesn't snow much in Tokyo.

The television doesn't work.

## Unit 16_ 조동사 can/could

### Dialogue

A: 무엇을 도와드릴까요?
B: 10달러 지폐좀 바꿔주실래요?
A: 물론이죠. 여기있어요.

### Unit Test

**1.**
1. He can swim.
2. He can ride a horse
3. He can't drive.
4. He can ski.

**2.**
1. Can, help
2. can taste
3. can't come
4. can speak
5. can't tell

**3.**
1. Can I sit here?
2. You can park here.
3. It can't be true.
4. Could I have a cup of coffee?
5. Could I have your name?
6. I couldn't say a word.
7. My mother can't speak English.

### Writing Pattern Practice

**1.**
I can ski.
He can speak French very well.
I can't make spaghetti.

**2.**
Can I park here?
Can I ask your name?
Can I use the phone?
You can sit here.
You can swim in the pool.

**3.**
It can't be true.
It can't be possible.
He can't be married.

**4.**
I couldn't say a word.

Ted couldn't attend the meeting.
We couldn't sleep well.

**5.**
I could go to the party.
He could be at home.
It could be Cathy's bag.

**6.**
Could you help me?
Could you give me a ride home?
Could you change a ten-dollar bill?

## Unit 17_ 조동사 may/might

P.75

### Dialogue

A: 질문 하나 해도 될까요?
B: 물론이죠.
A: 여기서 White 박사님과 만나기로 했는데요. 어떻게 만나뵐 수 있을까요?
B: 지금 아마 회의실에 계실 거예요.

### Unit Test

**1.**
1. May    2. may    3. may not

**2.**
1. I might see a movie.
2. Leo might be here soon.
3. Mark might be at home.
4. It might snow this afternoon.
5. There might be some misunderstanding.

**3.**
1. I might not be home until tomorrow.
2. It might not rain tomorrow.
3. There might not be anybody in there.
4. Susan might not come back to Korea.
5. It might not be cold tonight.

### Writing Pattern Practice

**1.**
May I take your order?
May I ask a question?
May I leave a message?
May I sit here?
May I have your name?

14

You may use my pen.
You may park here.
You may use my phone.
You may not smoke here.

**2.**

I may go to Japan.
I may be absent.
You may be tired.
Your coat may be in the closet.
Jack may come here.
They may stay here for a week.

**3.**

I might go to Europe.
I might be late.
You might be bored.
You glasses might be on the desk.
Jenny might be in her room.
It might snow tomorrow.
It might be true.
They might get here tomorrow.
There might be some milk in the fridge.

## Unit 18_ 조동사 will/would

| P.78

### Dialogue

A: 이 카트가 망가졌어요. 좀 도와 주실래요?
B: 물론이죠. 들어다 드릴께요.

*ma'am : 성인 여자를 높여서 부르는 말로 굳이 해석할 필요 없다.

### Unit Test

**1.**
1. won't   2. will   3. will   4. will   5. won't

**2.**
1. Will you hand it to me? - Will you buy me some flowers?
2. The door won't open. - This car won't move.
3. Will you come to the meeting? - I will eat a sandwich for lunch.
4. This hat will be in the closet. - That will be 10 dollars each.
5. Will you drink some wine? - Will you have some cake?

**3.**
1. Would you like to go out to eat ?

2. Would you like to eat some cake?
3. Would you like to eat some ice cream?
4. Would you like to go out for a walk?
5. Would you like to play tennis?

**4.**
1. 'd rather          2. 'd rather not
3. 'd rather          4. 'd rather not
5. 'd rather

### Writing Pattern Practice

**1.**

I will eat spaghetti for lunch.
I will go home now.
Sally won't be late.

**2.**

He won't listen to me.
The window won't open.
My ring won't come off.

**3.**

Will you have some Coke?
Will you do me a favor?

**4.**

That will be the most popular movie this summer.
That will be $20.
That will be a great painting.

**5.**

When I was young, I would study hard.
He would often go swimming.

**6.**

Would you have dinner with me?
Would you spell that?

**7.**

I'd like to eat out.
Would you like some tea?
Would you like to go for a walk?

**8.**

I'd rather stay home.
I'd rather not go there.
Would you rather take a taxi?

## Unit 19_ 조동사 shall/should/ had better

### Dialogue

A: 우리 내일 일 끝내도 될까요?
B: 안돼. 오늘 마쳐야해. 서둘러야해.
A: 커피마시면서 조금 쉬었다하죠, 그럴래요?
B: 아니, 시간이 별로 없어. 그냥 계속 일하지.

### Unit Test

**1.**

| | |
|---|---|
| 1. should | 2. should |
| 3. shouldn't | 4. shouldn't |
| 5. shouldn't | 6. should |
| 7. shouldn't | 8. shouldn't |
| 9. shouldn't | 10. should |

**2.**

| | |
|---|---|
| 1. 'd better | 2. 'd better not |
| 3. 'd better not | 4. 'd better |
| 5. 'd better | |

**3.**

1. Shall we take a break?
2. You should not lie.
3. She should see a doctor.
4. You had better be quiet.
5. You had better not cry.

### Writing Pattern Practice

**1.**

Shall I sit here?
Shall I close the window?
Shall we dance?
Shall we talk about it later?

**2.**

Let's go for a walk, shall we?
Let's eat dinner, shall we?
Let's take a break, shall we?
Let's leave now, shall we?

**3.**

You should see a doctor.
You should be there on time.
You shouldn't watch too much TV.
Should I dress up?

**4.**

You should be tired.
Tim should be at his office at this hour.
The remote control should be next to the television.

**5.**

You'd better watch out.
You'd better take the subway.
You'd better not be absent.
You'd better not be late.
You'd better not cry.

## Unit 20_ 조동사 must/ have to/ have got to

P.84

### Dialogue

A: 다이어트 해야겠어. 나 60kg 넘게 나가.
B: 아니야. 그럴 필요 없어, 딱 좋은 것 같은데.
A: 진심이야?
B: 물론이지.

### Unit Test

**1.**

| | |
|---|---|
| 1. must not | 2. must not |
| 3. must | 4. must not |
| 5. must not | 6. must |

**2.**

1. You must not stay here.
2. I have to get up early.
3. Jack cannot be at work.
4. It must be true.
5. You must stay up all night.

**3.**

1. You have got to wait here.
2. Must I finish this by tomorrow?
3. Does Kim have to work on Saturdays?

### Writing Pattern Practice

**1.**

You must fasten your seatbelt.
Must we study English?

**2.**

You must not drink and drive.
You must not park here.

16

**3.**

It must be true.

Jack must be in his room.

You must weigh over 50kg.

There must be a lot of people here on Friday night.

**4.**

Gary can't be married.

It can't be true.

**5.**

I have to go right now.

Jin has to study.

Do you really have to leave now?

We had to attend the meeting.

Susie will have to go and see Mrs. Wilson.

**6.**

You don't have to wait for me.

You didn't have to pay for it.

**7.**

You've got to do your homework.

I've got to go.

Have you got to go now?

**8.**

You've got to be joking.

That bag has got to be expensive.

James has got to be at home.

## REVIEW 1

**1.**

① like → likes

② rain → rains

③ 'm knowing → know

④ Are you liking → Do you like

⑤ 're understanding → understand

⑥ don't → doesn't

⑦ doesn't → don't

⑧ speaks → speak

⑨ is → be

⑩ 'd like to → 'd like

**해설**

**1.**

① everybody는 항상 단수 취급한다.

② 주어가 3인칭 단수인 현재형 문장은 동사원형에 -

(e)s를 붙인다.

③ know는 진행형을 쓸 수 없는 동사다.

④ like는 진행형을 쓸 수 없는 동사다.

⑤ understand는 진행형을 쓸 수 없는 동사다.

⑥ 주어가 3인칭단수인 현재형문장의 부정은 「주어 +doesn't+동사원형」이다.

⑦ 주어가 복수일 때 현재형문장의 부정은 「주어 +don't+동사원형」이다.

⑧ 조동사 다음에는 항상 동사원형이 와야한다.

⑨ 조동사 다음에는 항상 동사원형이 와야한다.

⑩ 「'd like to+동사원형」이고「'd like+명사」임을 유의한다.

**2.**

① John is downstairs.

② They are doctors.

③ I'd rather take a taxi.

④ The window won't open.

⑤ You'd better not be absent.

**3.**

① 너는 여기에 주차해도 좋아.

② 그것은 20불입니다.

③ 그것이 가능할 리 없다.

④ 너는 50Kg 이상 나감에 틀림없디.

⑤ 너는 농남하고 있음에 틀림없다.

**4.**

① John isn't upstairs.

② We don't watch television often.

③ You'd better not go there.

④ I can't make spaghetti.

⑤ We are tired.

⑥ You must turn left here.

⑦ It could be true.

⑧ I'd rather stay here.

## REVIEW 2

1. ④   2. ④   3. ④   4. ⑤   5. ④   6. ①

7. 그들이 그것을 가지고 있음에 틀림없다.

**해설**

1. ① am→ are    ② walk→ walks

③ plays→ play  ⑤ will you?→ shall we?

2. ④ snows→ snow

3. ④번은 can이 능력의 뜻이고 나머지는 허락의 뜻이다.

4. ⑤번은 must가 의무/금지의 뜻이고 나머지는 강한 추측의 뜻이 된다.

5. must be(강한추측)의 부정은 can't be를 써야 한다.
6. have to가 들어있는 문장의 의문문은 「Do/Does+주어+have to+동사원형?」이다.
7. must는 '꼭 ~을 해야 한다' 와 '~임에 틀림없다'의 두 뜻으로 주로 쓰이는데 문맥상 강한 추측으로 쓰였음을 알 수 있다.

**해석**

한국 사람들은 인스턴트 국수를 매우 좋아합니다. 라면이라는 인스턴트 국수는 세계적으로 인기입니다. 그들이 얼마나 라면을 좋아하는지 아십니까? 한국 가게에서는 100가지 이상의 라면을 살 수 있습니다. 소고기나 야채 라면, 닭이나 오징어 라면, 그리고 맵거나 순한 맛의 라면을 찾을 수 있습니다. 두껍거나 얇은 라면을 찾을 수 있습니다. 어떤 종류의 라면을 먹기를 원하든지 한국에는 틀림없이 있을 것입니다.

## Chapter 04 | 시제

### Unit 21_ 현재시제

P.92

#### Dialogue

A: 네 남자친구에 대해 얘기해봐.
B: 잘 생기고 모두에게 친절해. 항상 다른 사람들을 행복하게 만들고 친구들도 많아.

#### Unit Test

**1.**

come→comes  go→goes  eat→eats
drink→drinks  get→gets  take→takes
have→has  dream→dreams  sleep→sleeps
sit→sits  stand→stands  say→says
pay→pays  buy→buys  cry→cries

**2.**

|  | /s/ | /z/ | /iz/ |
|---|---|---|---|
| eats | o |  |  |
| likes | o |  |  |
| comes |  | o |  |
| kisses |  |  | o |
| sleeps | o |  |  |
| buys |  | o |  |
| finishes |  |  | o |
| goes |  | o |  |
| wants | o |  |  |
| listens |  | o |  |

**3.**

speaks, takes, listens, works, has, practices, speaks, studies.

**4.**

1. Mark speaks five languages.
2. Water boils at 100℃
3. I walk to school.
4. The sun sets in the west.
5. You speak English well.

#### Writing Pattern Practice

**1.**

I get up early.
I come from Canada.
You have a lot of money.
We live in Hawaii.
We go to the same school.
They speak English well.
Tom and Mary go to church.

**2.**

I don't have much money.
I don't exercise.
You don't have a girlfriend.
You don't study hard.
We don't eat meat.
We don't work.
They don't come from Canada.
My parents don't live in Korea.

**3.**

Jane takes a shower every day.
Jack drives to work every day.
Water freezes at 0℃.
Water boils at 100℃.
That store opens at 9.
The sun rises in the east.

**4.**

Cindy doesn't eat pork.
David doesn't exercise.
My sister doesn't drink Coke.
It doesn't snow in Hawaii.

### Unit 22_ 현재진행시제

P.95

#### Dialogue

A: 너희 가족은 지금 무엇을 하고 있니?

B: 우리 아버지는 커피를 마시고 계셔. 아버지는 커피를 좋아하시거든. 어머니는 점심으로 오믈렛을 만들고 계셔. 어머니는 요리를 정말 잘 하시지. 그리고 우리 형은 TV를 보고 있어. 그는 TV를 정말 좋아해.

## Unit Test

**1.**

| | |
|---|---|
| vacuum → vacuuming | cry → crying |
| snow → snowing | live → living |
| go → going | stop → stopping |
| swim → swimming | open → opening |
| rain → raining | die → dying |
| begin → beginning | play → playing |

**2.**

1. is taking some pictures.
2. is eating some ice cream.
3. is walking the dog
4. is singing.
5. are playing badminton.

**3.**

1. She is taking a shower.
2. Cindy likes coffee,
3. I'm not watching it now.
4. I'm looking for my bag.
5. He plays soccer very often.

## Writing Pattern Practice

**1.**

I'm taking a shower.
I'm going to school.
My brother is talking on the phone.
Jim is smoking.
It's snowing.
The sun is shining.
My mother and I are cleaning the house.
We're eating breakfast.
They're playing badminton.

**2.**

I'm not sleeping.
I'm not talking on the phone.
You aren't doing your homework.
You aren't exercising.
Terry isn't cleaning his room.
Kathy isn't bothering her brother.
It isn't raining.

They aren't having a party.

**3.**
Am I bothering you?
Are you eating breakfast?
Are you taking a shower?
Is Monica listening to the radio?
Is John watching TV?
Is it raining?
Are they sweeping the floor?
Are they fighting?

### Unit 23_ 과거시제

| P.98

## Dialogue

A: 휴가 어땠니?
B: 정말 좋았어.
A: 뭐했는데?
B: 우리 가족과 함께 제주도를 갔었어.
우리는 해변에 갔었는데, 정말 재미있었어.

## Unit Test

**1.**

| | | |
|---|---|---|
| 1. woke up | 2. got up | 3. washed |
| 4. brushed | 5. took off | 6. ate |
| 7. put on | 8. went | 9. studied |
| 10. had | 11. played | 12. came |
| 13. drank | 14. watched | 15. told |
| 16. slept | | |

**2.**

went, left, arrived, swam, watched, were, had, came

**3.**

| | |
|---|---|
| 1. snowed | 2. washed |
| 3. flew | 4. ate |
| 5. worked | |

## Writing Pattern Practice

**1.**

I was with my friends.
You were fat.
Daniel was late this morning.
We were in Busan last week.

**2.**

I wasn't with Ted last night.

You weren't thin.
David wasn't absent.
It wasn't hot yesterday.
They weren't here.

**3.**

Was I late?
Were you at the party?
Was it sunny yesterday?
Were they tired?

**4.**

I saw a movie with my friends.
You bought a new coat.
Liz went shopping.
We did our homework.
My parents left for Japan.

**5.**

I didn't do my homework.
I didn't sleep well last night.
You didn't clean your room.
It didn't rain.
We didn't get up early.

**6.**

Did I bother you?
Did I wake you?
Did you brush your teeth?
Did Julia call you last night?

## Unit 24_ 과거진행시제

### Dialogue

(형사) 어젯밤 11시 뭐하고 계셨습니까?
(혐의자1) 차 몰고 집에 가고 있었어요.
(혐의자2) 자고 있었어요.

### Unit Test

**1.**

1. I was watching a movie.
2. Jinny was driving home.
3. My uncle was riding a horse.
4. We were doing our homework.
5. My daughter was talking on the phone.

**2.**

1. was having breakfast.
2. was driving to work.
3. was working.

**3.**

1. I was wearing a hat.
2. The girl was eating ice cream.
3. It was raining.
4. We were living in Italy.
5. Leo and I were playing tennis.

### Writing Pattern Practice

**1.**

I was thinking about you.
I was wearing a hat.
You were sleeping.
Molly was eating pizza for lunch.
My friends and I were having a party.
Jack was vacuuming the floor.
Leo and I were playing tennis.
It was snowing.

**2.**

I wasn't studying.
I wasn't thinking about the test.
You weren't exercising.
Tom wasn't cleaning the room.
Kate wasn't bothering her brother.
They weren't having a party.
They weren't waiting for you.

**3.**

Were you eating breakfast?
Were you taking a shower?
Were you looking for this pen?
Was Monica listening to the radio?
Was Jack watching TV?
Was the girl eating ice cream?
Was it raining?
Were they fighting?

## Unit 25_ 현재완료시제

### Dialogue

A: 디즈니랜드 가봤니?
B: 아니, 하지만 사진에서 본 적있어. 정말 크지?
A: 응, 우리 가족은 모두 둘러보는데 일주일 걸렸어.

## Unit Test

**1.**
1. have just finished
2. have been
3. has waited for you
4. have turned off
5. has rained
6. have been
7. has tried
8. has got
9. have known
10. has been cold

**2.**
1. has left home
2. has bought glasses.
3. has broken his leg

**3.**
1. T
2. F(has begun→began) 또는 (at 3 o'clock 삭제)
3. F('ve finished→finished) 또는 (yesterday 삭제)
4. T          5. T

## Writing Pattern Practice

**1.**
I've just had dinner.
I've already finished my homework.
Jane has just left.
I haven't decided yet.
Have you just got(ten) home?
Has Cindy already left?

**2.**
I've tried Mexican food.
You've seen the movie 'Titanic'.
We've been to Disneyland.
James hasn't tried bungy jumping.
Have you (ever) been to Florida?

**3.**
I've waited for you for an hour.
Ted has worked here for 20 years.
It has rained for a week.
We've known each other for 10 years.
We haven't seen Mr. Kim for a year.
How long has it rained?
How long have you known each other?

**4.**
I've had enough.
I've lost my book.
Janet has gone to the United States.
Nancy has left for New York.
Have you finished your homework?

## Unit 26_ 미래시제

P.108

### Dialogue
A: 이번 금요일 생일파티를 할 거야. 올거니?
B: 물론, 가야지.
A: 좋아. Jack과 Michael도 온대.

### Unit Test

**1.**
is going to take a shower.
are going to play tennis.
is going to rain.

**2.**
1. will
2. will
3. will
4. will
5. won't
6. will
7. will
8. won't
9. won't
10. will

**3.**
1. It will rain.
2. We will win the game.
3. I am going to eat a sandwich for lunch.
4. Jim is leaving tonight.
5. We aren't going to the party.

### Writing Pattern Practice

**1.**
I'll go to Chicago next week.
I'll miss you.
Mom, I won't let you down.
You'll be fat.
It'll be sunny.
We'll win the game.
What will you do?
Will you come on time?
Will you join us?
Won't you help me get up?

**2.**
I'm going to swim.
I'm not going to eat dinner.
We're going to see a movie tonight.
My aunt is going to have a baby.
What are you going to do?
Are you going to be at home?
Is it going to rain?

**3.**
I'm leaving tonight.

Kate is getting married next week.
David is getting here in an hour.
We aren't going to the party.
What are you doing tonight?
Are you coming tonight?

## REVIEW 1

**1.**

① He exercises every day.
② I ate dinner
③ We haven't eaten(=tried) Thai food.
④ Will it rain?
⑤ Are you going to have a party?

**2.**

① 너는 뚱뚱했었어.
② 너는 잠을 자고 있었니?
③ 너는 파리에 가본 적이 있니?
④ 나는 방금 여기에 도착했어.
⑤ 눈이 올까?

**3.**

① take → taking
② Did you your → Did you do your
③ watch → watching
④ sees → see
⑤ be → been

해설

① be동사와 일반동사를 이어서 쓸 수 없다. 진행형은 「주어+be동사+동사-ing」이다. ② 일반동사가 들어간 문장의 과거의문문은 「Did+주어+동사원형?」인데 동사가 빠져있다. ③ be동사와 일반동사를 이어서 쓸 수 없다. 진행형은 「주어+be동사+동사-ing」이다. ④ 조동사가 들어간 문장의 의문문은 「조동사+주어+동사원형?」이다. ⑤ 현재완료 문장의 의문문은 「Have/Has+주어+과거분사?」이다.

**4.**

① Does Sue get up early?
② I didn't lose my keys.
③ We took a vacation.
④ Jane has had lunch.
⑤ Did Shakespeare write many plays?
⑥ I won't go to bed early.
⑦ Are they going to invite Karen?
⑧ I have told him.
⑨ It is going to rain.
⑩ I haven't started my new job.

## REVIEW 2

1. ②   2. ④   3. ①   4. ⑤   5. ②   6. ④
7. ②

해설

1. ① be동사와 일반동사를 이어서 사용할 수 없다.
   ③ 현재완료문장의 의문문은 주어가 3인칭 단수일 경우「Has+she/he/it+과거분사?」이다.
   ④ be동사와 일반동사를 이어서 사용할 수 없다.
   ⑤ 일반적인 사실을 나타낼 때 항상 현재형문장을 쓴다.
2. ④ 현재진행형시제는 과거부사와 쓰일 수 없다.
3. '다음 주에 그녀는 뉴욕에 가 있을 것이다.' 라는 미래 문장이다.
4. 'Amy는 지난주에 영화를 두 번 보러갔다' 라는 과거 문장이다.
5. 'Richard를 만나봤니, 아니면 내가 너에게 소개해 줄까?' 라는 현재완료 문장이다.
6. B가 '전화 통화를 하고 있었어요.' 라고 과거진행형으로 대답을 했으므로 같은 시제로 물어봐야한다.
7. 2000년 전의 발렌타인데이에 대해 설명하고 있으므로 과거형을 써야한다.

해석

2월14일 발렌타인데이에 세계 대부분의 사람들은 사랑을 축하한다. 로마의 젊은 남자와 여자는 2천년 전에 사랑을 축하했다. 하지만 남자와 여자들은 카드, 꽃다발 또는 초콜릿 등을 서로 주고받지 않았다. 여자들은 그들의 이름을 단지 안에 넣고 남자들은 단지 안에서 한 개의 이름을 뽑아내면 그 남자는 1년 동안 그 이름을 가진 여자의 남자친구가 되어야 했다. 다행히도 우리는 더 이상 그렇게 하지 않는다.

# Chapter 06 | 부정사와 동명사

## Unit 27_ 명사 역할을 하는 to 부정사

| P.116

### Dialogue

A: 너는 무엇을 하기를 원하니?
B: 나는 테니스를 치고 싶어.
A: 밖에 좀 추운데. 우리 안에서 탁구 치면 어떨까?
B: 좋아.

### Unit Test

**1.**

1. to see
2. not to be
3. to stay
4. to be
5. to rain
6. not to travel
7. to do
8. to be
9. to be
10. to drive

**2.**

1. to eat
2. to drive
3. to ask
4. to be
5. to turn off

**3.**

1. I decided to sell my car.
2. What do you want to do?
3. I tried to do my best.
4. I hate to be late.
5. Jane decided to go to Italy.
6. Would you like to eat a sandwich?
7. Rita hopes to be a singer.

## Writing Pattern Practice

**1.**

It's fun to be with my friends.
It's exciting to learn English.
It's important to exercise every day.
It's difficult to make spaghetti.
It's not easy to catch a taxi here.
It's hard to quit smoking.
It's impossible to get there on time.

**2.**

I want to go bowling.
Tess needs to clean her room.
Jane decided not to leave.
Rita hopes to be a singer.
I'd like to eat spaghetti.
Don't forget to turn off the light.
It started to rain.
I like to eat out.
Jane hates to clean her room.
I tried to do my best.
Would you like to eat a sandwich?

**3.**

My goal is to become a doctor.
I want you to come to my party.
Do you want me to become a singer?
I told you to come on time.
My mother always tells me to study hard.

## Unit 28_ 형용사 역할을 하는 to 부정사

### Dialogue

A: 나 목말라.
B: 마실 것 갖다 줄게.
　뭐 원하니?
A: 물을 원해.
B: 여기 있어.

### Unit Test

**1.**

1. 명사　　2. 명사　　3. 명사　　4. 형용사
5. 형용사　6. 형용사　7. 형용사　8. 형용사
9. 명사　　10. 명사　　11. 명사　　12. 명사
13. 명사　14. 명사　15. 형용사

**2.**

1. I need something to eat.
2. You have a lot of things to do.
3. Jane bought some books to read.
4. Bob has no time to sleep.
5. You need a friend to rely on.
6. We had no time to have lunch
7. They had no time to see a movie.
8. There is something to eat in the fridge.
9. Do you have any homework to finish?
10. I'll get you something to drink.

### Writing Pattern Practice

**1.**

something to do
I have something to do.
something to read
I need something to read.
food to eat
There is no food to eat.
money to spend
He has a lot of money to spend.
friends to meet
I have some friends to meet today.
water to drink
Give me some water to drink.

**2.**

chairs to sit on
There are no chairs to sit on.
a friend to study English with

I need a friend to study English with.
a friend to have lunch with
I want a friend to have lunch with.
something to write with
I need something to write with.
something to write on
Please give me something to write on.
someone to talk to
I need someone to talk to.
a house to live in
Do you have a house to live in?
a roommate to live with
I want a roommate to live with.

## Unit 29_ 부사 역할을 하는 to 부정사

P.122

### Dialogue

A: 만나서 반가워요.
B: 나도 만나서 반가워요.
A: 말씀 많이 들었어요.
B: 좋은 얘기였으면 좋겠네요.

### Unit Test

**1.**
1. 부사　　2. 부사　　3. 명사　　4. 형용사
5. 명사　　6. 형용사　7. 부사　　8. 부사
9. 부사　　10. 부사　　11. 부사　　12. 형용사
13. 형용사 14. 명사　　15. 형용사

**2.**
1. That book was fun to read.
2. I came here to see you.
3. You were lucky to get a new job.
4. I am happy to see you here.
5. She went out to see her friends.
6. You were foolish to say that.
7. Are you waiting to see the doctor?
8. The movie was difficult to understand.
9. I'm working at two jobs to make a lot of money.
10. I turned on the TV to watch the news.

### Writing Pattern Practice

**1.**
I came here to see Henry.
I tried not to be late.
He did his best to win the game.

Mandy went shopping to buy a coat.
Charlie went to Tokyo to learn Japanese.
What do I need to open an account?

**2.**
It's nice to meet you.
It was good to hear from you.
I'm glad to hear the news.
I'm happy to hear that.

**3.**
You were foolish to do something like that.
You must be a genius to solve the problem.
My father was lucky to get a new job.

**4.**
He grew up to be a great singer.
Her mother lived to be eighty.

**5.**
This book was fun to read.
This river is very dangerous to swim in.
That movie was difficult to understand.

## Unit 30_ to 부정사의 의미상 주어

P.125

### Dialogue

A: 생일 축하해!
B: 고마워. 내 생일을 기억하다니 다정하구나.
A: 선물을 열어보지 그래?
B: 알았어. 스웨터네. 내가 딱 원했던 거야.

### Unit Test

**1.**
1. you　2. you　3. She　4. me　5. you
6. them　7. me　8. you　9. her　10. me

**2.**
1. of　2. for　3. of　4. for　5. of
6. of　7. for　8. for

**3.**
1. It's kind of you to help me.
2. It's unusual for him to make jokes.
3. Is it possible for you to come here on time?
4. It was careless of him to say that.
5. It's important for her to study hard.

24

## Writing Pattern Practice

### 1.

These pants are too big for you to wear.
This tea is too hot for me to drink.
It's impossible for him to get up early.
It's difficult for them to come here right away.
It's time for us to go to bed.
It's important for you to be on time.
This vacuum cleaner is hard for me to use.
It's impossible for her to speak English fluently.

### 2.

It was sweet of you to remember my birthday.
It was careless of him to say that.
It's kind of you to help me.
It was nice of you to e-mail me.
It was stupid of her to do that.
It was rude of you to yell at him

### 3.

I want to go out.
I want you to come on time.

### 4.

It's good to be diligent.
It's not a good idea to skip that class.

---

## Unit 31_ to 부정사를 이용한 다양한 표현

| P.128

### Dialogue

A: 나 영어를 잘 못하는 것 같아.
B: 아니야, 네 영어는 대화 나누기에 충분해.
A: 정말 그렇게 생각해?
B: 물론이지. 걱정하지마.

### Unit Test

### 1.

1. To make matters worse   2. Strange to say
3. To tell the truth

### 2.

| | |
|---|---|
| 1. too, to | 2. enough, to |
| 3. too, to | 4. enough, to |
| 5. too, to | 6. enough, to |
| 7. enough, to | 8. enough, to |

### 3.

1. Her English is good enough to become an English teacher.
2. That coat is too expensive to buy.
3. They are old enough to get married.
4. I was too surprised to say a thing.
5. It's too far to walk there.

## Writing Pattern Practice

### 1.

to make matters worse
To make matters worse, I fell down on my way here.
to tell the truth
To tell the truth, I don't want to sell my house.
strange to say
Strange to say, but I don't want to make much money.

### 2.

I'm too tired to go out.
It's too cold to play soccer outside.
Tim is too young to drive.
That coat is too expensive to buy
It is too far to walk there.
I was too surprised to say a thing.
The shelf is too high to reach.
This bag is too heavy to carry.

### 3.

You're old enough to see that movie.
Your English is good enough to be understood.
They are old enough to get married.
Sam is rich enough to buy a BMW.
The boy is smart enough to understand this book.
She's tall enough to be a model.

---

## Unit 32_ 동명사의 역할

| P.131

### Dialogue

A: 1교시에 왜 늦었어?
B: 늦잠잤어.
A: 그럴 줄 알았어.
B: 매일 일어나는 것은 너무 어려워.

## Unit Test

**1.**
1. 현   2. 동   3. 현   4. 동   5. 동
6. 현   7. 동   8. 현   9. 현   10. 현

**2.**
1. 주   2. 주   3. 목   4. 주   5. 전   6. 목   7. 전

**3.**
1. I don't mind helping you.
2. It started raining.
3. I enjoy visiting other countries.
4. She prefers traveling by car.
5. Eating less is good for your health.
6. It stopped snowing.
7. They kept walking.

## Writing Pattern Practice

**1.**
Exercising every day is good for your health.
Being kind to everyone is not easy.
Getting up early every day is difficult.
It was nice talking to you.
Getting there in an hour is impossible.

**2.**
I like playing soccer.
I hate eating alone.
The car needs repairing.
I enjoy seeing all kinds of movies.
He quit smoking.
Eating less is good for your health.
It started snowing.
It stopped snowing

**3.**
My hobby is watching movies.
My part time job is cooking in a restaurant.
My favorite sport is playing tennis.

**4.**
Thank you for helping me.
I feel like dancing.
I'm used to sleeping on the bus.
I don't mind helping you.
I'm looking forward to seeing you.

## Unit 33_ 목적어로 쓰이는 부정사와 동명사

P.134

### Dialogue
A: 뭐가 잘못됐지?
B: 몰라. 울음을 멈추지 않아.
A: 배고픈 것 같은데.
B: 아, 밥 먹이는 걸 잊었다.

### Unit Test

**1.**
1. to drink  2. crying  3. smoking  4. to eat

**2.**
1. exercising          2. going
3. to eat              4. to see
5. moving              6. to study
7. to fly

**3.**
1. F   2. T   3. T   4. F   5. T

**4.**
1. Everybody stopped talking.
2. Don't keep bothering me.
3. I gave up trying to lose weight.
4. I decided not to go out.
5. Don't forget to give me a call.

### Writing Pattern Practice

**1.**
I want to eat pizza.
I decided not to leave for Japan.
I didn't expect to see you here.

**2.**
I finished working.
I don't mind helping you.
I enjoy learning English.

**3.**
I like to watch movies.
= I like watching movies.
I love to cook.
= I love cooking.
I prefer to watch soccer games.
= I prefer watching soccer games.
I hate to be alone.

= I hate being alone.
It started to snow.
= It started snowing.
It began to rain.
= It began raining.
I continued to talk.
= I continued talking.

**4.**
Remember to go to see a doctor today.
I remember seeing him once before.
Don't forget to give me a call.
I forgot about calling you.
I forgot to call you.
I tried eating Mexican food.
I tried to help him.

## REVIEW 1

**1.**
① I want to go out.
② Playing the piano is my hobby.
③ I enjoy sleeping.
④ Jane needs to buy a coat.
⑤ I'm used to taking a shower in the morning.

**2.**
① 나의 목표는 가수가 되는 것이다.
② 너는 그런 일을 하는 것 보니 어리석었다.
③ 이 책은 읽기에 재미있었다.
④ 나는 전에 그를 봤던 것을 기억한다.
⑤ 나는 너에게 전화할 것을 잊었다.

**3.**
① seeing → to see      ② go → to go
③ are → be             ④ read → to read
⑤ talk → talk to(=talk with)
⑥ going → to go
⑦ enough old → old enough
⑧ seeing → to see
⑨ to open → opening
⑩ to work → working

**해설**
① hope은 to 부정사를 목적어로 취한다.
② want는 to 부정사를 목적어로 취한다.
③ to부정사는 「to+동사원형」이다.
④ '읽을 책'은 'a book to read' 이다.
⑤ '말할 사람'은 'someone to talk to(=with)' 이다.
⑥ 「too ~ to ...」는 '너무 ~ 해서 ... 할 수 없다' 는

뜻이다.
⑦ 「형용사+enough」 어순임을 유의한다.
⑧ expect는 to 부정사를 목적어로 취한다.
⑨ mind는 동명사를 목적어로 취한다.
⑩ finish는 동명사를 목적어로 취한다.

**4.**
① to see           ② to exercise
③ working          ④ gambling
⑤ to study         ⑥ eating
⑦ changing         ⑧ to leave
⑨ to go            ⑩ wearing

## REVIEW 2

1. ①   2. ③   3. ③   4. ⑤   5. ②
6. ④   7. ⑤   8. ④   9. ①

**해설**
1. 보기의 to 부정사는 부사역할을 한다. ②-형용사역할, ③-명사역할, ④-명사역할, ⑤-형용사역할
2. 보기의 동명사는 목적어역할을 한다. ①-주어역할, ②-전치사의 목적어역할, ④-주어역할, ⑤-전치사의 목적어역할.
3. ①-feel like~ing, ②-be used to~ing, ④-~nice talking, ⑤-~is to be~.
4. 의미상의 주어 앞에 전치사 of를 쓸 때는 형용사가 사람의 성질을 나타내는 경우이다.
5. 주어자리이므로 주어자리에 들어갈 수 있는 명사, 동명사, 대명사 중에 하나를 선택해야한다.
6. '밖에 너무 추워서 축구를 할 수 없다' 라는 뜻이므로 「too~to~」구문을 이용한다.
7. ⑤번은 주어역할이고 나머지는 형용사역할을 한다.
8. ④번은 부사역할이고 ①, ③번은 목적어자리에서 명사역할, ②번은 주어자리에서 명사역할, ⑤번은 형용사역할을 한다.
9. 각각 형용사, 부사역할을 하는 to 부정사의 to가 필요하다.

**해석**
사람들은 보드게임을 매우 좋아한다. 왜냐하면 재미있기 때문이다. 어떤 게임은 짧고 어떤 게임은 하루 종일 걸린다.
우리는 두명 또는 가끔 여덟 명 까지 게임을 할 수 있다. 많은 종류의 보드 게임이 있다. 우리는 말을 옮기기 위해서 카드를 뽑거나 주사위를 던진다. 이기거나 지거나 매우 재미있다. 미국에서 가장 인기 있는 보드 게임 중의 하나는 모노폴리이다. 그것은 한국의 부루마블과 유사하다.

P.140

## Dialogue

A: 유모차에 앉아 있는 아기를 봐.
B: 정말 귀엽다!
A: 우리를 보고 웃고 있어.
B: 응, 그러네. 웃는 모습이 예쁘다.

## Unit Test

**1.**

1. crying  2. dancing  3. watching

**2.**

1. child  2. woman  3. baby  4. concert  5. man

**3.**

1. 주격보어                 2. 목적격보어
3. 목적격보어               4. 목적격보어
5. 주격보어

**4.**

1. My work is tiring.
2. The man sitting on the bench is Ted.
3. Do you know the woman sitting on the stage?

## Writing Pattern Practice

**1.**

the smiling baby
Look at the smiling baby.
a boring movie
I saw a boring movie last night.
an interesting person
My sister is an interesting person.
a boring concert
It was a boring concert.

**2.**

the man smiling over there
Look at the man smiling over there.
the girl playing the piano
The girl playing the piano is my daughter.
the man sitting on the bench
Do you know the man sitting on the bench?
the man standing over there
The man standing over there is my boyfriend.

**3.**

I'm taking a shower.
I'm feeding the dog.
You're studying hard.
My father is washing his car.
We're having a party.
The movie seems interesting.

**4.**

I saw you walking with Kate.
I saw John cheating.
I heard a baby crying last night.
Did you hear them fighting?
I kept you waiting.

P.143

## Dialogue

A: 그동안 어떻게 지냈어?
B: 일하느라 바빴지.
A: 새로운 일은 어때?
B: 좋아. 정말 만족해.

## Unit Test

**1.**

1. broken  2. fallen  3. interested

**2.**

1. leaves  2. cars  3. university  4. song  5. book

**3.**

1. 주격보어                 2. 주격보어
3. 목적격보어               4. 주격보어
5. 목적격보어

**4.**

1. Look at the parked cars.
2. He looked satisfied with his new job.
3. Hotels have rooms filled with sheets and towels.

## Writing Pattern Practice

**1.**

a used car
Eric bought a used car.
fallen leaves
There are some fallen leaves on the ground.
the broken door

Look at the broken door.

**2.**

the cars parked on the street
Look at the cars parked on the street.
one of the languages spoken in many countries
English is  one of the languages spoken in many countries.
the university attended by Britney Spears
This is the university attended by Britney Spears.
a book written by O'Henry
I bought a book written by O'Henry.

**3.**

I'm tired.
I'm bored.
I'm embarrassed.
I'm excited.
I'm interested.
I'm confused.
I'm disappointed.
I'm surprised.
I'm shocked.
I'm satisfied.
I'm depressed.

**4.**

I found the store closed.
I want my shoes repaired.
I heard my name called.

Unit 36_ 분사구문

**Dialogue**

A: 지난 밤에 어디 갔었어? 여러 번 전화했는데.
B: 자고 있었어. 피곤해서 일찍 잠자리에 들었어.

**Unit Test**

**1.**

1. Shocked  2. Turning  3. Not having  4. Tired
5. doing  6. Working  7. Watching  8. Putting on
9. Not knowing  10. Written

**2.**

1. Talking to you  2. Having ho time
3. Going straight  4.Waving his hand

**3.**

1. Singing  2. Not having  3. Excited

**Writing Pattern Practice**

**1.**

Seeing me, he ran away.
Hearing the news, I was surprised.
Going into my room, I turned on the TV.
Having no time, I hurried up.

**2.**

Turning right, you'll see a bank.
Listening to music, you should not study.
Chewing gum, he kept talking.

**3.**

Not having lunch, I was hungry.
Not having a car, she walked here.

**4.**

(Being) tired at work, I came home early.
Written in French, I can't read that book.

REVIEW I

**1.**

① girl playing the piano
② cars parked on the street
③ man playing soccer in the field
④ man sitting on the bench
⑤ woman standing (over) there

**2.**

① 나는 그가 춤추고 있는 것을 봤다.
② 나는 아기가 울고 있는 것을 들었다.
③ 나는 너를 계속 기다리게 했다.
④ 나는 서가에 소설책들이 가득 차 있는 것을 발견했다.
⑤ 밝게 웃으며 그는 내게 걸어왔다.

**3.**

① walked → walking    ② watch → watching
③ excited → exciting   ④ take → taking
⑤ bored → boring
⑥ interesting → interested
⑦ pleasing → pleased
⑧ Eaten → Eating
⑨ Knowing not→ Not knowing
⑩ Finished → Finishing

① 「지각동사 see+목적어+동사/동사-ing」
② 「지각동사 watch+목적어+동사/동사-ing」
③ excite는 '신나게 하다' 뜻으로 '그 이야기가 신나게 한다' 라고 써야한다.
④ 현재 진행형 문장으로 현재분사를 써야한다.
⑤ bore는 '지루하게 하다' 뜻으로 '그 영화가 지루하게 했다' 라고 써야한다.
⑥ interest는 '흥미를 느끼게 하다' 뜻으로 주어의 느낌을 말할 때는 「be동사+과거분사」형태로 써야한다.
⑦ please는 '내가 기쁘다' 라고 할 때는 be pleased의 형태를 쓴다.
⑧ As I ate too much, I couldn't eat another bite. 라는 문장을 분사구문을 포함한 문장으로 바꾼 것이다. 접속사와 주어를 생략하고 동사에 ~ing를 붙이면 Eating too much, ~라고 써야 한다.
⑨ 분사구문의 부정은 분사 앞에 not을 붙인다.
⑩ After she finished her homework, she went to bed.이라는 문장을 분사구문을 포함한 문장으로 바꾼 것이다. 접속사와 주어를 생략하고 동사에 ~ing를 붙이면 Finishing her homework, ~라고 써야 한다.

**4.**

① shocking        ② boring
③ embarrassed     ④ exciting
⑤ depressing      ⑥ interested
⑦ disappointed    ⑧ Being mean
⑨ Not feeling     ⑩ Listening

## REVIEW 2

1. ⑤  2. ⑤  3. ①  4. ③  5. ①  6. ④  7. ④

1. ⑤번은 목적격보어로 쓰인 현재분사이고 나머지는 명사를 꾸며주는 현재분사이다.
2. ⑤번은 현재완료 문장에 쓰인 과거분사고 나머지는 명사를 꾸며주는 과거분사다.
3. ② bored→boring  ③ Eaten→Eating
   ④ interested→interesting
   ⑤ Knowing not→Not knowing
4. '내차가 온통 움푹 들어갔다. 나는 그것이 고쳐졌으면 좋겠다' 라는 문장이다. dent는 '움푹 들어가게 하다' 라는 뜻으로 '움푹 들어갔다' 라고 하려면 be dented를 써야한다. 그리고 목적어 it과 repair와의 관계가 '수리당하다' 라는 수동관계이므로

repaired를 써야한다.
5. ①번은 과거형이고 나머지는 과거분사로 쓰였다.
6. 그녀는 멀리 살아서 크리스마스에 거의 못 온다.
7. Isn't it surprising?(surprise:놀랍게하다, 놀랍지 않나요?) You must be interested.(interest: 흥미를 주다, 너는 흥미가 있음에 틀림없다.)

당신은 육지에서 가장 무거운 동물이 무엇인지 아십니까? 그것은 코끼리입니다. 바다에서 가장 무거운 동물은요? 그것은 바다표범입니다. 숫 바다표범은 4000kg까지 무게가 나갑니다. 그것은 차의 두배 무게죠. 놀랍지 않습니까? 당신은 그것들이 무엇을 먹는지에 흥미로워 할 것임에 틀림없습니다. 이상하게도 그들은 큰 것들을 먹지는 않습니다. 그들은 낙지, 오징어, 그리고 홍합을 먹습니다. 그들은 자주 한끼로 그것들을 많이 먹습니다.

# Chapter 08 | 수동태

## Unit 37_ 능동태와 수동태

P.152

### Dialogue

A: 뭐야?
B: 몰라. 일본말로 쓰여 있어.
A: 어디보자. 너 Akiko 생일파티에 초대 되었어.
B: 정말? 그거 좋은데.

### Unit Test

**1.**
1. Ellis is loved by everybody.
2. Frogs are eaten by snakes.
3. I was bitten by a mosquito.
4. This cake was made by my mother.
5. I was used by my boss.

**2.**
1. Is Jinny loved by everyone?
2. Jinny was loved by everyone.
3. Jinny will be loved by everyone.
4. Jinny has been loved by everyone.

**3.**
1. is spoken        2. are imported
3. was invited      4. was stolen

5. was made

**4.**

1. That building was built 100 years ago.
2. When were you born?
3. This cake was made for Michael.

## Writing Pattern Practice

**1.**

Jane is loved by everybody.
I was bitten by a mosquito.
This cake was made by my mother.

**2.**

English is spoken in many countries.
The window is broken.
The letter was written in Chinese.
I was born in Seoul.
Rome wasn't built in a day.

**3.**

I'm helped by many people.
You aren't allowed to park here.

**4.**

When were you born?
This house was built 10 years ago.

**5.**

You will be punished.
The store will be closed at 9 pm.
The meeting will be held this Friday.

**6.**

Dinner is being made.
The bread is being baked.
The car is being towed away.

**7.**

The secret has been kept for a long time.
The Pizza has been delivered.

## Unit 38_ 수동태표현

| P.155

### Dialogue

A(엄마): 뭔가 냄새 좋은데.
B: Mary가 케익 만들고 있어요. 파티에 가져간대요.
A: 너도 파티에 초대 받았니?
B: 네. 정말 기대되요.

## Unit Test

**1.**

1. John was run over by a truck
2. My baby should be taken care of by me.
3. The pizza can be delivered by them
4. This work may be done by me.
5. The baggage was picked up by a man.

**2.**

1. That song is liked by young people.
2. The letter wasn't written in English.
3. This room isn't cleaned everyday.
4. Was she surprised at the news?
5. Are people interested in movies?

**3.**

1. to  2. in  3. with  4. with  5. at(by)

**4.**

1. Many stars can be seen in this weather.
2. When was the car towed away?
3. The problem can't be solved.

## Writing Pattern Practice

**1.**

That movie is not liked by young people.
The letter wasn't written in English.
It was not made in Italy.
The problem has not been solved.

**2.**

Was it painted by Picasso?
Will the thief be caught soon?
Where was the child found?
When was that book published?

**3.**

Jane was run over by a truck.
David was laughed at by his classmates.
The baby is being taken care of a baby-sitter.

**4.**

This work can be done right away.
The car may be parked over there.

**5.**

The mountain is covered with snow.
I'm interested in sports.
Are you satisfied with your job?
I was surprised at/by the news.

All of us are pleased with the result.

## REVIEW 1

**1.**
① The store was closed at 6.
② That song is loved by young people.
③ The book will be published soon.
④ I was bitten by a mosquito.
⑤ Mangos are not grown in Korea.

**2.**
① 나는 파티에 절대 초대받지 못한다.
② 그 문제는 해결될 수 있다.
③ 너는 음악에 관심 있니?
④ 그것은 미국에서 만든 것이니?
⑤ 그 아기는 베이비시터에 의해 보살핌을 받고 있다.

**3.**
① born → was born    ② spoken → is spoken
③ grow → grown      ④ cancel → canceled
⑤ catch → caught     ⑥ a car → by a car
⑦ speak→spoken      ⑧ love → loved
⑨ write → written    ⑩ visit → visited

**해설**
① '나는 홍콩에서 태어났다.' 라는 수동태문장으로 I 와 born 사이에 was를 써야한다.
② '중국에는 무슨 언어가 쓰이는가?' 라는 수동태문 장으로 language와 spoken 사이에 is를 써야한 다.
③ '오렌지가 한국에서 재배되는가?' 라는 수동태문 장으로 grow대신 grown을 써야한다.
④ '그 회의가 취소되었다.' 라는 수동태 문장으로 cancel 대신 canceled를 써야한다.
⑤ '도둑이 잡히지 않았다.' 라는 수동태 문장으로 catch 대신 caught을 써야한다.
⑥ 'John이 차에 치었다.' 라는 수동태 문장으로 a car 앞에 by가 필요하다.
⑦ '멕시코에서는 스페인어가 사용되는가?' 라는 수 동태 문장으로 speak대신 spoken을 써야한다.
⑧ '매운 음식은 태국에서 사랑받는다.' 라는 수동태 문장으로 love대신 loved를 써야한다.
⑨ 'Harry Potter는 Joan K. Rolling에 의해 쓰여졌 다.' 라는 수동태 문장으로 write대신 written을 써야한다.
⑩ '디즈니랜드는 많은 사람들에 의해 방문되어져 왔 다.' 라는 수동태문장으로 visit 대신 visited를 써 야한다.

**4.**
① in  ② by  ③ for  ④ by  ⑤ in
⑥ at  ⑦ with  ⑧ in  ⑨ by  ⑩ by

## REVIEW 2

1. ②  2. ①  3. ⑤  4. ②  5. ②  6. ②
7. ③  8. ②

**해설**
1. be satisfied with '~에 만족하다'
   be covered with '~로 덮여있다'
   be pleased with '~에 만족하다, 기뻐하다'
2. ② speak → spoken  ③ build → built
   ④ fire → fired  ⑤ cook → cooked
3. ⑤번 문장은 '다이아몬드반지가 발견되지 않았다' 라는 수동태문장으로 find 대신 found를 써야한다.
4. '야구는 대부분의 나라에서 행해진다.' 라는 수동태 문장으로 빈칸에 is played를 써야한다.
5. '이 단어가 어떻게 발음 되는지 아니?' 라는 수동태 문장으로 빈칸에 is pronounced를 써야한다.
6. '어디에서 태어났니?' 는 'Where were you born?' 으로 수동태문장을 쓴다.
7. '많은 사람들이 사고에서 부상을 당했다' 라는 수동 태 문장으로 빈칸에 were injured를 써야한다.
8. '~로 가득 차다' 는 'be filled with' 를, '~를 검사 받다' 는 '~be checked' 를 쓴다.

**해석**
우리는 비행기를 타기위해 공항에 간다. 공항은 서로 다른 나라에서 온 비행기들로 가득 차 있다. 어떤 것은 이륙하기를 기다리고 어떤 것은 착륙을 기다리고 있 다. 비행기가 착륙할 때는 안전을 위해 조심스럽게 검 사 받는다. 타이어와 엔진을 검사받는다. 연료도 다시 채워진다. 모든 것이 검사되면 새로운 탑승객이 (비행 기에) 오른다.

# BASIC
## English
## Grammar
*for Speaking & Writing*